ESSAYS ON JOHN

ESSAYS ON JOHN

C. K. Barrett

THE WESTMINSTER PRESS
PHILADELPHIA

Published by The Westminster Press®
Philadelphia, Pennsylvania

PRINTED IN THE UNITED STATES OF AMERICA
9 8 7 6 5 4 3 2 1

Library of Congress Cataloging in Publication Data

Barrett, C. K. (Charles Kingsley), 1917–
    Essays on John.

    Includes Index.
    1. Bible. N.T. John—Criticism, interpretation,
etc.—Addresses, essays, lectures. I. Title.
BS2615.2.B345   226'.506   82-2759
ISBN 0-664-21389-8   AACR2

CONTENTS

ACKNOWLEDGEMENTS

The publishers acknowledge the following sources for the essays in this volume:

'Christocentric or Theocentric?' first appeared in *La Notion Biblique de Dieu* edited by J. Coppens, published by Editions J. Duculot (1976).

Thanks are due to Verlag Herder, Freiburg, for permission to reprint ' "The Father is greater than I" ', first published in *Neues Testament und Kirche, Festschrift für Rudolf Schnackenburg* (1974), and also ' "The flesh of the Son of Man" ', first published in German in *Jesus und der Menschensohn, Festschrift für Anton Vögtle* (1975).

'The Theological Vocabulary of the Fourth Gospel and of the Gospel of Truth' first appeared in *Current Issues in New Testament Interpretation, Studies in honor of Otto A. Piper*, published by Harper & Row (1962).

The four papers 'Symbolism', 'Sacraments', 'Paradox and Dualism' and 'History' were first given in their present form as lectures at the Waldensian Faculty of Theology, Rome, in 1980, and are being published in Italian in the Faculty's series *Brevi Studi*.

'Jews and Judaizers in the Epistles of Ignatius' first appeared in *Jews, Greeks and Christians, Festschrift for W. D. Davies*, published by E. J. Brill (1976).

'John 21.15–25' was a University Sermon delivered at St Mary's, Oxford, in 1979, and has not previously been published.

PREFACE

In the Preface to *Essays on Paul* (SPCK, 1982) I mentioned some of
the reasons by which I had been persuaded to republish a number
of pieces that had previously appeared elsewhere and were to some
extent paralleled in commentaries that I had written. The same
reasons apply to the studies contained in this new volume, but with
perhaps greater force. One has never been published, one has been
published only in German, and four have been published only in
Italian. None can be said simply to reduplicate anything that
appears in my Commentary on John.

Like the *Essays on Paul*, the *Essays on John* are connected with
persons and places which it is both a duty and a pleasure to recall.
Four appeared originally in Festschrifts, and I am glad to renew my
salutations to Otto Piper, whom I have unfortunately never met in
person, to Rudolf Schnackenburg and Anton Vögtle, outstanding
German Catholic theologians from whom I have learnt much, and
to W. D. Davies, one of my oldest friends in the New Testament
world. 'Christocentric or Theocentric?' was given at the Jubilee
meeting of the Colloquium Biblicum Lovaniense in 1974. The four
papers on Symbolism, Sacraments, Paradox and Dualism, and
History and Theology have been given, in whole or in part, as
lectures in several places, and have developed with time. They
were first given at the Perkins School of Theology, Dallas, as the
Willis M. Tate-Willson Lectures, and delivered most recently in
Italian at the Waldensian Faculty of Theology in Rome. They are
appearing in the series *Brevi Studi* published by the Faculty. Individual lectures have been given in South Africa, at Kiel, and perhaps
elsewhere. They evoke many pleasant memories of much kindness
and hospitality, and of instructive discussions, for which my gratitude remains.

Last of all I have added a University Sermon, preached at St
Mary's, Oxford, in May 1979. I include this piece partly because it
says a few things I am glad to repeat, but also as a symbol of the
fact that New Testament theology, as I understand it, is a practical

exercise, and the only foundation for Christian proclamation, whether in universities or elsewhere.

Durham University C. K. BARRETT
September, 1981

ABBREVIATIONS

BHT	*Beiträge zur historischen Theologie*, Tübingen
BZNW	*Beiheft zur Zeitschrift für die neutestamentliche Wissenschaft und die Kunde der älteren Kirche*, Berlin
CD	*Damascus Rule*
EV	*Evangelium Veritatis* (Gospel of Truth)
HNT	*Handbuch zum Neuen Testament*, Tübingen
JThS	*Journal of Theological Studies*, Oxford
LXX	The Septuagint
1*QS*	*Community Rule* (Qumran Scroll)
SBL	Society of Biblical Literature
SNTS	Studiorum Novi Testamenti Societas
ZNW	*Zeitschrift für die neutestamentliche Wissenschaft und die Kunde der älteren Kirche*, Berlin

1

CHRISTOCENTRIC OR THEOCENTRIC? OBSERVATIONS ON THE THEOLOGICAL METHOD OF THE FOURTH GOSPEL

The three main divisions of R. Bultmann's treatment of Johannine theology[1] deal with *Der johanneische Dualismus, Die κρίσις der Welt* and *Der Glaube*. There is a clear parallel with R. Bultmann's 'anthropological' exposition of Paul's Gospel, and it is unnecessary to point out that his understanding of John is based upon the view that what John offers us is a Christian reinterpretation of the gnostic myth, which if it is to make sense for us must be demythologized in existential terms. The final subdivision of this part of R. Bultmann's *Theologie, Der Glaube als eschatologische Existenz,* makes this particularly clear; and so far as John's thought can be presented in terms of anthropology it is hard to think of a better portrayal of it than this. In what follows I hope not to forget the great debt that we owe to R. Bultmann for this insight.

In the last twenty years, however, things have changed, and as an index of the change I note the headings under which Johannine theology is expounded in H. Conzelmann's *New Testament Theology*[2] – a book I cite partly because of its excellence and partly because in general layout and in other ways it is notably similar to R. Bultmann's. After substantial paragraphs on *Die Christologie, Der Vater und der Sohn, Die Sendung des Sohnes* and *Die Selbstdarstellung Jesu: ἐγώ εἰμι,* H. Conzelmann winds up with very brief treatment of *Welt und Mensch, Die Gemeinde in der Welt* and *Die Eschatologie –* these last three themes take up only six and a half pages. The change of balance is unmistakable, though it would of course be absurd to suggest either that R. Bultmann had no interest in, or said nothing about, Christology, or that H. Conzelmann omitted to discuss John's view of the nature of faith and Christian life. Indeed, H. Conzelmann opens his discussion of Christology with the words (p. 363): 'Man kann sagen, die gesamte johanneische Theologie sei Christologie, aber ebensogut auch, sie sei Soteriologie (bzw. Anthropologie).' He goes on, however, to distinguish between

Paul and John on precisely this issue. Paul makes use of the concept
of wisdom but does not personify it. 'Das ist[3] ... eine Identi-
fizierung in semitischem Stil, nicht eine wirkliche Personifizier-
ung ... Bei Johannes dagegen ist der Logos a priori als Person
gedacht.' The identification of John's theology with Christology had
been made earlier and more explicitly (though as it were in passing)
by F. C. Grant:[4] 'The basis of John's theology – i.e. of his Christology – is not Paul's teaching but the whole broad foundation of
early Gentile Christianity . . .'.

Has this movement from anthropology to Christology gone far
enough? Or, to put the matter in another way, has the emphasis
upon the figure of Jesus Christ gone too far? The question may be
approached as follows. No one has done more to swing the interpretation of Johannine theology from anthropology to Christology
than E. Käsemann. Thus he writes:[5] 'Der Ausgangspunkt ist nicht
die Anthropologie, deren Hoffnung vorweggenommen wird. Der
Ausgangspunkt ist die Christologie und deren Realität, die wie in
den neutestamentlichen Hymnen im weltweiten Siege über alle
Feinden gesehen wird.' A footnote attached to this sentence makes
the point that the theme of new birth in John 3, for which R.
Bultmann provides an existential interpretation, 'setzt jedoch Jesu
Erhöhung voraus ... So ist das Geheimnis der Wiedergeburt zutiefst
das Geheimnis des Menschensohns als des inkarnierten Logos.' E.
Käsemann returns to the theme, which indeed he scarcely leaves, on
p. 62: 'Die Frage nach dem Zentrum der christlichen Botschaft ist
auch uns auferlegt. Von Johannes haben wir zu hören, dass das
die Frage nach der rechten Christologie ist.' So far so good. John
does insist that we should believe that Jesus is the Christ, the Son of
God, and there are for him no anthropological, psychological processes that are independent of Jesus. It is, however, at this point (on
p. 62) that E. Käsemann adds, 'Wir müssen zugleich darauf
reagieren, dass er das nicht anders als in der Weise eines naiven
Doketismus zu sagen vermochte.' It is here that one begins to ask
whether the christological interpretation of John has not gone too
far. Does John present us with 'das Bild des über die Erde schreiten-
den Gottes Jesus' (p. 154)? It may be that a thoroughly christocentric interpretation of John is bound to arrive at this conclusion,
for that John means to speak about God is certainly true, and it is
equally true that he tells the story of Jesus as he walks the earth. It
is, however, something like a *reductio ad absurdum* of Christocentricity,

for it was not John's intention (even if it turned out to be the result of his work) to depict a God who only appeared to be a man. There may be a measure of artificiality in his references to the weakness, weariness and ignorance of Jesus, but the very artificiality is an underlining of John's attempt to say, Jesus was truly a man. It is this sort of consideration that leads me to put my question the other way and ask whether the development in Johannine interpretation has gone far enough. That it was right to go on, without abandoning anthropology (this I think is important), to speak in terms of Christology, would probably be agreed by most students of the Gospel. It seems clear to me that we must now, without abandoning either anthropology or Christology, go on to speak of theology in the strict sense of the term. John is writing about, and directing our attention to, God.[6]

John directs our attention to God; but he does so by writing a Gospel. We are to inquire into his purpose and method in doing this, and that means that we must investigate his theology of the historical Jesus. This is much more than a christological question in the traditional sense of the term, for the question we are asking is not one that could conceivably be answered in terms of a 'two-natures' theory. Such a theory could not be adequate to deal with the functional character of New Testament Christology, including John's Christology, and the theological significance of the Gospel material does not lie only – perhaps even does not lie mainly – in the metaphysical make-up of the God-man person, but in the whole context of his activity. By writing a Gospel John draws our attention to the significance of what Jesus said and did. From this point of view it is quite irrelevant whether Jesus actually spoke the words and performed the actions reported in the Gospel; it is, so John tells us, as a speaking and acting historical person that he claims our attention, and it is our task to inquire how the whole complex of teaching, action and human personality are related to God and contribute to our knowledge of God.

The writing of a Gospel also makes it clear that, for John, Jesus stands in the centre of his understanding of God. This appears from the form of the book, also from the details it contains. Great though differences in other respects may be, John shares completely with the Synoptic Gospels their absolute concentration on the figure of Jesus. John the Baptist may be mentioned more frequently in the Fourth Gospel, but this is only in order that it may be made unmistakably

clear that Jesus must increase while John diminishes (3.30). The
Jews, and in a different way the disciples, appear as a foil against
which Jesus stands out more clearly. John differs from the Synoptic
Gospels in providing more explicitly a theological framework within
which this dominating person must be understood: 'The Word was
God . . . and the Word became flesh' (1.1, 14). Within this framework the story progresses, and we read how Jesus called disciples,
performed miracles, was rejected and killed, and subsequently returned to his disciples; we hear him pronounce long discourses, in
which he speaks of his relation with the Father, of the glory whence
he came and to which he returns, of the life that he bestows and of
the Paraclete whom the Father will send at his request and in his
name. More explicitly than the Synoptic Gospels, John tells the
story of the Son of God who is the Saviour of the world, and Grüne-
wald's famous picture of John the Baptist who points to the crucified
Redeemer is no bad portrayal of John the Evangelist: 'Behold the
Lamb of God who takes away the sin of the world.' To say this is
not, I repeat, to affirm the historicity of the several sayings and
actions attributed to Jesus in the Fourth Gospel, but it is incon-
ceivable that John should have written the kind of book he did write
if he had not wished to attach unique theological significance to the
historical figure of Jesus, or rather perhaps (as he might have pre-
ferred to say), had not seen theological truth of unique importance
arising out of that historical figure.

There can be no doubt then that for John the historical figure of
Jesus was central for his understanding of God; central, but not
final. The things said and done in the Gospel are indispensable,
but they are not complete; it was not possible for the whole truth to
be communicated by such a medium. 'I have still many things to
tell you, but you cannot bear them now' (John 16.12). The content
of the teaching of Jesus was limited by the capacity of his hearers,
even of his disciples, to understand what he said; it was limited also
by the circumstances of his mission, which could not be both in
progress and complete at the same time. The disclosure, like the
offence that accompanies it, will be complete only when Jesus
returns to the glory he had before the incarnation: 'Does this offend
you? What then if you see the Son of man ascending where he was
before?' (John 6.61f.).

The vital penultimacy of the historic ministry of Jesus is brought
out in the Synoptic Gospels by means of eschatology. The Kingdom

of God, though adumbrated in the exorcisms and other miracles, is still to be revealed in power. The Son of man who now lives a humble and homeless life, exercising an authority which is not acknowledged, the Son of man who in the end is rejected and killed, will come in the glory of his Father with the holy angels. The sufferings of the people of God will end when God gathers together his elect and many come from the east and the west, the north and the south, to join in the feast of the Kingdom. Marriage and death will give rise to no more problems. Heaven and earth shall pass away but the words of Jesus will retain their validity when the whole family of the people of God assemble in the age to come. This simple, chronological way of expressing the conviction that the historic ministry of Jesus, though in a sense God's last word, is not in itself the last act in his dealings with the human race, is reproduced in John, though on a small scale. It is of course possible to remove from the Gospel as redactional glosses all references to a last day.[7] To some extent discussion of this literary problem is a strife over words, for someone has incorporated these references in the Gospel as it has been transmitted to us, and if this person was not John I then he was John II – or John III or IV or V; and in my view he was neither an ecclesiastic nor a fool (if we are to distinguish between these characteristics), but understood what the Gospel was intended to convey. I have written about this matter elsewhere and must not now repeat myself, except to say that these passing, undeveloped references to a 'last day' are best explained as designed to meet precisely the point that we are dealing with here. Neither sacramental nor mystical communion is in any real sense an end: whatever I know or experience today, I shall not at the last day rise up of my own accord but only if the Son of God raises me up. What is true of the moments of religious experience is true also of the historic moment of the ministry of Jesus. It is not enough to look back to it as a point in history, viewing it either as an act of redemption universally effective *ex opere operato* or as a full communication of all truth; it points forward to another day that truly is a last day.

The theme of futurist eschatology runs deeper into Johannine thought than is often supposed; it is, however, by no means the only theme that is relevant to our discussion. More characteristic of John is his use of the Holy Spirit to make the same point. The essential proposition is stated in the bluntest terms in 7.39: 'This [the outflow of living water] he said about the Spirit, which those who believed in him were to receive (ἔμελλον λαμβάνειν); for there was not yet Spirit, for Jesus had not yet been glorified.' A further act of divine revelation waited upon the close of Jesus' ministry. This is worked out more fully in the Paraclete sayings in the last discourses. In 14.25f. the contrast is made explicitly: 'These things I have spoken to you while remaining with you' – this of course refers to the teaching of Jesus during his ministry. 'But the Paraclete, the Spirit of truth whom the Father will send (πέμψει, future) in my name, he will teach (διδάξει, future) you all things and will bring to your remembrance (ὑπομνήσει, future) all the things that I have said to you.' Both the connection and the distinction are to be noted. The Paraclete belongs to the time which, relative to the ministry of Jesus, is future; in contrast with what Jesus has done he will teach all things (πάντα). But he will do so by bringing to the minds of the disciples what Jesus has already said. The sayings in chapter 16 underline these points. The coming of the Paraclete is dependent on the departure of Jesus; only if he goes can the Paraclete come (16.7). When the Paraclete comes, he will guide the disciples into all truth[8] – presumably they have not yet reached it (16.13); but, again, he will do so not by completely fresh revelation but by application and elucidation of what was already present in Jesus and his words (16.13ff.). God's work is done in Jesus, yet it will not be complete until a stage later than that of the ministry of Jesus. The same truth is stated differently in 17.20: 'Not for these only do I pray, but also for those who believe in me through their word.' A subsequent generation of believers is envisaged; compare 20.29: 'Blessed are those who have not seen [the historic acts of revelation], yet have believed.'

So far we have used only chronological considerations: the last day and the Paraclete in different ways indicate that the historical work of Jesus is not the end of God's self-disclosure. There is a good deal more to say about the nature of Jesus' ministry. In several respects the person of Jesus himself is made to appear as in some sense secondary.

Thus, in the first place, Jesus appears as one who is sent. An expression constantly recurring on his lips is 'He (or the Father) who sent me', ὁ πέμψας με (πατήρ).[9] Another characteristic group of passages is found in chapter 17, where repeatedly it is emphasized simply that Jesus has been sent – we are not told on what mission; it is the being sent that is important. Thus eternal life is said to consist in knowing God and Jesus Christ whom he sent (17.3). The merit of the disciples is simply that they believe that God sent him (17.8, 25). It is hoped that the world will come to know and believe that God sent Jesus (17.21, 23). Occasionally but less frequently the mission of the Son is given a specific content, most comprehensively in 3.17: 'God sent not his Son into the world to judge the world, but that the world through him might be saved.' It corresponds with the idea of sending that Jesus declares his intention to do the will of God. This is his very life: 'My food is to do the will of him who sent me, and to accomplish his work' (4.34). For 'doing the will', $\pi o\iota\epsilon\hat{\iota}\nu$ $\tau\grave{o}$ $\theta\acute{\epsilon}\lambda\eta\mu\alpha$, of God see also 5.30; 6.38, 39, 40. Only at 6.39 is there a hint at the content of the will of God, which Jesus does, and it is therefore not surprising that E. Käsemann (*Wille*, p. 45) thinks that 'doing the will of God' should be distinguished from moral obedience. This must, however, be put together with the parallel expressions $\tau\grave{o}$ $\check{\epsilon}\rho\gamma o\nu$ $\alpha\mathring{v}\tau o\hat{v}$ $\tau\epsilon\lambda\epsilon\iota o\hat{v}\nu$ (4.34; 5.36; 17.4), $\pi o\iota\epsilon\hat{\iota}\nu$ (10.37, 38; 14.10, 12; 15.24), $\dot{\epsilon}\rho\gamma\acute{a}\zeta\epsilon\sigma\theta\alpha\iota$ (5.17; 9.4) and such vivid metaphors as 18.11, $\tau\grave{o}$ $\pi o\tau\acute{\eta}\rho\iota o\nu$ $\grave{o}$ $\delta\acute{\epsilon}\delta\omega\kappa\acute{\epsilon}\nu$ $\mu o\iota$ $\acute{o}$ $\pi\alpha\tau\acute{\eta}\rho$, $o\mathring{v}$ $\mu\grave{\eta}$ $\pi\acute{\iota}\omega$ $\alpha\mathring{v}\tau\acute{o};$ The ministry of Jesus meant that he turned his back upon those courses of self-regarding action that come naturally to mankind and subordinated his will to that of his Father. That this subordination was expressed not in terms of 'Do this! Do that!', but more generally in hearing and keeping the Father's word is consistent with John's style, and does not rob the subordination of the one will to the other of moral value. For the moment, however, our point may be put in a pair of simple questions. Jesus was sent: by whom? Jesus was obedient: to whom?

A second, related, observation is that Jesus in his ministry manifests dependence. It is frequently repeated that he does not speak or act of himself ($\dot{a}\pi'$ $\dot{\epsilon}\mu\alpha\upsilon\tau o\hat{v}$: 5.30; 7.17, 28; 8.28, 42; 12.49; 14.10). The theme is stated in great detail in chapter 5. The Son can do nothing of himself ($\dot{a}\phi'$ $\dot{\epsilon}\alpha\upsilon\tau o\hat{v}$, 5.19) but only what he sees the Father doing. If he executes judgement and gives life to the dead, this is because these privileges have been granted him by the Father. Again a simple question suggests itself, and it has already been answered. Jesus was dependent: on whom?

Thirdly, the work of Jesus is represented as revelation. This is made clear from the beginning. It is implicit in the use of the word $\lambda\acute{o}\gamma o\varsigma$ (1.1, 14), and the last verse of the Prologue sums up the whole: $\theta\epsilon\grave{o}\nu$ $o\mathring{v}\delta\epsilon\grave{\iota}\varsigma$ $\dot{\epsilon}\acute{\omega}\rho\alpha\kappa\epsilon\nu$ $\pi\acute{\omega}\pi o\tau\epsilon.$ $\acute{o}$ $\mu o\nu o\gamma\epsilon\nu\grave{\eta}\varsigma$ $\upsilon\acute{\iota}\acute{o}\varsigma$[10] . . $\dot{\epsilon}\xi\eta\gamma\acute{\eta}\sigma\alpha\tau o$

(1.18). The theme thus sounded in the Prologue is repeated in the body of the Gospel. Corresponding to the Prologue is the passage that closes the public ministry (12.36–50), which includes, and indeed focuses on, the words ὁ θεωρῶν ἐμὲ θεωρεῖ τὸν πέμψαντά με (12.45). The last discourses make the same point in almost the same words (14.9, ὁ ἑωρακὼς ἐμὲ ἑώρακεν τὸν πατέρα), and the whole is wound up in the prayer that precedes the Passion (17.26, ἐγνώρισα αὐτοῖς τὸ ὄνομά σου καὶ γνωρίσω). Jesus himself is directly visible to the physical eye, but truly to see him (as not all men do) is to see one who otherwise is invisible. The term *God* may point either to the invisible Father who is revealed, or to the visible Son who reveals him, for John is at pains to point out that the revealer is himself God (1.1 and perhaps 1.18). Whether, however, the word θεός bears precisely the same meaning in the two cases is a question to be discussed. We may add to our list of rhetorical questions: Jesus reveals – whom? Behind this lies the general observation that the Johannine Christology is a Christology of mediation.

To minimize the figure of Jesus would certainly be to misunderstand John, to whom E. Käsemann rightly applies the famous words of Zinzendorf: 'Ich habe nur eine Passion. Das ist er, nur er' (*Wille*, p. 85). For John, as I have said, Jesus is central; yet he is not final. I may refer to the two sets of passages that I have discussed elsewhere,[11] which are represented respectively by the statements 'I and the Father are one' (10.30) and 'The Father is greater than I' (14.28). This is an antinomy that cannot be disposed of by source criticism; it is itself part of John's Christology, and it may lead us now to a further consideration of John's theological method, and, in turn, of his theological purpose. For merely to speak of 'mediation' answers no questions and poses a good many. In what sense is Jesus a mediator? Is his mediation a matter of function or of being? Does he mediate in the sense of setting up a relation, or in conveying something, such as life, or truth, from the one party to the other? How is he related to God and to man, between whom he mediates?[12]

It may help us to grasp John's method if we begin by noting the contrast between mediation in John and mediation as the concept is handled elsewhere. This contrast I shall first state and then illustrate – it is evidently impossible in one short essay to do more than illustrate it. It is, broadly speaking, true to say that the great exponents of mediation in John's immediate environment, such as

Philo, start with a concept, almost a definition, of God, and then ask how such a being as they have defined can have any relation with existence outside himself. How can pure being (Philo delights to speak of τὸ ὄν) be related to contingent being? How can a God who is defined as pure goodness (and therefore incapable of evil) and as all-powerful (and therefore able to put all his good purposes into effect) create a universe in which so much evil manifestly exists? How can that which is beyond knowledge come to be known by finite beings of limited intelligence? How can pure spirit have fellowship with beings who are at least in part material? How can such a God love and redeem creatures who are manifestly unworthy to be loved and on the whole unwilling to be saved?[13] Here are the problems posed by the theological presuppositions of Philo and the Gnostics; their elaborate systems of mediation were designed to resolve them, and the mediatorial figures are invoked, one may say, imagined, to serve this purpose. John, on the other hand, begins with his Mediator, who is simply given him in the Christian tradition – a double tradition flowing in the not always distinct channels of historical tradition, conveying deeds and words attributed to Jesus, and christological tradition, confessing faith in the heavenly κύριος. Both traditions are represented in the Fourth Gospel, and it appears that John found that he could not adequately represent them without speaking about God – a God who needed no definition, save that he was the God of the biblical tradition, who, high and lifted up though he was, was the Creator of all things, an active participant in human affairs and ready at all times to dwell with him that is of a lowly and contrite spirit.

To illustrate this difference we may glance at the use made by Philo and by John of a familiar Old Testament narrative, Jacob's dream, recorded in Genesis 28. Philo refers to this elsewhere, but gives a detailed interpretation in *De Somniis* 1.1–188. Characteristically, his interpretation is manifold and not consistent with itself; I shall make no attempt to trace out the variations that occur, though the very fact that they exist is significant. Philo is freely allegorizing an event for whose historicity he has no concern (save when he is pointing out the moral lesson taught by the sleeper's avoidance of luxurious bedding); John does not exercise this kind of freedom in respect of history. Starting from the words 'He came to a place' (ἀπήντησε τόπῳ), Philo notes that τόπος may signify simply space (χώρα), or the θεῖος λόγος or αὐτὸς ὁ θεός (*De Somniis* 1.62). The last two are sharply distinguished, and Philo argues in passing that Genesis 22.3f. refers to both, the Logos and ὁ πρὸ τοῦ λόγου θεός (65; contrast John 1.1). When Abraham reaches the divine word 'he does not actually reach Him Who is in very essence God' (66: οὐ φθάνει πρὸς τὸν κατὰ τὸ εἶναι θεὸν ἐλθεῖν). All Abraham learns at this point through the Logos is the utter remoteness of God (67: he was far from τοῦ ἀκατονομάστου καὶ ἀρρήτου καὶ κατὰ πάσας ἰδέας ἀκαταλήπτου θεοῦ). The λόγος, subsequently differentiated into λόγοι (69), who may be ἄγγελοι (115), does, with the δυνάμεις (162f.), provide a means by which man may approach God, so that Jacob becomes Israel (ὁρῶν θεόν). God says to the soul, ἀποστρέψω σε εἰς τὴν γῆν ταύτην (180; Gen. 28.15), I will bring you back from your wandering into the realm of immortality. Philo now proceeds to a violent interpretation of the text. Jacob declares (Gen. 28.17), ὡς φοβερὸς ὁ τόπος οὗτος. He is confronted with the question 'as to where, and whether at all *in* anything the Existent Being is' (184: ποῦ καὶ εἰ συνόλως ἔν τινι τὸ ὄν). Jacob sees the truth and corrects his error: διόπερ εὐθὺς ἀνέκραγεν, 'This is not' (Gen. 28.17); this that I supposed, 'that the Lord is in some place' (Gen. 28.16), is not so; for according to the true reckoning He contains, but is not contained (οὐκ ἔστι τοῦτο, ὃ ἐδόξασα, ὅτι ἔστι κύριος ἐν τῷ τόπῳ. Περιέχει γάρ, ἀλλ᾽ οὐ περιέχεται κατὰ τὸν ἀληθῆ λόγον, 185).[14] Yet the world surrounding Jacob was in truth πύλην τοῦ πρὸς ἀλήθειαν οὐρανοῦ (186), for the κόσμος νοητός is perceived only by contemplating the κόσμος αἰσθητός (187f.).

With this brief snatch from a lengthy exposition we may compare the passing allusion–it is no more–in John 1.51. How far contemporary Jewish exegesis influenced John's use of the Old Testament must remain doubtful. R. Schnackenburg's[15] extreme scepticism perhaps hardly allows sufficient weight to the unusual ἐπὶ τὸν υἱὸν τοῦ ἀνθρώπου. His main point is surely right. 'Heaven opens above the Son of Man, so that what is a vision of the future in the Synoptics is already present in John ... the Son of Man on earth is the "gate of heaven" (cf. Gen. 28.17), the place of the presence of God's grace on earth, the tent of God among men (cf. 1.14)' (p. 321). But why 'upon the Son of man' in the place where Genesis says ἐπ᾽ αὐτῆς (on the ladder)? John surely is concerned not only to make a christological point in a straightforward ontological proposition, but to emphasize movement, traffic, intercourse. It is true that he does not quote the words of Genesis 28.13, ὁ δὲ κύριος ἐπεστήρικτο ἐπ᾽ αὐτῆς, but the movement of the angels (who are ἄγγελοι τοῦ θεοῦ) implies something of the kind. Thus Jesus as the Son of man becomes the means by which men have communion *with God*. Nathanael has been impressed by Jesus' supernatural knowledge of his whereabouts (1.47ff.). He (and others – ὄψεσθε, plural) will see more than this; they will find that when they look understandingly at Jesus they will see no mere θεῖος ἀνήρ[16] but a direct link with the supreme God. There are greater things than are contained in the confession σὺ εἶ ὁ υἱὸς τοῦ θεοῦ, σὺ βασιλεὺς εἶ τοῦ Ἰσραήλ, even though Nathanael may at first have intended this as the highest evaluation he could think of. John is saying, in effect, Look at the historical Jesus, the Son of man, and you will find your thoughts carried up the heavenly ladder to God himself.

There is thus a fundamental difference between John and other religious writers who are concerned with the theme of mediation between the supreme God and men – the mediation of knowledge and of substance, whether this be called life, salvation, or some other term. Along with the difference, however, goes the fact that John finds himself obliged to use what is to some extent at least the same framework of thought and concept as his contemporaries. He does not use identically the same theological method, because written into his is the historical framework of the work of Jesus, and not even when (for example) Philo expounds an event such as Jacob's dream does he tie himself to history; but he does use a closely related method. This fact leads to not a few of the problems and ambiguities that occur in the Fourth Gospel.

We may, for example, return here to the alleged docetism of the Gospel, and, as I have said above, recognize the artificiality of some of John's references to the humanity of Jesus – though it must also be recognized that there is no artificiality about death, and that the Johannine Jesus shares with mankind the human property of dying. The analogy, or one of the analogies, that John chooses to use in setting forth his picture of Jesus is the Philonic *logos*,[17] and this *logos*, which owes much to earlier Greek thought, especially to Stoic-Platonic eclecticism, and is also well on the way to Gnosticism, is a divine emanation which on the one hand is to be distinguished from the supreme God, and on the other is certainly not man – related perhaps to empirical man as the νοητός to the αἰσθητός, but not more closely. The model was not without value but at the same time was not without danger, for it was not John's intention to write about a divine-human hybrid, but about a real man who was unique in that when men looked at him with the eye of faith they saw the invisible God. How far John was successful in using the model without being dominated by it, how far he allowed it to lead him into making statements that did not correspond with what he really wished to say, will doubtless continue to be disputed. The important thing is to recognize the method, with both its usefulness and its limitations. It was useful in that it provided a means of expressing mediation, a means by which the invisible God could communicate knowledge of himself, and himself, to men; limited in that of the Philonic *logos* you could not truly say (what John is careful to say by way of qualification in his Prologue) either θεὸς ἦν ὁ λόγος or ὁ λόγος σὰρξ ἐγένετο.

Here I may mention again[18] the apparent clash between such statements as 'I and the Father are one' and 'The Father is greater than I'. John finds himself obliged to make these two sets of statements about the same person, because he must make it clear that God in his revelation is truly God; that Jesus reveals not a secondary deity but the Most High God. Yet he is *Deus revelatus*; not the whole abyss of Godhead, but God known.

There are other themes that could be taken up here. One is the much discussed Johannine use of the ἐγώ εἰμι formula. Sometimes (for example at 6.35) these words are provided with a complement; in these passages there is no problem.[19] Nor is there any serious problem in 4.26; 6.20; 18.5, 8, where a complement is easily inferred from the context.[20] The difficult passages are 8.24, 28, 58; 13.19; and of these 8.58 soon falls out of the discussion, for the main sense here is that of the continuous being of the Son – he exists before Abraham, now, and for ever. In the remaining passages (and in some of those I have dismissed) it is often supposed that John is taking up the divine name of the Old Testament (Exod. 3.14: *I am that I am*),[21] so that Jesus is claiming to be God. It is not always noted that this interpretation is inconsistent with the passages themselves. This is particularly clear in 8.28, where with the knowledge that ἐγώ εἰμι there goes, included in the same ὅτι clause, 'and I do nothing of myself, but speak as the Father taught me'. It is simply intolerable that Jesus should be made to say, 'I am God, the supreme God of the Old Testament, and being God I do as I am told.' The context of 13.19 is similar. Having prophesied what is to come in order that, when the prophecy is fulfilled, 'You may believe that ἐγώ εἰμι', Jesus goes on in the next verse to declare not only 'He who receives anyone I send receives me' but also 'He who receives me receives him who sent me.' The juxtaposition is perhaps not quite as sharp as in chapter 8, but it is again intolerable that Jesus should be made to say, 'I am God, and I am here because someone sent me.' The meaning of 8.24 is determined by that of 8.28, but there is no explanatory context because John intends that the un-explained ἐγώ εἰμι shall provoke and be taken up by the question, σὺ τίς εἶ; (8.25). If a translation of ἐγώ εἰμι in these verses is sought I should be inclined to offer the colloquial English, 'I'm the one', that is, 'It is at me, to me, that you must look, it is I whom you must hear.' This corresponds with John's view of the person of Jesus, and harmonizes well with such passages as Isaiah 45.18–25. The sense would be not, 'Look at me because I am identical with the Father', but 'Look at me for I am the one by looking at whom you will see the Father' (14.9), 'since I make him known' (1.18).

One further theme may be taken up at this point. It has been maintained that John represents Jesus in the Hellenistic manner as a θεῖος ἀνήρ. The evidence for this class of beings is perhaps less clear-cut than one could wish,[22] but it is easy to observe and list in John such properties as wise teaching, convincing argument, the gathering of disciples, the working of miracles, and so on. Jesus undoubtedly appears as an impressive spiritual personality, who exercises powers that are more than human, and it is not unreasonable to suppose that in his portraiture John was dependent on more than the primitive tradition about Jesus (though this certainly represented him as teacher and wonder-worker). But let us return to the en-counter between Jesus and Nathanael. Jesus first puts on the im-pressive show of the θεῖος ἀνήρ, who is able by means of his supernatural vision to disclose Nathanael's character and move-ments (1.47f.). Nathanael is duly impressed, but Jesus, as we have seen, goes on to speak of himself not as a being complete in himself at whom men may gaze in admiration, but as a ladder, a link between men and God, to whom he is related, to whom he is perhaps equivalent in that he effects his presence, but from whom he is to be distinguished, as the ladder is distinguished from the upper floor from which it is let down and to which it is the only means of access. Jesus is too humble to be a conventional θεῖος ἀνήρ; he is too humble because he is more than a θεῖος ἀνήρ.

A different kind of illustration of John's method is provided by a study of what gnostic exegesis made of his Gospel. The old Philonic hybrid *logos* returns, as the Revealer is seen to be only in appearance a man, and yet not fully God. 'The Valentinians insist that the reality which the pneumatics apprehend is essentially indescribable and ineffable. They call it the "depth", the "abyss", the "Father". . . . So the *logos*, who mediates between the Father and other beings, himself is only an "image" of the Father.'[23] The docetic strain of gnostic exegesis hardly calls for illustration; see for example Clement, *Excerpta e Theodoto*, 61.3, where the blood and water that flow from the side of the dead Jesus (John 19.34) represent the flow of passions ($\pi\acute{a}\theta\eta$) from the things in which passion is mingled ($\dot{\epsilon}\mu\pi\alpha\theta\epsilon\hat{\imath}s$) for the preservation of those that are free from passion ($\dot{a}\pi\alpha\theta\epsilon\hat{\imath}s$). Jesus is not very man, and it is not very God that is encountered in him.

Finally we may raise the question of John's purpose in writing his Gospel. This question has often been answered, and naturally enough, by reference to the Prologue, in which John appears to define his own programme, or to 20.30f., than which nothing could be more explicit: 'These have been written that you may believe that Jesus is the Christ, the Son of God.' It would be absurd to deny that these passages convey important insights into John's intention, and if I cite another passage it is with a view rather to supplementing than to supplanting them. I suggest, however, that it may be profitable to consider John 4.19–26 as a further summary of what John intended to achieve in writing his book. The Father himself seeks men who will worship him in Spirit and in truth: this then was God's purpose in the incarnation, and John certainly wrote with the intention of furthering the divine purpose, whatever that may have been. The main themes of his Gospel appear in this paragraph, and this essay may move to its end with a brief survey of them as the paragraph itself discloses them.

Verse 19 begins with the picture of the $\theta\epsilon\hat{\imath}os\ \dot{a}v\acute{\eta}\rho$, who not only offers the Samaritan woman living water – true teaching and thereby salvation – but is able to tell her the details of her past husbands and present paramour, and so to awaken the hope that he may be able to tell the secrets of true worship. Indeed, he will do so, but they do not amount to a case for either Jerusalem or Gerizim against the other. Verse 20 shows awareness of the internal disputes of Judaism, or of Judaism with its nearest neighbour, but these are mentioned only to show that the claims of each rival are now outmoded. The

eschatological fulfilment of the biblical tradition is now at hand
(ἔρχεται ὥρα, verse 21), and the disputes and privileges of Judaism
are alike left behind in realization. The privileges had been real. In
Judaism God, otherwise unknown, had been known: We worship
what we know.[24] Inaccessible to philosophy and natural religion he
had himself spoken in the law and the prophets, and his word was
salvation. Hence it is that salvation proceeds from the Jews to the
world at large.

Verses 23, 24 take the matter forward in two respects. First we
learn that the hour of fulfilment has arrived: ἔρχεται ὥρα καὶ νῦν
ἐστιν. That which replaces Jerusalem and Gerizim as the point of
contact between God and man is simply the person of Jesus, the Son
of man who is the ladder between heaven and earth (1.51). Where
he is, true worship, that is, a living contact with God, is possible.
This means both that the Church, in and on behalf of which John
writes, is the new people in whose midst God dwells, and also that
the historical Jesus is the true mediator. This is the more important
in view of the second point made in verses 23f.: πνεῦμα ὁ θεός. It
will be remembered that John has just referred to the Father; he is
therefore not subsuming the whole of the Godhead under what we
speak of as the third person of the Trinity. That is, he uses πνεῦμα
here in a way different from that of, say, 7.39. Perhaps the most important explanatory cross-reference is 3.8: τὸ πνεῦμα ὅπου θέλει πνεῖ,
καὶ τὴν φωνὴν αὐτοῦ ἀκούεις, ἀλλ᾽ οὐκ οἶδας πόθεν ἔρχεται καὶ ποῦ ὑπάγει.
Πνεῦμα is invisible, known only through its sound (φωνή) and its
effects. The proposition 'God is Spirit' means that he is invisible and
unknowable;[25] that is, it repeats the proposition of 1.18: 'No one has
ever seen God.' The hour for disclosure, however, has now come,
and he is known through his sound, his speech, which is apprehended not by all men but by the elect. The word φωνή bears this
sense in John: see 1.23, where the Baptist describes himself as the
φωνή of one crying in the wilderness; 5.25, 28, which claim that the
dead will hear and be quickened by the φωνή of the Son, verses
which are taken up in 11.43 by the φωνὴ μεγάλη with which Jesus
summons Lazarus from the tomb; 10.3, 4, 5, 16, 27, which tell how
the sheep of the flock hear and recognize the Shepherd's voice;
12.28, 30, the voice from heaven which came, though Jesus did not
himself need it in view of his continual communion with the Father,
for the benefit of the bystanders. With these passages we must put
18.37: 'Everyone who is of the truth (ἐκ τῆς ἀληθείας) hears my

voice' ($\mu o \upsilon$ $\tau \hat{\eta} s$ $\phi \omega \nu \hat{\eta} s$), and 5.37f.: 'Neither have you ever heard his voice ($\phi \omega \nu \grave{\eta} \nu$ $\alpha \grave{\upsilon} \tau o \hat{\upsilon}$) nor have you seen his face, and you do not have his word ($\lambda \acute{o} \gamma o \nu$) abiding in you.'

God, then, is $\pi \nu \epsilon \hat{\upsilon} \mu \alpha$: the invisible God whom no one has ever seen, but who has uttered his voice and sent his Word into the world, so that to all who are of the truth the Word may make him known. It is here that the other sense of $\pi \nu \epsilon \hat{\upsilon} \mu \alpha$ makes itself felt, for *the* Spirit, the Paraclete, brings home to men the truth revealed in Jesus (14.26; 16.14). God is $\pi \nu \epsilon \hat{\upsilon} \mu \alpha$, and men must worship him in Spirit and in truth, $\acute{\epsilon} \nu$ $\pi \nu \epsilon \acute{\upsilon} \mu \alpha \tau \iota$ $\kappa \alpha \grave{\iota}$ $\acute{\alpha} \lambda \eta \theta \epsilon \acute{\iota} \alpha$. Some commentators are at pains to point out that the disavowal of Jerusalem and Gerizim does not in itself imply the rejection of all formal acts and places of worship, and this is true enough, but John makes it clear that the relation with God which worship is intended to express consists simply in hearing the word he speaks in the historical Jesus and in being directed through this word to himself.[26]

This theme is picked up in verse 25 in the word $\acute{\alpha} \nu \alpha \gamma \gamma \epsilon \lambda \epsilon \hat{\iota}$. To understand this verse it is not necessary to examine in detail what the Samaritans believed (or did not believe) about the Messiah. It is doubtful whether John was deeply interested in such matters. For him the Messiah is the Revealer and Redeemer, with the stress in this verse (and perhaps elsewhere) on revelation. The woman knows that he will disclose all things, that is, all the truth about God. Jesus replies: 'I am the one' – the Messiah who will tell you all things.

This is indeed the message of the Gospel. The whole truth ($\acute{\alpha} \pi \alpha \nu \tau \alpha$) about the invisible and unknown God is declared in the historical figure to which John points in his not literally historical narrative. The figure of Jesus does not (so John in effect declares) make sense when viewed as a national leader, a rabbi, or a $\theta \epsilon \hat{\iota} o s$ $\acute{\alpha} \nu \acute{\eta} \rho$; he makes sense when in hearing him you hear the Father, when in looking at him you see the Father, and worship him.

NOTES

1 *Theologie des Neuen Testaments*, 2. Lieferung, first published in 1951 (Tübingen), pp. 349–439.
2 *Grundriss der Theologie des Neuen Testaments*. Munich 1967.
3 Conzelmann has referred to the use of *wisdom* in 1 Corinthians 1.20ff., 30.
4 *The Gospels, their Origin and their Growth* (London 1957), p. 167.
5 *Jesu letzter Wille nach Johannes 17* (Tübingen [3]1971), p. 41.
6 This was clearly seen and stated by E. C. Hoskyns, *The Fourth Gospel*, ed.

F. N. Davey. London 1940. See, e.g., p. 120: 'The theme of the Fourth Gospel is the non-historical that makes sense of history, the infinite that makes sense of time, God who makes sense of men and is therefore their Saviour'; and especially perhaps the *Introductory Essay* by F. N. Davey, e.g. p. xlvi, 'The truth made known in history is the truth *of God*: it is not, that is to say, the truth of observable history in relation to other points in observable history, but the truth of observable history in relation to Him whom *no man hath seen at any time.*'

7 R. Bultmann, for example, considers the references to 'the last day' in 6.39, 40, 44, 54 to be due to an ecclesiastical redactor. I have commented briefly on this view in *New Testament Essays* (London 1972), pp. 56f., 66f. See also the 2nd edn of my commentary, ad loc.

8 It makes little difference to the point at issue here whether we read εἰς τὴν ἀλήθειαν πᾶσαν or ἐν τῇ ἀληθείᾳ πάσῃ; the Paraclete has the whole of truth for his sphere of operation.

9 4.34; 5.23, 24, 30, 37; 6.38, 39, 44; 7.16, 18, 28, 33; 8.16, 18, 26, 29; 9.4; 12.44, 45, 49; 13.20; 14.24; 15.21; 16.5.

10 P66 has greatly strengthened the case for reading μονογενὴς θεός here.

11 ' "The Father is greater than I" (John 14.28): Subordinationist Christology in the New Testament' in *Neues Testament und Kirche, für Rudolf Schnackenburg*, ed. J. Gnilka (Freiburg 1974), pp. 144–59; in this volume, pp. 19–36.

12 See H. Clavier, 'Mediation in the Fourth Gospel' in *SNTS Bulletin*, 1 (1950), pp. 11–25.

13 There are many suggestive observations on these matters in H. Braun, *Wie man über Gott nicht denken soll.* Tübingen 1971.

14 I use the Colson-Whitaker translation of this problematical passage.

15 R. Schnackenburg, *The Gospel according to St John*, vol. i (Eng. trans., New York and London 1968), pp. 321f. Cf. the treatment of this point on p. 109–11.

16 See p. 13.

17 I do not mean to imply that John's use of the word λόγος is identical with Philo's, but that it is impossible to read the word in John without recalling the Philonic λόγος.

18 See p. 8 and note 11.

19 I do not mean that there is no serious theological work to do on these passages.

20 On 4.26 see p. 16; the meaning clearly is, 'I am the Messiah'. At 6.20 (cf. Mark 6.50), Jesus says, 'It is I – the person whom you know'. At 18.5, 8 he says, 'I am the person you have named, Jesus of Nazareth'.

21 אהיה אשר אהיה. The LXX, ἐγώ εἰμι ὁ ὤν, is not so helpful. See also Isaiah 43.25; 45.18; 46.4, 9; 47.8; etc.

22 For an excellent account of the material and a balanced view of the parallels and differences, see Elwyn Jones, *The Concept of the Θεῖος Ἀνήρ in the Graeco-Roman World with special reference to the first two centuries* AD. Unpublished Durham Ph.D. thesis 1973.

23 E. H. Pagels, *The Johannine Gospel in Gnostic Exegesis*, SBL Monograph Series, vol. 17, (Nashville and New York 1973), p. 119.

24 Note the neuter of the relative pronoun, ὅ. It is not claimed that even Jewish worship was adequate worship of the God who in verse 24 is said to be Spirit, and is revealed in the person of his Son.

25 Save, perhaps, among the Jews, in the sense given and limited by the neuter pronoun of verse 22; see note 24.

26 See further, pp. 111–13.

2

'THE FATHER IS GREATER THAN I'
John 14.28
SUBORDINATIONIST CHRISTOLOGY
IN THE NEW TESTAMENT

Fides catholica haec est: ut unum Deum in Trinitate, et Trinitatem
in unitate veneremur ...
    Patris, et Filii, et Spiritus sancti una est divinitas, aequalis gloria,
coaeterna majestas.
    Qualis Pater, talis Filius, talis Spiritus sanctus ...
    In hac Trinitate nihil prius aut posterius, nihil maius aut minus:
sed totae tres personae coaeternae sibi sunt et coaequales ...
    Qui vult ergo salvus esse, ita de Trinitate sentiat.

On this basis, does the Fourth Evangelist qualify for salvation? The
question is a serious one. Not all the branches of Christendom make
formal dogmatic or liturgical use of the Quicumque vult, but many
more adopt the homoousion of Nicaea, and the main stream of
Christian tradition (from which there have indeed been some notable
divergent branches) has adopted the view that the divine Persons,
being divine, are essentially equal.

> Three Persons, equally divine,
>   We magnify and love (Charles Wesley).

But is this the view of the New Testament? The title of this essay
quotes John 14.28; other parts of the Fourth Gospel will be introduced into the discussion. The New Testament as a whole provides
more material than can be handled in one short essay, but not only
is the question under discussion not confined to one Gospel, apart
from the exegetical problems of particular passages, it arises out of
modern New Testament study in general. What do we understand
by the term Jesus Christ? What do we know of his own understanding of his own person? I have put this question in historical form,
and it is indeed a historical question of unusual difficulty. We have
no immediate knowledge of Jesus in the form of writings that go

back to his own hand; we know him only through the testimony of devotees, who undoubtedly placed him on the divine side of reality. Does this fairly represent the truth? Does it fairly represent what he himself believed to be the truth? Or has the tradition forced him, or its picture of him, into a pattern that he would have rejected? A parallel of a negative kind would be provided by an attempt to estimate the character and intentions of the Emperor Tiberius on the basis of the writings of Tacitus alone. For Tacitus, Tiberius was an ogre; anything that seemed virtuous was hypocrisy, or a stage on the road to evil.[1] There is other evidence, which serves to control Tacitus's *ex parte* account; and when the account itself is critically examined, when, for example, the actual number of executions is counted and set beside the wholesale indictment of Tiberius's rule as a reign of terror, it is seen to bear witness against itself. The historian has, with very considerable but not complete success, printed his own conception upon the traditional material he was handling. Modern study of the Gospels, recognizing that the Evangelists and their predecessors in the use of the tradition reverenced the person of Jesus as in some sense divine, inquires whether a similar process may not have occurred in the New Testament. Is it possible to trace beneath the theologizing of the Gospels, not an untheological tradition, for it is now fairly generally recognized that there was no untheological tradition about Jesus, but a tradition bearing a different theological stamp from that which subsequently was imposed upon it?

It is not the intention of this essay to pursue this inquiry in general terms. It is mentioned here only to illustrate the kind of provocation (*Anstoss*)[2] which study of the New Testament provides for theological thinking, and to introduce a particular theme of some importance within the larger task. The Fourth Gospel has often been taken as the bastion of orthodox Christology: the Synoptists might possibly give us leave to think of a human Christ, a venerated teacher and leader who was perhaps the best of men but not God, but John, according to whom Jesus declares 'I and the Father constitute a single unit of being' (10.30), surely permits no such reduced belief. Is this view legitimate? Or does the Fourth Gospel also compel the critical reader to look afresh at traditional Christology, and thereby constitute a provocation to Christian thinking? It is never wise to run away from problems, and a firm look at the provocation may be as salutary for theology today as it has been in the past. 'Just as Hippolytus and Tertullian had used St John's Gospel as their main weapon against Sabellianism, just as Novatian had used it against those who said that the Son is a mere man, so now Alexander uses it against the extreme subordinationism of Arius. If it is St John's Gospel which raises the questions which these heresies sought to solve, it is the same Gospel which provides the basis for the answers which the Church gave to them.'[3] It may still be true that the Fourth Gospel not only raises dangerous questions but also contributes to their solution.

One respect in which the Gospel raised questions that were later to divide the Church was in the use of the word Logos. In the light of the disputes of later centuries it is easy to forget that this word, as a christological title, occurs in only two verses of the Gospel (1.1, 14). Partly, perhaps, for this reason later use was not governed by John's, and indeed probably sprang from other sources. Already in the second century the apologists were, not wholly consciously, drawing on Greek philosophical rather than biblical usage, and the result was an unmistakable tendency to subordinationism. 'Dieser Logos ist zur Zeit und zum Zweck der Weltschöpfung von Gott kausiert . . . Justin nennt den Logos das πρῶτον γέννημα τοῦ θεοῦ, προβληθὲν . . . πρὸ πάντων τῶν ποιημάτων.'[4] It is this background that enables Justin to say that the Logos a θεὸς ἕτερός ἐστι τοῦ τὰ πάντα ποιήσαντος θεοῦ, ἀριθμῷ, . . . ἀλλ' οὐ τῇ γνώμῃ (Dialogue 56.11).[5] Two hundred years later, in the alliance between Athanasius and the Western theologians, the Father–Son relationship was to overthrow both the logos-concept of Alexandria and the word-wisdom concept of Antioch. 'If Alexandrian theology in the third century demonstrates the inadequacy of the Logos-concept as the basis for interpreting the witness of St John's Gospel to the Father–Son relationship in the godhead and to the fullness of the divinity and humanity in Jesus Christ, Antiochene theology as we see it represented in Paul of Samosata demonstrates the inadequacy of the Hebraic Word-Wisdom concept. Of the three ante-Nicene traditions, only Western theology understood St John's intention that the central concept for Christology must be that of the Father–Son relationship; because of this clearer understanding of St John's intention and its stronger emphasis on the faith of the Church as expressed in the rule of faith, the Western tradition appears to have been more representative of the faith of the majority of Christians everywhere.'[6] But λόγος is part of the Christology of the Fourth

Gospel; one may well ask whether subordinationism is also a part, or an unintended and unjustified inference, to which John inadvertently gave occasion by not integrating the concept of the Logos with that of the Son.

Many of the relevant data have been clearly set out by J. E. Davey in his study[7] of the dependence of Jesus on the Father, and a long quotation may be permitted. 'The real Christ of the Fourth Gospel lives in absolute dependence at every moment upon the Father ... Christ depends upon the Father for his *power* [John 5.19] ...; for His *knowledge* [8.16] ...; for His *mission* [7.28] ...; for all necessary *instructions* [14.31] ...; for His *message* [7.16] ...; for *life* [5.26] ...; for the *destinies* of life [18.11] ...; for His *authority* [17.2] ...; for *love* [10.17] ...; for His *glory* [17.24] ...; for His *disciples* [6.37] ...; for *testimony* [5.37] ...; for the *gift of the Spirit* [3.34] ...; for *all other gifts* [17.7] ...; for *guidance* [11.9] ...; for *union* and *communion* with the Father [8.29] ... And the same dependence is manifested in Christ's *obedience* [4.34] ...; and witnessed to by His *prayers* (cf. John 17.15) and by His *titles*, Son, Light of the World, Life, Truth, The Way, The Door, The Vine, etc., which rest ultimately upon God as Father, as Light (1 John 1.5), as True, as the End (John 14.6), as the Husbandman (John 15.1), and so forth.'[8] Davey goes on to claim that these features are not simply a function of the earthly, human, life of Jesus. 'The human traits in John's picture of Jesus, weariness, thirst, tears, etc., imply a creaturely dependence during the life of Christ in the flesh; but even *John's* picture of the Eternal Son in Himself retains the same subordinationist note – cf. John 14.28 ... Indeed, there is no doubt that for *John* the dependence of Christ upon the Father is not confined to His life upon this earth; it reaches back into His preexistence (17.24) and forward into His exalted life as the Risen One (14.16).'[9]

Davey's list of passages could be considerably extended (and he himself extends it in the detailed discussion that follows the passages I have quoted). Not only could the references for (for example) the mission and the message of the Son be multiplied,[10] further categories could be introduced, such as Jesus' prophetic zeal (2.17) and his being sealed by God (6.27). An important passage not yet mentioned is 20.17, where Jesus, both associating himself with the disciples ('my brothers'[11]) and distinguishing himself from them (my ... my ... your ... your), speaks of 'my Father' and 'my

God', still, after the resurrection,[12] recognizing the divine being as one to whom he owes obligation. As Son he has a Father; may we add, as man he has a God?

It is further to be observed that those notable Johannine passages that seem at first sight to proclaim most unambiguously the unity and equality of the Son with the Father are often set in contexts which if they do not deny at least qualify this theme, and place alongside it the theme of dependence, and indeed of subordination. It will be important to look briefly at some of these passages. They follow a regular pattern.

The first is the Prologue, 1.1–18.[13] This opens with the bald statement, which John evidently intends to govern the understanding of his Gospel throughout: θεὸς ἦν ὁ λόγος (1.1). The fact that θεός is anarthrous does not make it mean something less than God:[14] the Word is not indeed the whole content of deity, yet he is (not divine in a secondary sense but) God. In the same sentence, however, he is differentiated from God (in that he exists πρὸς τὸν θεόν), and this differentiation is underlined in 1.2.[15] It receives clearer definition in verse 14; the λόγος is the μονογενής (cf. verse 18). As such he occupies the position of an honoured friend (εἰς τὸν κόλπον; cf. 13.23), and serves the purpose of executive agent and revealer. Indeed, though the themes of creation and regeneration are sounded in the Prologue (1.3, 12f.), that of revelation is central: note the stress on light,[16] the beholding of glory (ἐθεασάμεθα, verse 14), the revelation of grace and truth (comparable with the revelation of Torah through Moses, verse 17) and especially the concluding words of the Prologue, which sum up its import, ἐκεῖνος ἐξηγήσατο (v. 18). Thus what is said in the Prologue about God is absolute; the only clear affirmation about him is that in his proper being he is unknowable, for the οὐδεὶς ἑώρακεν of verse 18 implies more than invisibility to the physical eye. But the λόγος, the μονογενής, is essentially visible, perceptible, the agent of communion on behalf of the invisible and unknowable God, for whom he acts. Thus he is God (v. 1), but God in his knowability, in his revelation, and in this function, he, who is πρὸς τὸν θεόν (vv. 1, 2), is παρὰ πατρός (v. 14), God's agent.[17]

A second passage is the miracle and discourse of 5.1–47. The miracle of 5.1–9a forms a suitable starting-point for what follows; '. . . sie, als Geschichte eines Sabbatbruches, die Ständigkeit des Offenbarerwirkens symbolisch darstellt'.[18] Jesus' reply to the charge

of Sabbath-breaking, in which he compares himself with his Father
(v. 17), leads naturally to the further charge that he is ἴσον ἑαυτὸν
ποιῶν τῷ θεῷ (v. 18). These words are of course John's own formulation (though it is probable that they reproduce Jewish arguments
against Christians), and John, who has already in the Prologue
written θεὸς ἦν ὁ λόγος, will have had no hesitation in accepting their
import, except that he would regard the ποιῶν as mistaken: the Son
did not and did not need to make himself equal to God – he was
equal to God. But the discourse immediately proceeds, as the Prologue did, not to withdraw but to qualify and expand the astounding
proposition that Jesus was equal to God, and in the ensuing paragraph occur some of the verses most strongly insistent on the
subordination of the Son. The theme is set out in verse 19, and for
our purpose it is scarcely necessary to go beyond this verse. The Son
is not an independent, spontaneous source of activity; his work is
entirely derivative, both in its form and its content. He does only
what he sees the Father doing, and would indeed not be able to do
this if the Father had not granted him the privilege of having life in
himself (v. 26). Once this essential proviso is granted, no honour is
too high: it is the Father's own intention that all men should
bestow equal honour on the Son, but this honouring is evidently
contingent upon the Father's will. The power to raise the dead and
authority to pass judgement are divine attributes,[19] and the Son
enjoys them; yet the first division of the discourse closes (v. 30) with
the reiterated proposition that the Son can do nothing of himself.
This is followed by further exposition of the same theme in terms of
μαρτυρία (vv. 31–47). As in the Prologue, God recedes into the realm
of unknowability; he might have been known in the activities, which
are proper to him, of raising the dead and passing judgement, but
he has abdicated these functions. Resurrection tends to fade out of
the picture since the believer has already passed out of death into
life (v. 24); so far as it remains, it, like judgement, is entrusted to the
Son (vv. 21f., 25, 27ff.). Thus the Father is known as Lord and
Judge only through the revelation provided by the Son – who
reveals the Father because he does precisely as he is told (v. 30). He
does the things God does, but in a secondary, dependent relationship.

A third passage that may be considered here is 10.22–39,[20] which
includes the claim, ἐγὼ καὶ ὁ πατὴρ ἕν ἐσμεν (v. 30),[21] and the
charge, similar to that of 5.18, that σὺ ἄνθρωπος ὢν ποιεῖς σεαυτὸν

θεόν (v. 33). The paragraph opens with the demand that Jesus shall
say plainly whether he is the Christ. To this there is no direct
reply,[22] but an appeal to the works of Jesus which bear witness to
who and what he is. This evidence the Jews fail to perceive because
they do not belong to Jesus' sheep (v. 26). This explanation turns the
line of thought back (v. 27) to the allegory of sheep and shepherd,
and the fate of those who do not belong to the flock suggests the
safety of those who do: They shall never perish, and no one shall
snatch them out of my hand (v. 28). This is restated in the next
verse in the form, No one is able to snatch them out of the Father's
hand. The restatement is preceded by a sentence which presents
notorious textual problems, but may be rendered as, My Father is
greater than all,[23] and it makes little difference as far as we are
concerned whether 'greater than all' is masculine or neuter. It includes the single comparison of 14.28, The Father is greater than I.
The unity referred to in verse 30 is now seen to relate specifically to
the safe care in which the elect are guarded. Christ and the Father
are one in that, whether the one or the other is considered, the
elect are safe under their care. It would thus be wrong to read too
much Christology out of the ἕν ἐσμεν.[24] There is, moreover, more to
follow, for after the charge of blasphemy Jesus replies by quoting
Psalm 82.6, ἐγὼ εἶπα, θεοί ἐστε. Scripture itself describes as θεοί
those to whom the Word of God came;[25] how then is he at fault if he
describes himself as the Son of God? It may be that the argument is
directed so sharply *ad hominem* that it is not to be given serious theological attention.[26] It is bound, however, to affect the value assigned
in this context to the word θεός, and involves a considerable reduc-
tion in the claim ascribed to Jesus. Jesus is indeed one with God;
but the nature of his unity with the Father, which is not discussed
here as it is in chapter 1 and chapter 5, is such as to accommodate
a real distinction between the two divine figures.

To accommodate rather than to obliterate; though the latter
seems to be the view of E. Käsemann.[27] It is true, Dr Käsemann
argues, that we read repeatedly in the Fourth Gospel that the
Father sent the Son, but this sending is to be interpreted in terms of
the Jewish *šljḥ*-principle, that the one sent is as he who sent him; and
the 'sending' formula alternates with claims that the Son is one with
the Father. It is the latter, he says, that give the former their
christological meaning. 'Jesus ist der himmlische Gesandte, der aus
der Einheit mit dem Vater handelt und nach 1.18 als dessen

"Exeget" in einzigartiger Würde alles, was sonst gesandt gewesen sein mag, übertrifft. Eine wirklich subordinatianische Christologie lässt sich von hier aus keinesfalls ableiten' (p. 31). He adds, however, 'Isoliert man die Formeln von der Sendung durch den Vater und der Einheit mit ihm, kommt man zum Subordinatianismus oder Ditheismus. Sie sind korrelat und komplementär, weil nur beide gemeinsam den Sachverhalt umschreiben, dass Jesus nichts als der Offenbarer, andererseits aber der einzige Offenbarer Gottes ist und darum selbst auf Erden ganz auf Gottes Seite gehört' (pp. 31f.). Of this conclusion it may be said that correlation and complementariness are not in themselves more illuminating terms than the 'paradox' that Dr Käsemann rejects as an account of the majesty and humiliation of Christ.[28] The purpose of the present examination of the subordinationist element in John's thought is not to deny the existence of another element (which is sufficiently proved by the first verse of the Gospel), but to inquire into the way in which the two elements are correlated, and the way in which the Johannine correlation is related to the historical Jesus. It is true that 'Im 4. Evangelium beherrscht Jesu Herrlichkeit aber die Darstellung so sehr im ganzen und von vornherein, dass die Einordnung der Passionsgeschichte zu einem Problem werden muss' (p. 22). Yet the problem is there, and the solution of the problem is, as Dr Käsemann clearly shows, a crucial one for the interpretation of Johannine theology. How hard this problem is, and how easy it is to misunderstand the correlation, is shown by Dr Käsemann on pp. 55–64, and he is right in stressing the revelational and soteriological aspects of the unity of the Son with the Father. 'Nur als Gottes Offenbarer bleibt er mit dem Vater eins . . . Seine Einheit mit dem Vater hat soteriologische Funktion' (p. 55); but does not subordination also share the functions of revelation and salvation? Are they not functions of subordination? The functions of a subordinate? So, essentially, O. Cullmann: The Logos is God, 'aber nur insofern er sich offenbart'.[29] As Dr Cullmann observes, the Bible deals only with God *revealed*; and this means that the agent of revelation is a subordinate agent.

That a subordinationist element is to be found in the Fourth Gospel has not escaped its readers in the past, and, indeed, did not escape its earliest students. By orthodox readers it was explained along two lines.[30]

1 The subordinationist passages were taken to refer to the

human nature of Christ. Classical expression is given to this view in
the *Tome* of Leo (*Ad Flavianum, Epistola* 4): Non eiusdem naturae
est, dicere, 'Ego et Pater unum sumus', et dicere, 'Pater maior me
est'. Quamvis enim in Domino Jesu Christo, Dei et hominis, una
persona sit, aliud tamen est, unde in utroque communis est con-
tumelia, aliud unde communis est gloria. De nostro enim illi est
minor Patre humanitas; de Patre illi est aequalis cum Patre divinitas.
This line of interpretation is not much earlier than Leo. It appears
in Augustine:[31] Quid itaque mirum vel quid indignum, si secundum
hanc formam servi loquens, ait Dei Filius: Pater maior me est; et
secundum Dei formam loquens, ait idem ipse Dei Filius: Ego et
Pater unum sumus? Unum sunt enim secundum id quod Deus erat
Verbum: maior est Pater, secundum id quod Verbum caro factum
est. – With many more neat epigrammatical pronouncements. This
kind of interpretation, however, is neither the earliest, nor the
predominant one.

2   Most patristic writers take the view that some kind of distinction is to be sought between the Father as Father and the Son as
Son, independently of the circumstances of the incarnation. This
view was already clearly expressed by Tertullian in his discussion in
Adversus Praxean. All Tertullian's references to the Fourth Gospel in
this tract (including the extended treatment in cc. 21–5) are worthy
of study; we may note especially the discussion of 14.28 in c. 9 (cf.
c. 14), and several references to 10.30 which was one of Praxeas's
(few – see c. 20) proof-texts. Tertullian writes: Pater enim tota
substantia est, Filius vero derivatio totius et portio, sicut ipse
profitetur: 'Quia Pater maior me est' ... Sic et Pater alius a Filio,
dum Filio maior; dum alius, qui generat, alius qui generatur; dum
alius, qui mittit; dum alius qui facit; dum alius, per quem fit.[32] In
c. 22, discussing 10.30, Tertullian argues that though used by
Praxeas the verse is in fact contrary to Praxeas's monarchian position. It contains an intimation of two beings, duorum esse significa-
tionem, whose unity is not in person (as if John had written unus,
masculine), but in some substance (unum, neuter). Compare c. 25,
ad substantiae unitatem, non ad numeri singularitatem. Tertullian
has no difficulty in showing that the Fourth Gospel teaches a distinction between the first and second Persons; the question is whether,
from the standpoint of christological orthodoxy, he proves too much,
namely that the Son is distinct from the Father through being in-
ferior to him. That Origen, notwithstanding his doctrine of eternal

generation, fell into this error is hardly open to doubt, though Tixeront[33] is perhaps no more than fair when he refers to circumstances which, 'si elles ne le justifient pas complètement, atténuent singulièrement la gravité des accusations portées contre lui'. Origen had, however, contributed, though it may be unwillingly, to the beginnings of Arian Christology, and it is the more striking that both Alexander of Alexandria[34] and Athanasius[35] adopt essentially the same exegesis. That the Father is greater than the Son belongs to their proper being and intrinsic relationship. On these lines, perhaps, the nihil maius aut minus of the Quicumque vult might be defended as not inconsistent with the maior me of the Fourth Gospel.

But is either of these patristic lines of interpretation satisfactory? Westcott[36] attempts to combine them in the observation, 'So far then as it was fit that the Son should be Incarnate and suffer, and not the Father, it is possible for us to understand that the Father is greater than the Son as Son, in Person but not in Essence.' He is on firmer ground with the note, 'It appears to be unquestionable that the Lord here speaks in the fulness of his indivisible Personality'; and this observation provides not a basis for but the fundamental criticism of both lines of patristic exegesis.[37] Most of the 'subordinationist' material that we have reviewed (see pp. 22–6) cannot be interpreted in terms of the eternal relations between the Persons of the Trinity; it belongs within the setting which John himself is careful to provide for it, namely that of the historic ministry. It will suffice to note that this is true of the passage on which most of the discussion has concentrated. 'You heard that I told you, I am going away, and coming to you. If you loved me, you would have rejoiced that I am going to the Father, for the Father is greater than I.' The historic Jesus is on his way not to death but through death to one who is greater than he; the occasion of his death should for this reason be for his disciples a cause not of cowardly fear (14.27), but of rejoicing. The historical setting is essential to John's point. Similar observations could be made with regard to most of the 'subordinationist' passages. But if a historical[38] setting is implied, the 'alternating' kind of exegesis which makes Jesus speak now out of his human, now out of his divine, nature, is intolerable,[39] unless we are to give up altogether the idea that he was a real person, whom other real persons may hope, though partially, to understand.

This criticism does not mean that we have nothing to learn from

the patristic exegesis; only that we cannot be content with it as it ← N 13
stands. I turn now to modern interpretation, and in particular to the
inference drawn by J. E. Davey from the material he adduces from
the Gospel. According to him, only two possibilities are open: 'the
one that we have a strong historical conviction and tradition at
work, and that the portrait is substantially correct in its psychological presentation in this field; the other that we have here a very
thorough working out, in the form of a religious fiction, of an
Alexandrian conception of Christ as the Logos, the eternal image of
God and agent of His will, Who is conceived of as assuming flesh for
a time but as still retaining this eternal position of metaphysical and
automatic dependence upon the mind and purposes of the invisible
God.'[40] There is something to be said for each alternative, and for
Davey's preference for the former; it is, however, impossible to be
satisfied with either. The various possibilities, as Davey discusses
them, are interrelated. Of his general examination[41] of the historical
value of the Fourth Gospel, this is not the place to speak; the present
writer can only confess that he has not been convinced by Davey's,
or by other more recent attempts to show that John is, or was ever
intended to be, in the ordinary sense, a historical document.
Davey's argument that the 'dependence' material goes back to the
history of Jesus himself, and accurately describes a genuine feature
of his life and religious experience, turns to a great extent upon his
rejection of what he regards as the only alternative to it. Christ, he
claims, is a middle term between God and men – 'the ratios God:
Christ, and Christ: men, are strictly parallel and proportionate'
(p. 87); so far it could be said that Christ occupies the position of the
Philonic Logos. This, however, is simply not (apart from a few
verses in the Prologue) what Logos means in John. John does
(Davey believes) modify history in a docetic direction,[42] but this is
without special reference to the Logos conception. 'The material
here is not Alexandrian, but rather Christian in the widest sense'
(p. 87). It is thus that Davey believes himself to be thrown back
upon his historical solution.

It will be seen that in this argument Davey virtually assumes that
the Johannine Logos will be either Philonic or Christian in origin.
But Johannine discussion was already tending to leave this field
when Davey wrote. For 'Alexandrian' and 'Philonic', Bultmann,
and many others, have substituted 'gnostic'. Where much could be
quoted, I refer to one characteristic and important passage in

Bultmann's Commentary.[43] The unity of Jesus with the Father (says Dr Bultmann) is not a moral union, nor is it adequately explained in terms of the Old Testament prophets. '... auch ist das autorisierte Reden Jesu nicht durch die Kategorien der Erwählung, Berufung und Inspiration interpretiert, sondern durch *die Begriffe des gnostischen Mythos*. Dieser redet von der Sendung eines präexistenten Gottwesens, das in seiner metaphysischen Wesensart Gott gleich ist und von ihm entsandt wird, um im Auftrage und der Ausrüstung des Vaters und in Einheit mit ihm sein Offenbarungswerk zu vollbringen. Hier ist die Offenbarung nicht auf die intermittierende Inspiration, sondern auf die Wesensgleichheit des Gesandten mit Gott gegründet, die eine dauernde ist' (p. 188). Bultmann goes on to show that John historicizes this mythological material, and claims that all the language that describes the relationship between the Father and the Son, including passages that we have described as 'subordinationist', shows that 'Vater und Sohn nicht als zwei getrennte Personen betrachtet werden können, deren Tun einander ergänzt, wobei – wie im Mythos – der Vater im geheimnisvollen Hintergrund des Ungeschichtlichen bleibt, oder die in der Intention ihres Wollens einig wären; sondern ... dass das Wirken von Vater und Sohn *identisch* ist' (p. 188).

Justice is thus done to the equality sayings, but it is not done to the subordinationist sayings, and we are left looking for further clues that may help us to co-ordinate the glimpses of truth that have appeared in both ancient and modern exegetical work.

One such clue may be found in the Marcan theme of the Messianic Secret, which, in its Marcan form, is notoriously absent from John.[44] This is not the place for a discussion of what is in itself one of the most important and most difficult problems in the New Testament. It has long been recognized that the theme, as the Evangelist presents it, is a theological one. 'Die Idee des Messiasgeheimnisses ist eine theologische Vorstellung';[45] but is Wrede equally convincing when he sets beside this positive statement the corresponding negative one, 'ein geschichtliches Motiv kommt wirklich gar nicht in Frage?' I think he is not; and note here only one fact of fundamental importance. In Mark, Jesus is addressed as Rabbi, either in transliteration (9.5; [10.51]; 11.21; 14.45) or in translation (4.38; [5.35]; 9.17, 38; 10.17, 20, 35; 12.14, 19, 32; 13.1; [14.14]). This was not made up by the Church, which thought of Jesus in other terms. Yet Jesus was cast out by his own people, and executed by the Romans as a rebel. That is, he was addressed by a term, and, it seems, consistently permitted himself to be addressed by a term, that concealed rather than disclosed the true meaning and character of his mission. It was not false, for he did teach; he was not an armed rebel; whether or not he was a false prophet was and must remain a matter of opinion. But if, as seems certainly true, he allowed himself to be addressed as Teacher, there was an element of secrecy, of concealment, about his work. This element Mark (or his predecessors) has thought through into a major theologoumenon. The process involved both theological development, in terms of the doctrine of election and the theory of a divine hardening, and the creation of ostensibly historical statements – notably commands, incapable of fulfilment, that secrecy should be maintained (e.g. Mark 5.43). It is too often assumed that theological processes operating within the gospel tradition were independent of and inconsistent with the raw material of the tradition itself. Sometimes this was so, but it was not necessarily always so, and it seems not to have been so in regard to the Messianic Secret. A genuine element in the historical tradition was drawn out and developed theologically, and the theological development then reacted upon the historical tradition. When we read Mark in the form in which the Evangelist has given it to us we see, and are intended to see, Messiahship veiled behind a cover of artificial Non-Messiahship, or at least of speciously denied Messiahship. When we press into the tradition, working back through the theological development and its 'historical' side-effects, we see something that is both more significant and less clear cut – an undefined authority veiled behind an aversion to the use of all titles, including messianic titles.

The Fourth Gospel, as I have said, does not reproduce the Messianic Secret in its Marcan form; it carries the theological development a stage further, expressing the conviction that, however clearly Jesus may state the truth, those who are not 'his sheep' will not hear his voice (10.26).[46] It may be, however, that in this development we can find a clue to the subordinationist material in John. That we are dealing here with a theological theme is surely manifest. I have already noted that Dr Bultmann's theory of John's use of the gnostic myth of the Revealer enables him to explain the sayings that stress the unity and equivalence of the Son with the Father, but not the subordination of the revealing Son to the revealed Father. This suggests that[47] the extent of the Johannine theological operation has not yet been fully grasped. There could hardly be a more christocentric writer than John, yet his very Christocentricity is theocentric.[48] From one point of view the aim of the book is that men may believe that Jesus is the Christ, the Son of God (20.31); yet it is a profounder truth that the aim of the actions the book describes is that men may worship the Father in Spirit and in truth (4.21, 23). This leads, when the Gospel is read 'in the flat', to two sets of sayings, which, as the patristic exegesis shows, it is not easy to harmonize into a smooth christological formula. Alexandrian and Antiochene, even Arian and Athanasian, can pick out their texts and use them to support their own christological theories.

It is natural, and not in the end wrong, to describe the result in the language of paradox: one speaks of majesty veiled in humility.[49] To this exposition of Christology Dr Käsemann objects: 'Dialektische Formeln wie die vom Paradox zwischen Niedrigkeit und Hoheit geben dem Verständnis einen so breiten Spielraum, dass sich das Verschiedenartigste darunter vereinen lässt ... Ein wirkliches Paradox zwischen Niedrigkeit und Hoheit des irdischen Jesus kann nur behauptet werden, wenn ernsthaft von angefochtener, der Welt, dem Leiden und dem Tode ausgesetzter Menschheit Jesu gesprochen werden muss.'[50] This condition, he claims, is lacking. Jesus is not in this Gospel represented as exposed, powerless, to such distress. 'In Wahrheit ändert er nicht sich selbst, sondern nur seinen jeweiligen Ort' (p. 34). This is, however, a very substantial concession. There is a good deal of difference between 'the glory which I had with thee before the world was' (17.5), and the place in which Jesus is exposed to condemnation and death. Dr Käsemann is right in pointing (pp. 27ff.) to the artificiality of some of the Johannine references to the earthly circumstances of Jesus' life, but this is the same kind of artificiality that enters into the Marcan presentation of the Messianic Secret. Every theologian, including Mark and John, is concerned with a mystery, a secret, and every theologian owes a duty to his reader, the duty of making his subject-matter as clear as he can. He is thus caught, inevitably, in cross-fire. Either he is true to his theme, and retains its mysteriousness at the expense of his reader; or he does his duty to his reader and plays false to his theme by simplifying its mystery. Mark simplified the theme of Messiahship, with the result that the Marcan Jesus issues orders that no one ever thought of obeying (e.g. 1.44f.; 5.43) and teaches in a manner calculated to prevent his hearers from understanding what he meant (4.11f.). John – may we not say? – simplifies the theme of the relation of Jesus to God by presenting him in a somewhat inhuman humanity, and as both claiming and denying equality with the Father. If we know anything at all about the historical Jesus we know that he was the sort of man Dr Käsemann describes – exposed and vulnerable to the world, to suffering and to death, and that in this situation he 'endured the cross, despising the shame' (Heb. 12.2). We know too that for the primitive Church, which in one generation produced the dynamic Christology of Paul and in little more the highly sophisticated Christology of the Fourth Gospel, he had the value of God. The sense in which this man can have the value of God is the theme and problem of all Christology, and John has both clarified it and obscured it by the use of gnostic categories. It is probably true to speak both of a projection of gnostic terminology and concepts on history, and of a projection of history on a theological screen; both processes can be found in John. It is a further projection on a later theological screen when we read in the famous dogmatic text quoted at the beginning of this essay, 'Aequalis Patri secundum divinitatem, minor Patre secundum humanitatem'. This is not a recognizable picture of a living person, and the processes of biblical study and of dogmatic theology alike require us in our generation to return once more, so far as we are able, to the living person, and thus to renew the theological operation that fixes in new terminology the paradox of the living and dying man who is God. We shall not perform the task better than our fathers, even when we do it differently, and the Johannine Christology which emerged towards the end of the first century has lessons as well as provocation for us.

This short essay makes no claim to discuss the problem fully, still less to present a new Christology; at most it offers a few observations on the theme as it is suggested by some of the material in one of the books of the New Testament. The rest of the New Testament has its own contribution to make, and abler minds must consider the whole. But the times call for the task. The old quest of the historical Jesus, as Schweitzer described it, was a reaction against dogmatic Christology; it was abandoned, but a new quest has taken its place. The new quest calls for a new Christology, or, better perhaps, a new thinking-through of the raw materials of all Christology. It may be that the next generation will find the right formulas, reminded by a better understanding of the historical Jesus that the New Testament, and not least the Fourth Gospel, is in the end about God.

NOTES

1 Tacitus, *Annales*, 6.51: While Germanicus and Drusus still lived, he concealed his real self, cunningly affecting virtuous qualities ... As long as he favoured (or feared) Sejanus, the cruelty of Tiberius was detested, but his perversions were unrevealed. Then fear vanished, and with it shame. Thereafter he expressed only his own personality – by unrestrained crime and infamy.

2 For the significance of this word see the 'Grusswort' by J. Gnilka in the *Festschrift* for R. Schnackenburg, from which this essay is taken.

3 T. E. Pollard, *Johannine Christology and the Early Church*, SNTS Monograph Series 13 (Cambridge 1970), p. 164.

4 F. Loofs, *Leitfaden zum Studium der Dogmengeschichte*, 5. Aufl. hrsg. von K. Aland, (Halle 1951), 1. Teil p. 91.

5 'Der in seiner Überweltlichkeit depotenzierte Gott' in Loofs, *Leitfaden*, p. 92. On the whole, the apologists kept their understanding of the 'Kausiertheit' (Loofs) of the Logos under control.

6 Pollard, *Christology*, p. 116.

7 J. E. Davey, *The Jesus of St John*. London 1958.

8 Davey, *Jesus*, pp. 77f.

9 Davey, *Jesus*, pp. 78f.

10 Evidence is easily found in the concordance under the words ἀποστέλλειν, πέμπειν, λόγος, ῥῆμα, etc.

11 There is some evidence for the omission of 'my', but this is due to unwillingness to accept the association. C. H. Dodd in *Studies in the Gospels. Essays in Memory of R. H. Lightfoot*, ed. D. E. Nineham (Oxford 1955), p. 19; also *Historical Tradition in the Fourth Gospel* (Cambridge 1963), p. 324, takes the brothers to be those of 7.3; an unlikely identification, in view of 20.18.

12 T. Zahn, *Das Evangelium des Johannes* (Leipzig ³⁺⁴1912), p. 675: '... der Vater im Himmel ... auch ihm sein Gott sei, nicht nur in den Stunden der Angst ... sondern auch jetzt noch, da er als ein Überwinder des Todes in göttlicher Freiheit lebt und sich erzeigt (14.28).'

13 For a fuller discussion of the Prologue see C. K. Barrett, *New Testament Essays* (London 1972), pp. 27–48.

14 The matter is discussed in the standard commentaries.

15 See O. Cullmann, *Die Christologie des Neuen Testaments* (Tübingen 1957), pp. 272f.

16 If it is said in verse 4 that ἐν αὐτῷ ζωὴ ἦν this leads up to the identification of ζωή with φῶς; there is but one source of light for all men – see verse 9.

17 Cf. παρὰ θεοῦ, said of the Baptist in verse 6.

18 R. Bultmann, *Das Evangelium des Johannes* (Göttingen ²1950), p. 184.

19 See, for example, C. K. Barrett, *The Gospel according to St John* (London 1956), pp. 216f.; 2nd edn (1978), p. 260.

20 The point is missed by Bultmann because he divides up and rearranges the paragraph.

21 C. H. Dodd, *The Interpretation of the Fourth Gospel* (Cambridge 1953), p. 27, notes, without affirming that this is John's meaning, that this unity is the goal of the Hermetic τέλειος ἄνθρωπος. For many further parallels see W. Bauer, *Das Johannesevangelium*, ad loc.

22 See p. 31.

23 On the text see Barrett, *John*, p. 317; 2nd edn, pp. 381f., now also J. N. Birdsall, *JThS* 11 (1960) pp. 342ff.

24 For patristic interpretation of this saying see p. 27.

25 The reference may be to the giving of the Law on Sinai.

26 Bultmann, *Johannes*, p. 297.

27 *Jesu letzter Wille nach Johannes 17* (Tübingen [3]1971), especially pp. 21–64.

28 Käsemann, *Wille*, p. 32. And see p. 32; also pp. 98–115.

29 Cullmann, *Christologie*, p. 317; cf. pp. 272–5.

30 See M. F. Wiles, *The Spiritual Gospel* (Cambridge 1960), pp. 122–5, and, for the changing attitude of Cyril of Alexandria, p. 131. See also the discussion and development of Cyril's point by M. J. Lagrange, *Évangile selon Saint Jean* (Paris [8]1947), p. 395.

31 *Tractatus in Joannis Evangelium*, 78.2.

32 Cf. c. 12: Qui si ipse deus est, secundum Johannem 'deus erat sermo', habes duos: alium dicentem, ut fiat; alium facientem. Alium autem quomodo accipere debeas, iam professus sum; personae, non substantiae nomine; ad distinctionem, non ad divisionem. Ceterum etsi ubique teneo unam substantiam, in tribus cohaerentibus: tamen alium dicam oportet, ex necessitate sensus, eum, qui jubet, et eum, qui facit. Also c. 15: Pater enim sensu agit. Filius vero, qui [quod?] in Patris sensu est, videns, perficit.

33 J. Tixeront, *Histoire des Dogmes*, i, *La Théologie Anténicéenne* (Paris [11]1930), p. 309.

34 'We do not reject his divinity, however, but we ascribe an accurate and complete likeness to the image and expression of the Father, but we hold that the property of unbegottenness belongs only to the Father (τὸ δὲ ἀγέννητον τῷ πατρὶ μόνον ἰδίωμα παρεῖναι), even as the Saviour says, "My Father is greater than I".' Quoted by Pollard, *Christology*, p. 155.

35 *Contra Arianos*, 1.58: 'The word "greater" expresses a priority, not in any order of time, and a pre-eminence, not as to plenitude of essence, but in consequence of the Son's eternal generation from the Father.'

36 B. F. Westcott, *The Gospel according to St John*. London 1903, ad loc.

37 R. E. Brown, *The Gospel according to John, xiii–xxi* (New York 1970), p. 655: 'Would the Evangelist think of a distinction between Jesus speaking as man and Jesus speaking as God? More particularly is such a distinction appropriate in the Last Discourse where more than anywhere else the Jesus who speaks transcends time and space?' Brown, citing P. Borgen, goes on to make the important point that the Jewish šljḥ-principle implies the subordination of the agent to the sender.

38 This is not intended to imply anything positively or negatively about the

    historicity of John's material.

39 See Barrett, *Essays*, p. 65. Cullmann virtually gives up the attempt to explain the paradox, while insisting on its existence: *Christologie*, pp. 273, 309.

40 Davey, *Jesus*, pp. 79f.

41 Davey, *Jesus*, pp. 31–55.

42 Davey, *Jesus*, p. 87 – a notable anticipation of Käsemann, *Wille!*

43 Bultmann, *Johannes*, pp. 186–9.

44 Barrett, *John*, pp. 59f., 255. W. Wrede, *Das Messiasgeheimnis in den Evangelien* (Göttingen ³1963), pp. 203–6, makes little of the Fourth Gospel.

45 Wrede, *Messiasgeheimnis*, p. 66.

46 See also 10.24f., and cf. p. 25. However plainly Jesus speaks, those who are not his own will fail to understand and will think that he is concealing the truth.

47 Apart from the notorious problem of the form in, and the extent to which, the myth existed when John wrote.

48 See pp. 1–18.

49 See E. C. Hoskyns, *The Fourth Gospel*, ed. F. N. Davey (London 1940), pp. 85ff. (this passage was in fact written by F. N. Davey).

50 Käsemann, *Wille*, pp. 32f.

3

'THE FLESH OF THE SON OF MAN'
John 6.53

John 6.51–8 is one of the most discussed and disputed passages in the Fourth Gospel. Rudolf Bultmann is perhaps the most famous but not the first of those who have ascribed it to a redactor who, here and elsewhere, supplemented the Gospel in order to bring it into line with his own view of what a gospel ought to be. In particular, Bultmann thinks, he wished to conform the Gospel to current theological opinion in the Church so as to make it acceptable to official Christianity. It will be convenient to set out Bultmann's reasons for this view.[1] An account of the whole debate would be beyond my powers and the scope of this essay.

The verses in question 'refer without any doubt to the sacramental meal of the Eucharist' (op. cit., p. 218f.), and in them 'the Lord's Supper is ... seen as the φάρμακον ἀθανασίας or τῆς ζωῆς' (p. 219). This view is inconsistent with the Evangelist's thought in general, and in particular with what immediately precedes in chapter 6, for there the bread of life which the Father gives is the Son himself, the Revealer. 'He gives (v. 27) and is (vv. 35, 48, 51) the bread of life, in the same way that he gives the water of life (4.10) and is the light of the world (8.12), and as the Revealer gives life to the world (v. 33; cf. 10.28; 17.2) – to those, that is, who "come" to him (v. 35; cf. 3.20f.; 5.40), who believe in him (v. 35; and cf. 3.20f. with 3.18). In all of this there is no need for a sacramental act, by means of which the believer must make the life his own' (p. 219). Again, the eschatology of this passage, represented by verse 54 (κἀγὼ ἀναστήσω αὐτὸν τῇ ἐσχάτῃ ἡμέρᾳ) is inconsistent with Johannine eschatology, which, in Bultmann's view, is essentially realized eschatology. The believer already has eternal life (v. 47); he has passed already out of death into life (5.24). It is true that the inconsistent words appear also in verses 39, 40, 44, but in these verses too they are to be regarded as insertions by the ecclesiastical redactor. It is not claimed that the redactor's work can be separated from that of the Evangelist on purely stylistic grounds. For example, in the Jewish complaint of verse 52 ($\pi\hat{\omega}\varsigma$ $\delta\acute{\upsilon}\nu\alpha\tau\alpha\iota$...;) 'the editor clearly models himself on the Evangelist's technique' (p. 235, n. 4); Bultmann adds, however, that it is easy to see that it is no more than an insertion, since the misunderstanding is not based on the Johannine dualism. Verse 55, indeed, contains a kind of dualism, but it is the sacramental dualism of the mysteries, not John's. It is thus on theological grounds that Bultmann separates 6.51c–58 from the rest of the discourse on the bread of life.

I shall refer briefly to two developments of Bultmann's redactional theory. R. E. Brown[2] begins from the observation that the verses in question show general Johannine stylistic characteristics; these are sufficient to show that they 'belong to the general body of Johannine tradition' (op. cit., p. 286), but not more – an editor making additions would naturally take the trouble to make them in something like the Johannine manner. What makes Bultmann's theory, as it stands, unacceptable is the existence of eucharistic undertones in the miracle, in the transitional verses (vv. 22–4), and in the introduction to the discourse and the discourse itself (vv. 35–50). What is significant, however, is 'the very fact that the eucharistic element is primary in verses 51–8, while it is secondary in the rest of the chapter' (p. 286). This suggests that 'we have here two different forms of a discourse on the bread of life, both Johannine but stemming from different stages of the Johannine preaching' (p. 286).

A different turn to the discussion was given by G. Bornkamm,[3] who investigated the relation of the paragraph 6.60–71 to what precedes it. It has usually been assumed, for example, that the $\sigma\acute{\alpha}\rho\xi$ referred to in verse 63 must be interpreted christologically and indeed sacramentally with reference to the $\sigma\acute{\alpha}\rho\xi$ of the Son of man of verse 53; this assumption has undoubtedly caused commentators a good deal of trouble, for how can it be asserted both that to eat the flesh of the Son of man is indispensable if one would have life and that the flesh is of no avail? The difficulty, however, is removed if verses 51c–58 are recognized as an insertion; the way is then open for a different interpretation of $\sigma\acute{\alpha}\rho\xi$, in line with the $\sigma\acute{\alpha}\rho\xi$–$\pi\nu\epsilon\hat{\upsilon}\mu\alpha$ contrast of 3.6. The concluding paragraph of the chapter points back not to verses 51c–58 but to the earlier part of the discourse. This is confirmed by verse 62, where the greater mystery and offence are found in the $\mathring{\alpha}\nu\alpha\beta\alpha\acute{\iota}\nu\epsilon\iota\nu$ of the Son of man. The counterpart of this is to be sought (not in the 'eucharistic' passage but) in verses 33, 38, (41, 42), 50, 51a, which speak of a καταβαίνειν. It will follow that, in the original (or at least, in an earlier) form of the discourse, verse 51a was followed immediately by verse 60. A corollary of this conclusion is that the σκληρὸς λόγος (v. 60) was not the eucharistic material of verses 51c–58.

These suggestions have not gone uncriticized. Before Bultmann's commentary appeared, E. Schweizer[4] had sought to demonstrate the literary unity of the Gospel, and subsequently E. Ruckstuhl[5] has returned to the theme. But, as we have seen, the literary criteria are unlikely to be decisive, since it is allowed that the interpolator adopted Johannine style, and if he was even reasonably successful in this undertaking we can hardly expect to be able to distinguish a short stretch of eight verses from the original. Schweizer[6] has further argued that there are inadequate grounds for deciding the question of authenticity one way or the other. J. Jeremias[7] abandoned the view that 6.51c–58 was redactional in favour of the suggestion that in these verses the Evangelist used expressions from a pre-Johannine eucharistic homily, which began with the words explanatory of the bread (6.51c, ὁ ἄρτος ὃν ἐγὼ δώσω ἡ σάρξ μού ἐστιν ὑπὲρ τῆς τοῦ κόσμου ζωῆς). Most important, however, is the work of P. Borgen,[8] who shows that the discourse as a whole, including the eucharistic part, can be explained as a word-by-word midrashic exegesis, following accepted models, of the words, 'He gave them bread from heaven to eat' (v. 31; Ps. 78.24). If he is right, it follows at once that both parts (the sapiential in verses 35–50 and the eucharistic in verses 51–8) belong together.

Borgen's is a very effective argument; as far as form is concerned he makes it seem very probable that the whole discourse was produced by one author by the application of one method. The argument is, however, exposed to some objections: (1) It cannot be said that it is uniformly successful. There are some points, such as the explanation of the οὐ Μωϋσῆς ... ἀλλ' ὁ πατήρ μου ... of verse 32 in terms of the ... אלא ... לא midrashic form, where it seems hardly possible to question Borgen's conclusions, but some of the parallels are more forced. There are marks of midrashic exegesis throughout the discourse, yet the discourse as a whole is not simply a midrash. (2) In any case, the question remains: Why give a midrash (or quasi-midrashic exegesis) of Psalm 78? Surely, not simply as an exegetical exercise. What is the driving force behind the discourse? It does not seem enough to say that it was once delivered by the

Evangelist at the Lord's Supper – there must have been many such sermons that never reached the pages of gospels; or that it was an attempt to correct Jewish exegesis – for notwithstanding the ...לֹא ...אֶלָּא form (which does not continue throughout) it is not really polemical exegesis; or that it was aimed against docetism. J. L. Martyn[9] is nearer the truth when he says that it was designed to show that Jesus was the Mosaic Prophet-Messiah – and yet, beyond that, to show that such exegetical arguments supporting such neat propositions are in fact to be left behind. Jesus is beyond definition and not to be limited by such ready-made categories. He is, quite simply, the bread of life, that by which men live. The fact is that study of the *form* of the discourse can take us a long way towards understanding it but cannot take us all the way. Like most of the material in the Fourth Gospel it is to some extent susceptible of literary and historical analysis but cannot be fully assessed without theological evaluation.

There is, however, one literary question that remains to be considered. Most of the discussion of the question of redaction has proceeded on the assumption that the paragraph which may or may not be an original part of the Gospel is verses 51c (καὶ ὁ ἄρτος δὲ ...)–58 (... ζήσει εἰς τὸν αἰῶνα), and there is evidently something to be said for this assumption, since it is in verse 51c that the word σάρξ is for the first time introduced into the discourse. But division at this point is not entirely satisfactory, for it means that after one short sentence Jesus breaks off, the Jews ask their complaining question (v. 52: πῶς δύναται οὗτος ...;) and the discourse then resumes with a reiteration of the reference to σάρξ, expanded with further reference to the blood of the Son of man. It seems in fact to be John's method to break up his discourses by means of objections. This is undoubtedly true at verses 59, 60. There can be no doubt that verse 59 marks the end of a section: it locates the whole of the preceding discourse in the synagogue at Capernaum. Verse 60 therefore must be a new beginning, and it is marked by the complaint, σκληρός ἐστιν ὁ λόγος οὗτος, and the defection of a number of disciples. The same point can be made at the beginning of the discourse though there the position is more complicated because there is a conversation between Jesus and the Jews. The latter, however, initiate the discussion: 'When did you get here?' (v. 25). Jesus then introduces the theme of food which confers eternal life. This prompts a second question (v. 28) which leads to the true starting-point of the whole speech, verses 31f., in which the Jews make the fundamental quotation from Psalm 78, which implies the question: You speak of a continuing (μένουσα) food; it is written in the Old Testament, He gave them bread from heaven to eat; how can your claim be accommodated with this? Jesus replies (as Borgen has so well shown) by a new (though in form conventional) exegesis of the Old Testament passage quoted. In this reply he speaks of bread which (like the manna) comes down from heaven, and also says (v. 38) that he himself has come down from heaven. After this claim there is another fresh start in verse 41 with the complaining (ἐγόγγυζον) of the Jews, which is finally formulated in the question, πῶς νῦν λέγει ὅτι...; (v. 42). In response, Jesus embarks on a new elaboration of his thought. With these observations in mind it seems natural to end the next paragraph[10] with verse 51c, ὑπὲρ τῆς τοῦ κόσμου ζωῆς, and to begin a new one with verse 52, ἐμάχοντο...

It is worthwhile to notice that the same form can be observed elsewhere in the Gospel, though nowhere else is a long discourse punctuated quite so neatly as in chapter 6. Thus chapter 3 is set in motion by Nicodemus's proposition (3.2), 'No one can do the signs you do, unless God is with him.' This evokes in response the assertion that no one can see the Kingdom of God unless he is born ἄνωθεν. Here Nicodemus raises the perplexed and complaining question, πῶς δύναται...; (3.4); this becomes the cue for the discourse, which (if we take the text of 3.5 as it stands) makes a passing allusion to baptism and goes on to elucidate the process of regeneration in terms of the descent and ascent of the Son of man. In chapter 5 Jesus acts provocatively by healing a man on the Sabbath. The Jews complain (5.16), and he answers in christological terms (5.17). There is renewed complaint (5.18), and from this the discourse proceeds. Another example is provided by chapter 7. Jesus eventually appears in Jerusalem at the Feast of Tabernacles. The very fact of his presence and teaching provokes the characteristically expressed question (7.15): πῶς οὗτος γράμματα οἶδεν μὴ μεμαθηκώς; Jesus's reply leads up to the charge that his hearers are seeking to kill him. They take up this new point with the counter-charge (7.20): δαιμόνιον ἔχεις. Jesus replies. The Jews now raise a new objection (7.26f.): The origin of the Messiah will be unknown, whereas the origin of Jesus is well known. The chapter continues on these lines but the exchanges become so rapid that we are dealing here rather with a conversation than with a discourse developed in terms of objections to which responses are made. Further examples of the method can be found in chapters 8, 10, 12, and (*mutatis mutandis*, for here we have not the objections of the Jews but the remarks, often unintelligent, of the disciples) in chapters 13–16.

If it is correct to regard 6.52, and not 6.51c, as the beginning of a unit, certain consequences will follow, especially: (1) In the 'sapiential' part of the discourse on the bread of life there are not merely obscure eucharistic hints but an explicit reference to σάρξ. (2) What is said in verses 53–8 must be regarded as essentially a reply to the question πῶς . . .; (v. 52); that is, it provides some elucidation, or perhaps a special illustration, of the matter that precedes, explaining it in practical terms.

We turn then to the contents of verses 53–8, regarded as an answer to the question of verse 52, itself provoked by the final proposition of the earlier passage. Jesus announces that the bread he will give is his flesh; this leads to the question, How can this man give us flesh to eat? It is important to note that the question does not correspond exactly to what Jesus said. He refers to his flesh; the Jews speak of flesh.[11] The distinction is important, and must be borne in mind when we reach verse 63.[12] Throughout the paragraph, verses 53–8, Jesus continues to refer to 'my flesh' and the 'flesh of the Son of man'. By failing to see this point the Jews show that they are still in the position of those who (according to verse 26) sought Jesus not because they had seen signs (and recognized them as such) but because they had been satisfied with bread. Compare 2.19f., where men fail to understand that the temple Jesus speaks of, and will raise up, is the temple of *his body*. It is thus specifically the flesh *of Jesus* which is the bread of life; understand what he says as applying to flesh in general and his claims will fail to make sense. But in what sense or context is *his flesh* to be understood? The inclusion, in verses 53, 54, 55, 56, of references also to blood makes it very difficult to question[13] that the Eucharist is in mind; but to recognize this is one thing, to understand how John thought of the Eucharist another. It is the fatal weakness of Bultmann's exposition and critical handling of this passage that he assumes that because John alludes to the Eucharist he must understand it in a sense determined by the famous Ignatian φάρμακον ἀθανασίας, ἀντίδοτος τοῦ μὴ ἀποθανεῖν (Ignatius, *Ephesians* 20.2). Whether Ignatius meant by these words that a man needed only to consume the consecrated

bread and wine in order to be assured of immortality is a question
that cannot be taken up here; even if he did, this would not carry
with it the implication that John's thought was identical. Verses
53f. taken alone might suggest this: He who eats and drinks has
eternal life; he who does not eat and drink does not have life; that
which is eaten and drunk is therefore φάρμακον ἀθανασίας. This,
however, is a superficial logic, for it assumes that eating the flesh
and drinking the blood of the Son of man are to be simply identified
with eating and drinking consecrated bread and wine; but what
John means by eating and drinking the Son of man's flesh and
blood is a question that still has to be answered. How is an answer
to be found?

In the first place, verse 63 must be taken into account. The
questions raised by this verse are not stilled by saying that in it
flesh means simply a part or aspect of human nature, for it was
precisely this human σάρξ that the Logos became (1.14). The flesh,
however, that the Logos made his own is not mere flesh, which (as
a matter of common sense, not to say theology) John could not have
described as something that men must eat. Verse 63 in fact corrects
the mistake which we saw was made by the Jews in verse 52. *Flesh*
as a substance could provide at most a temporary good: the fathers
ate flesh in the desert, and it sustained their life for a time, but in the
end they died (v. 49). It is *the flesh of the Son of man*, the vehicle of the
Spirit and the mouthpiece of the Word, that sustains life for ever, or
rather, sustains life and also carries with it the promise of resurrection at the last day. The significance of this phrase I have discussed
elsewhere;[14] it is particularly important to note that it occurs in a
context that alludes to the Eucharist, for its effect is to rule out an
Ignatian interpretation of John's words. It is true that John says,
'He who eats my flesh and drinks my blood has eternal life'; but
precisely by adding, 'And I will raise him up at the last day', he
denies that the eating and drinking confer immortality. The eater
still has to be raised up at the last day; the Eucharist, indeed the
spiritual communion also to which it points, is not a recipe for
immortality.

It must be remembered that this concluding paragraph (vv.
53–8) of the discourse is an answer to the question πῶς . . .; (v. 52).
To facilitate his answer John introduces the Eucharist, to which his
attitude in general may be described as neither rejection nor sacramentarianism, but as one of critical acceptance. It would be hard to

find in John's age Christians who completely rejected the notion of
a common Christian meal linked in some way with the presence of
the Lord himself, and there were undoubtedly some[15] whose acceptance was uncritical in the extreme. That John should have
rejected the practice of holding a common meal is *a priori* improbable; that he should have been critical[16] of the way in which some
of his contemporaries observed the practice is *a priori* probable, and
is borne out by the evidence. The criticism is brought out, as we have
seen, explicitly but negatively by verse 63; verses 56, 57, 58 are perhaps even more important. Verse 56 insists that 'eating and drinking'
means mutual indwelling. We have in this verse an identity, and the
indwelling is as much an explanation of what 'eating and drinking'
means as vice versa; this simply takes up the earlier part of the
discourse. Verse 57 is more important still because (like, e.g., 17.18;
20.21) it draws a parallel between the relation of the believer to
Christ and the relation of Christ to the Father. There is only one
sense in which it can be said that Jesus the Son feeds upon the
Father; this is given by the words of 4.34, 'My food is to do the will
of him that sent me.' Jesus lives by and for the Father (διὰ τὸν
Πατέρα) who sent him; the believer lives by and for Jesus (δι'
ἐμέ) and thus 'eats and drinks' Jesus as Jesus 'eats and drinks' the
Father, in obedience and faith. Verse 58 makes the same point
negatively: the fathers in the desert ate the manna and the flesh of
the quails in a literal sense, but believers will eat οὐ καθὼς ἔφαγον οἱ
πατέρες. The whole discourse is about this kind of relation between
the believer and Jesus, this kind of feeding upon the bread of life.
The image of feeding, however, finds a focus in the Eucharist, and
John uses this, just as he uses that other focus, the miracle of the
loaves, but he is careful to show that each of these is not an end in
itself but points to a more significant kind of relation.

It is at this point that we may raise explicitly the question towards which this essay has been aimed. When John in 6.53 introduces
an unmistakable reference to the Eucharist he does so in terms of the
Son of man: ἐὰν μὴ φάγητε τὴν σάρκα τοῦ υἱοῦ τοῦ ἀνθρώπου. Why?
And what exactly does he mean in this context by *Son of man*?[17] It
will be well to recall that 'Son of man' occurs in two other verses in
the chapter: 6.27: τὴν βρῶσιν τὴν μένουσαν . . . ἣν ὁ υἱὸς τοῦ ἀνθρώπου
ὑμῖν δώσει; and 6.62: ἐὰν οὖν θεωρῆτε τὸν υἱὸν τοῦ ἀνθρώπου
ἀναβαίνοντα. It should also be noted that verse 54 contains a parallel
expression in which *the flesh of the Son of man* is replaced by *my flesh*.

This, however, is hardly a case for the application (even if it is right!) of Jeremias's rule,[18] that where parallel sayings occur, the one using 'Son of man' and the other not, the latter is more probably authentic. We are not dealing with a traditional saying transmitted in two forms but with Johannine composition. It would have been clumsy to repeat 'of the Son of man'; 'my' has the same meaning. This observation will apply not only to verse 54 but also to verses 55 and 56, though with diminishing force, as the reader tends to forget that Jesus is being defined as the Son of man. This very fact, however, makes it clear that it would have been easy in verse 53 also to write *my flesh*; why does John not do so? Several considerations contribute to an answer to this question.

1 It may be that John was affected by a tradition connecting the Eucharist and the Son of man. There is little trace of such a tradition in the Synoptic Gospels, in none of which is *Son of man* introduced into the words of institution. It is, however, very closely connected with them in Mark (and Matthew) where the prediction that the Son of man is departing[19] and the warning to his betrayer immediately precede (Mark 14.21; Matt. 26.24) the saying about the bread, τοῦτό ἐστιν τὸ σῶμά μου (Mark 14.22; Matt. 26.26). In Luke the order is reversed (22.19, τοῦτό ἐστιν τὸ σῶμά μου; 22.22, ὁ υἱὸς τοῦ ἀνθρώπου . . . πορεύεται). As a somewhat more remote connection, it may be mentioned that the Lucan supper narrative contains the Q saying in which Jesus promises (22.28–30) that those who have continued with him in his tribulations shall eat and drink at his table in his Kingdom, and shall sit on thrones judging the twelve tribes. The Matthean form of this saying (19.28) uses the term Son of man.

Another indirect connection is to be found in the simple fact of the eschatological content of the Last Supper and Lord's Supper material, as attested in the synoptic sayings about the Kingdom of God (Mark 14.25; Matt. 26.29; Luke 22.16, 18), and more particularly in the ἄχρι οὗ ἔλθῃ of 1 Corinthians 11.26 and the use of the Aramaic *Marana tha*, occurring at 1 Corinthians 16.22[20] and in the prescriptions for the celebration of the Eucharist in *Didache* 10.6. The hope for the coming of the Lord, which seems to have flourished not least in a eucharistic setting, was bound up in the tradition with the prophecy (or what was understood to be the prophecy) of the coming of the Son of man.

More important perhaps than any of these observations is the fact that it is precisely in the context, already referred to, in which Ignatius speaks of the Eucharist as φάρμακον ἀθανασίας (*Ephesians* 20.2) that he describes Jesus as Son of man. When the Christians come together to break bread it is ἐν μιᾷ πίστει καὶ [ἐν] ἑνὶ 'Ιησοῦ Χριστῷ . . . τῷ υἱῷ ἀνθρώπου καὶ υἱῷ θεοῦ. It is possible but not probable that Ignatius knew John as a piece of literature,[21] but that there was common Antiochene tradition known to both Ignatius and John is a not improbable hypothesis, and the Antiochene Eucharist may have associated the Son of man with the eucharistic elements. The *Acts of John* are more likely to be dependent on the Gospel than to offer independent evidence for the existence of a traditional connection between Son of man and Eucharist, but it is worthwhile to note that in John's eucharistic prayer (*Acts of John* 109) there occurs in a long list of adulatory epithets the phrase τὸν δι' ἡμᾶς λεχθέντα υἱὸν ἀνθρώπου.[22] Also dependent on John, but not unimportant because it shows how some at least interpreted the Gospel, is the *Gospel of Philip*. In the *Gospel of Philip*[23] the term flesh is explained. First, 1 Corinthians 15.50 is quoted: 'Flesh and blood shall not inherit the kingdom of God.' Philip continues:

> What is this which will not inherit? This which we have. But what is this which will inherit? That which belongs to Jesus with his blood. Because of this he said: He who shall not eat my flesh and drink my blood has no life in him. What is it? His flesh is the logos, and his blood is the Holy Spirit.

No difficulty was felt, we may note, though it was thought proper to remark upon it, in the fact that σάρξ is used in different senses. At an earlier point,[24] Christ as the dispenser of heavenly food is described as the perfect man.

> Man used to feed like the beasts, but when Christ came, the perfect man, he brought bread from heaven in order that man might be nourished with the food of man. (Compare *Philip* 100.[25])

Any traditional connection there may have been between Son of man and the Eucharist (or the Last Supper) is less important than the theological content and implications of the term, though these may be handled in shorter compass.

2 The Son of man is a suitable description for a figure who descends from heaven. The theme of descent runs throughout the discourse. It is suggested in the first instance by the descent of the

manna (Exod. 16.4; cf. Ps. 78.23f.), and the parallel and contrast with this are stated in characteristically ambiguous terms in 6.33, where ὁ καταβαίνων ἐκ τοῦ οὐρανοῦ may be 'he who comes down from heaven' or 'that (bread) which comes down from heaven'. In verse 35 Jesus makes it clear that he himself is the bread, and in verse 38 the logical implication is expressed in his καταβέβηκα – he has himself come down from heaven. The two points are put together in verse 41: ἐγώ εἰμι ὁ ἄρτος ὁ καταβάς. Verses 50f. make the same identification, verse 51c introduces the further identification of the bread with the flesh of Jesus and verse 58 resumes the whole. Descent is further implied in verse 62, for if the Son of man ascends to his former position he must at some point have descended from that position. Earlier pictures of a Son of man figure had usually described him in movement as ἐρχόμενος (Dan. 7.13; Mark 8.38; 13.16; 14.62; etc.), and this word does not in itself make clear whether he is coming or going, to heaven or earth, from heaven or earth. There is no need in this essay to attempt to settle the original meaning of Daniel 7.13; what is clear is that ἔρχεσθαι holds in itself a convenient ambiguity, and that this was made use of by Christians who alluded to the verse. It is, however, in John that the ambiguity is systematically exploited. The double movement of the Son of man is explicit in 3.13 (οὐδεὶς ἀναβέβηκεν ... εἰ μὴ ὁ ... καταβάς, ὁ υἱὸς τοῦ ἀνθρώπου). Only here and in 6.62 is the verb ἀναβαίνειν used, but immediately after 3.13 ἀναβαίνειν is replaced by ὑψωθῆναι (3.14), which recurs at 8.28 and 12.34; its double meaning (lift up on the cross – exalt to heaven) evidently appealed to the Evangelist. One aspect of ὑψωθῆναι is also covered by δοξάζειν (12.23; 13.31), and we should add 1.51, where the angels are said ἀναβαίνειν and καταβαίνειν on the Son of man.

It now becomes clear that, if it was John's intention to introduce into his discourse, in order to give it concreteness and to balance the sign that prompted it, an allusion to the Eucharist, and to identify the bread that comes down from heaven with the flesh and blood of a person, it would be natural for him to describe that person as the Son of man, who also descends from heaven. This observation harmonizes with the other two occurrences of 'Son of man' in the chapter. At 6.27 it is said that the Son of man will give you abiding food, and John adds, τοῦτον γὰρ ὁ πατὴρ ἐσφράγισεν ὁ θεός. God vouched for the Son of man (probably by giving him the Spirit, cf. 1.32f.) when he sent him on his mission, that is, when he came down from heaven. In 6.61f., Jesus asks, 'Does this offend you? What then if you see the Son of man ascending where he was before?' Some maintain that the scandal lies in the demand that men should eat the flesh and drink the blood of the Son of man, others that it is his descent.[26] But in truth these interpretations can hardly be separated. He descends in order to give his flesh and blood.

3 The last observation leads to a further point. The Son of man is a suitable term for a self-giving figure. The background of this hardly needs exposition. It is sufficient to quote Mark 10.45 ($\mathring{\eta}\lambda\theta\epsilon\nu$ $\acute{o}$ $vi\grave{o}s$ $\tauο\hat{v}$ $\mathring{a}\nu\theta\rho\acute{\omega}\pi ου$ . . . $δο\hat{v}ναι$ $\tau\grave{\eta}\nu$ $\psi υ\chi\grave{\eta}\nu$ $α\mathring{v}\tauο\hat{v}$) and to recall that in the Synoptic Gospels the predictions of the Passion are regularly cast in 'Son of man' sayings. The authenticity of these sayings is not a relevant question here; that they existed in tradition available when John wrote is beyond question. The synoptic Son of man gives himself for others; this is no less true of the Son of man in 6.53, especially if on the one hand we recall Jeremias's argument[27] that flesh and blood represent the whole human person (which will be true for John, whether or not Jeremias is right in seeing here the earliest form of the eucharistic words), and on the other note that verse 53 answers verse 52 which was provoked by verse 51, where Jesus speaks of his flesh as $\mathring{v}\pi\grave{\epsilon}\rho$ $\tau\hat{\eta}s$ $\tauο\hat{v}$ $κ\acute{o}σμου$ $ζω\hat{\eta}s$.

What is the outcome of these remarks, which have been prompted by, rather than focused upon, the use of 'Son of man' in John 6.53?

1 They help to demonstrate the unity of the chapter. The three references to Son of man cohere; what is more, the use of 'Son of man' in 6.53 introduces into verses 52–8 the theme of descent which is so characteristic of verses 35–50 and is implied by verse 62, but otherwise appears in verses 51–8 only at 58, which on any showing can be regarded as a summary of the discourse as a whole.

2 They suggest that a primary source of John's thought about the Son of man was the synoptic tradition rather than extra-biblical speculation about a heavenly man. It is true that the synoptic material has passed through John's mind and been transformed in the process. The notion of ascent and descent is shared but is by John inverted. In the synoptic tradition the Son of man after his suffering is exalted to heaven and comes from heaven as judge. In John[28] the first stage in the story is the descent of the Son of man from God to the world, the second is his ascent to where he was at the beginning. This means that the figure of the Son of man has virtually coalesced with that of the gnostic Revealer –

or of one so like the gnostic Revealer that it is not easy to distinguish them. John, however, does not relinquish that which is most characteristic of the synoptic Son of man: he gives himself for others.

NOTES

1 R. Bultmann, *The Gospel of John*, Eng. trans., Oxford 1971; also D. M. Smith, *The Composition and Order of the Fourth Gospel* (New Haven and London 1965), especially pp. 134–9.

2 R. E. Brown, *The Gospel according to John* (i–xii). New York 1966.

3 G. Bornkamm, *Geschichte und Glaube i* (*Gesammelte Aufsätze iii*). Munich 1968.

4 E. Schweizer, *Ego Eimi* . . . Göttingen 1939, ²1965.

5 E. Ruckstuhl, *Die literarische Einheit des Johannesevangeliums*. Freiburg i. d. Schweiz 1951.

6 E. Schweizer, in *Evangelische Theologie* 12 (1952–3), pp. 341–62, especially pp. 353–6.

7 J. Jeremias, in *Zeitschrift für die neutestamentliche Wissenschaft* 44 (1952–3), pp. 256f.

8 P. Borgen, *Bread from Heaven*. Leiden 1965.

9 J. L. Martyn, *History and Theology in the Fourth Gospel* (New York and Evanston 1968), pp. 116f., 138.

10 As, for example, Nestle, *Novum Testamentum Graece* and other familiar editions do.

11 P⁶⁶ B and a few other Greek manuscripts, supported by some of the versions, including the Latin and Syriac, add αὐτοῦ, probably by assimilation to the preceding verse.

12 See p. 43.

13 See pp. 84–92.

14 *New Testament Essays* (London 1972), pp. 52, 66–9.

15 Especially in Corinth; see especially 1 Cor. 10.1–13; 11.27–34.

16 As Paul was, over against the Corinthians. See note 15.

17 It is unnecessary to emphasize that in this essay no attempt is made to deal with the 'Son of man' problem as a whole.

18 *Zeitschrift für die neutestamentliche Wissenschaft* 58 (1967), pp. 164–170.

19 We may compare the Johannine sayings about the ἀναβαίνειν of the Son of man, especially 6.62.

20 Possibly, but not certainly, in a eucharistic setting; see C. K. Barrett, *The First Epistle to the Corinthians* (London 1968), p. 398.

21 See C. K. Barrett, *The Gospel according to St John* (London ²1978), pp. 110f.

22 Lipsius–Bonnet ii, 208. 2.

23 Pp. 104.32–105.7. Numbering according to Schenke.

24 Schenke 15; p. 103.10–14.

25 P. 123.15–21.

26 See pp. 38f.

27 J. Jeremias, *Die Abendmahlsworte Jesu* (Göttingen ⁴1967), pp. 191–4.

28 Except perhaps in ch. 5.

4

THE THEOLOGICAL VOCABULARY OF
THE FOURTH GOSPEL AND OF THE
GOSPEL OF TRUTH

That there exists a relation of some kind between the Fourth Gospel and non-Christian Gnosticism is scarcely open to question; exactly what this relation is, is one of the most disputed problems in current New Testament scholarship. It is even clearer and more certain that the Fourth Gospel, whatever its origin may have been, passed quickly into the hands of Christian Gnostics before it was recovered by the orthodox as their most powerful weapon in the struggle against gnostic heresy. Evidently the language of the Fourth Gospel is more gnostic than its thought, and the suggestion is probably correct that the Evangelist used gnostic terminology with the intention of rebutting gnostic ideas; but the processes by which this goal was reached remain obscure. A good deal of light, however, has been thrown upon them by the discovery of the so-called Gospel of Truth.[1] All that will be assumed about this document in the present essay is that it emerged from gnostic (probably Valentinian) circles about the middle of the second century; to discuss the question of its origin would occupy space which will be required for other matters. The aim of this essay is strictly limited. It will seek a clarification of the relation between Johannine thought and the Gnosticism of the Gospel of Truth by comparative examination of their theological vocabularies. The Fourth Gospel has a limited and distinctive vocabulary, which provides a useful means of investigation. It need not be said that in a sketch of this kind completeness cannot be achieved or even thought of; but the words discussed will be representative and important words, and on the basis of them some significant results may be obtained.

We shall consider first words characteristic of the Fourth Gospel but almost entirely absent from the Gospel of Truth; next, words that are used in both Gospels,[2] but with a marked difference in meaning. Finally, conclusions will be drawn.

I

1   The fundamental thought of John is that the Father *sent* the
Son to be the Saviour of the world; it is because he is sent that the
Son has authority, and because he is the Father's envoy that in him
and in his mission men encounter the Father himself. In turn, the
Son sends his disciples into the world, so that in them and their work
he himself is truly present. The centrality of this thought is represented by the fact that in John ἀποστέλλειν is used twenty-eight times
(ἀπόστολος once), and the synonym πέμπειν thirty-two times.[3]
   In *EV* the word 'send' (*jaw*) is used only once.

41.23–8

> The place to which they send out their thoughts, that place is
> their root, which lifts them up through all heights, even unto
> the Father.

The subject of *jaw* is the emanations; in their sending out their
thoughts there is no parallel to John. The word (*tiē*) which is here
rendered 'emanation'[4] is itself of uncertain meaning and not necessarily connected with sending. We conclude that this feature of
Johannine vocabulary is not represented in *EV*.
   2   In John the word 'glory' (δόξα) occurs eighteen times, and
'glorify' (δοξάζειν) twenty-three (twenty-two) times. The story of
Jesus can be told in terms of glory – he has laid aside but will
resume the glory he had with the Father before creation; he seeks
not his own glory but the glory of the Father, yet in his voluntary
humiliation and obedience, and pre-eminently in the disgrace of the
cross, he is glorified and manifests his glory (e.g., 2.11; 8.50; 12.23;
17.5). There is a characteristic Johannine paradox here;[5] but in
EV there is little of the language and none of the paradox of glory.
It is said of the little ones who have knowledge of the Father[6] that
'they were glorified, they glorified' (19.33f.). The emanations, or
pleromas, have not been deprived of the glory of the Father (42.3f.;
cf. 41.1, '. . . that he might glorify the pleroma').[7]
   Two passages recall more closely the Johannine use of glory.

23.26f. and 43.16ff.

> His (God's) glory, it (the knowledge of God) has exalted.
> His (God's) Spirit rejoices in him, and glorifies him in whom
> it exists

With these may be compared John 17.4 ($\dot{\epsilon}\gamma\dot{\omega}$ $\sigma\epsilon$ $\dot{\epsilon}\delta\delta\xi\alpha\sigma\alpha$) and 16.14 ($\dot{\epsilon}\kappa\epsilon\hat{\iota}\nu\sigma$, the Paraclete, $\dot{\epsilon}\mu\dot{\epsilon}$ $\delta\sigma\xi\dot{\alpha}\sigma\epsilon\iota$). But there is in *EV* no parallel to the thought that glory emerges out of the obedient fulfilment of the Father's will in humiliation and love.

3   The difference between John and *EV* is nowhere clearer than in their treatment of sin – or rather, in *EV*'s almost complete failure to treat the subject at all. In John, $\dot{\alpha}\mu\alpha\rho\tau\dot{\alpha}\nu\epsilon\iota\nu$ occurs three (four) times; $\dot{\alpha}\mu\alpha\rho\tau\dot{\iota}\alpha$, seventeen (eighteen) times; $\dot{\alpha}\mu\alpha\rho\tau\omega\lambda\dot{\delta}s$, four times. The ultimate barrier between man and God is sin (8.21; 9.41); hence it is sin that the Lamb of God must take away (1.29). It is thus particularly striking that the word 'sin' (*nabi*) occurs only twice in *EV*.

32.35–9

> (You) are to speak of the truth with those who seek it, and of the gnosis with those who, in their error (*planē*), have sinned. You are the children of the understanding of the heart.

Those who stand over against the sinners are 'children of understanding' – in a word, Gnostics. Sin is the result of error, *planē*. This transliterated Greek word is common in *EV*; it represents the enemy who seeks to destroy the Redeemer and must itself be destroyed (see 18.22ff.).[8] Error, however, is scarcely a real enemy. It is simply the negation of *gnosis* and is annulled by the communication of knowledge (e.g., 26.23–7).

35.25–9

> It (incorruption) followed him who had sinned, in order that he might come to rest. For forgiveness is that which remained for the light in defilement [due to *hulē*; cf. line 9], (namely) the word of the pleroma.

The meaning of this obscure passage seems to be that the forgiveness of sins is simply the release of the light-particles which are imprisoned in matter.

It can hardly be gainsaid that John's use of words of the $\dot{\alpha}\mu\alpha\rho\tau$- group[9] and *EV*'s preference for *planē* disclose a radical divergence between the two documents.

4   Study of the words dealing with judgement reveals a corresponding difference. John uses the verb $\kappa\rho\dot{\iota}\nu\epsilon\iota\nu$ nineteen times; the noun $\kappa\rho\dot{\iota}\mu\alpha$ once; and the noun $\kappa\rho\dot{\iota}\sigma\iota s$ eleven times. The theme of

judgement (like that of glory) is complex. God did not send his Son into the world to judge it (3.17), and the Son himself disavows the purpose of judging (8.15); yet the Father has committed all judgement to the Son (5.22), and the Son declares that it was for judgement that he came into the world (9.39). In this paradox a good deal of Johannine theology is contained.

25.25—26.15

In *EV* only one passage, and that a very obscure one, deals with judgement. The author uses an allegory based on jars (the word used is a transliteration of *skeuos*). No loss is incurred, but gain, when a number of old, unsound jars are broken and replaced by others which are full and perfect. He proceeds:

> For such is the judgement (*krisis*) which has come from on high, which has judged each one, a drawn sword with a two-edged blade[10] which cuts on one side and on the other. When the Word appeared, the Word which is in the hearts of those who pronounce it – and it was not only a sound but had taken a body – a great confusion reigned among the jars, for some had been emptied, others filled;[11] some were provided for, others were overthrown; some were purified, still others were broken to pieces.

There is here a certain amount of parallelism with John. The opening words may perhaps recall John 3.19; more important is the two-edged effect of the Word of God,[12] which empties and fills, shatters and purifies. But (and here we may recall what has been said about *sin*) the basis of this twofold operation is never laid bare as it is in John. The context (see 26.19) characteristically goes on to speak of error (*planē*) and of its destruction by *gnosis*. The reiterated Johannine emphasis on the theme of judgement is also wanting.

Two observations may be made about these words in regard to which there is a maximum of divergence between John and *EV*. First, the eschatological motif which runs throughout the New Testament, including John, is missing in *EV*. The sending of the Son, in fulfilment of the divine purpose, is an eschatological theme; so is judgement, and so is glory. It is true that the New Testament writers, and John in particular, speak of judgement as operating, and of glory as manifested, in the present as well as in the future, but they do so in virtue of the shift in 'centre of gravity' brought about by the historic mission of Jesus. They are in fact compelled to speak of his mission in these terms because their primary interpretation of it is eschatological. But *EV* views it in a different light.

Second, *EV* diagnoses the human situation which is the scene and occasion of the work of redemption in terms of ignorance rather than sin. This is not merely a linguistic difference but affects radically the substance of the two works.

2

In the following words, or groups of words, the difference in relative density of distribution is less marked, but difference in usage remains.

1   John does in fact speak of *love* much more frequently than does *EV*, but it would be impossible to say that the theme is absent, or virtually absent, from the latter. In John ἀγαπᾶν is used thirty-seven times, the noun ἀγάπη seven times. In addition, φιλεῖν is used thirteen times, and φίλος six times. On statistical grounds alone it would be impossible to question the centrality of love in the Evangelist's thought. Love exists within the Godhead, between Father and Son (3.35; 14.31). Love for the world led to the mission of the incarnate Son (3.16), who loved his own to the utmost (13.1). He required in turn that they should love him (14.21) and love one another (13.34). The meaning of this love appears in 15.13: it is most clearly manifested when the lover lays down his life for those whom he loves. The parallel with 10.11 (τίθημι) shows that the cross is in mind. Love (in John) is not acquisitive but gives itself utterly for and to the beloved.

This theme is perhaps not completely absent from *EV* (cf. 20.27–30) but it plays only a very small part. The evidence is as follows.

(a)   The Greek word ἀγάπη is three times transliterated. When the Word of God came forth,

23.30f.

His (the Father's) love became a body (*sōma*) upon him (the Word).

At first, this seems to be in close harmony with Johannine thought, because it appears to mean that it was God's love that caused the divine Word to assume bodily form. But the context, which speaks also of God's joy, glory, image and faith, shows that *EV* does not treat the body of Christ with John's realism or entertain the same radical view of God's love.

Towards its close, *EV* speaks of 'the true brothers, over whom is spread the love of the Father' (43.5ff.). Here too parallelism, but also devaluation of the idea of love, may be observed. In John also, Jesus loves *his own*; but *EV* knows little (but cf. perhaps 34.30f.) of God's love for the world, which forms a second focus in the Johannine pattern of love.

(b)   The Coptic word *maïe* is used (in different forms) four times. *EV* 30.31f., which refers to the beloved (*menrit*, adjective) Son need not detain us. In another passage the author speaks of God[13]

19.10–14

as one whom many people do not know, and who desires that they should know him and that thus they should love him.

There is nothing here that is contrary to Johannine thought, but the emphasis is different. Note (1) that God desires that men should love him – nothing is said of his love for men; (2) the close connection between knowledge and love, knowledge being the prior term – men must *know* and *thus* love.

In 26.33, it is said that all the emanations of truth love truth. Here should be noted not only the mythological language about emanations but also the essential kinship which is the ground of love: like loves like. So also in 34.1–4.

(c)   A different Coptic word (*wōshe*) is once rendered by 'love' in the English translation of *EV*.[14] The last words of *EV* (in this translation) run:

43.19–24

His children are perfect and worthy of his name, for they are children such as he, the Father, loves.[15]

The normal meaning of *wōshe* is 'will', hence 'desire'. It is perhaps rightly translated here, but if so this is highly significant for the doctrine of love, for in *EV* the Father loves his perfect children in the sense of *desiring* them; his love is not sacrificial but acquisitive.

2   There is no great difference between John and *EV* in the frequency with which each uses terms denoting *salvation*. In John σώζειν occurs six times, σωτήρ and σωτηρία once each. In *EV* the following passages come under consideration. In 16.36—17.1 the Coptic word *sōte* and a transliteration of *sōter* are used.

16.36—17.1

The Word is he whom they call the Saviour (*sōter*), for that is the
name of the work which he is to accomplish for the salvation
(*sōte*) of those who were ignorant of the Father.

Here it appears at once that the Saviour saves men from ignorance
(nothing is said of sin),[16] and does so (as the following pages show)[17]
by banishing error and oblivion and revealing the truth.

In four passages the root *ujeei* is used; 31.18 and 35.1 ('those who
wait for the salvation which comes from above') deal with salvation
in general terms.

31.16–19

He gave them thought and intelligence and mercy and salvation
and the spirit of strength.

The reference to thought and intelligence is significant, and so is the
following statement that when the Son 'caused punishments and
tortures to cease' (31.21f.) it was by destroying and confounding
them 'with the *gnosis*' (31.27).

The reference in 20.8 is more interesting. The divine work of redemption is expressed under the figure of a book,[18] the living book
of the living which was in the mind and in the thought of the
Father (19.35—20.1). Jesus accepted and endured suffering until
he should have taken possession of the book (20.10ff.). In the
meantime,

20.6–9

No one among those who believed in salvation was able to become
manifest as long as that book had not made its appearance –

that is, until after the death and victory of Jesus. So far as this means
that salvation became effective through the cross and resurrection,
it is in full accord with the New Testament, and in particular with
John. Significant differences, however, appear when we read on to
see what salvation means.

21.3–8

Those who are to receive the teaching, the living who are in-
scribed in the book of the living, they receive the teaching for

themselves alone. They receive it from the Father, they turn anew towards him.

These fortunate persons were registered in advance (21.23), and in due course their names were called (21.27). For those not registered, whose names were not called, there is no hope; they will be destroyed (21.30-7). This is a strictly amoral kind of predestination, quite different from John's.[19] It is never integrated into the work and person of Jesus, even though it is he who, after his suffering, takes the book (20.24), and it offers no parallel to the 'whosoever believeth' of John 3.16.

Salvation is mentioned in only one other passage, which should be quoted at length.

32.18-39

He laboured, even on the Sabbath, for the lamb whom he found fallen into a pit.[20] He saved the life of that lamb, having caused it to be lifted out of the pit – in order that you may know, in your hearts, what is that Sabbath in the course of which salvation must not remain inactive; in order that you may say of that day from on high which has no night, and of the light which does not fail, because it is perfect – that you may say then in your hearts that it is you who are this perfect day, and that it is in you that this light, which does not fail, dwells, that you may speak of the truth with those who seek it, and of the *gnosis* with those who in their error have sinned. You are the children of the understanding of the heart.

Lines 23ff. recall John 5.17; the Father does not cease from his redemptive work on the Sabbath – indeed (it is implied) his redemptive work in Christ *is* that which the Sabbath represents. So here. The saved enter into the life of the eternal day in which there is no night. This is the true Sabbath.[21] Notwithstanding, however, the close (probably literary) contact with John, the paragraph in its last lines runs out into unmistakably gnostic language.

3   After 'salvation' it is natural to take the term 'life'. This is very common in John ($\zeta\omega\dot\eta$ thirty-six [thirty-five] times; $\zeta\tilde\eta\nu$ seventeen times; $\zeta\omega\sigma\pi\omega\epsilon\tilde\iota\nu$ three times); it is much less common in *EV*, but the few passages provide some striking parallels.

In John it is said that the Son has life in himself (5.26); this is implied also in *EV*:

20.28ff.

He abases himself even unto death, though clothed with immortal life.

There is real parallelism here, but it is right to add that *EV* goes
on to describe the triumph of Christ as his divesting himself of 'these
perishable rags' (20.30f.). This is very different from the bodily
resurrection described in John.

By his death, Jesus made life available for men.

20.10–14

For this reason, Jesus, the merciful and faithful, patiently accepted the endurance of suffering until such time as he should
have taken possession of that book,[22] since he knew that his death
meant life for many.

This fundamentally Christian conception recalls many New Testament passages; but once more it appears that the suffering of Jesus
is completely external to those for whom he suffers, just as their
need is essentially external to themselves. It is not suggested that
their personal guilt leads to, or is removed by, the death of Jesus.

Other passages to be noted are 25.19 and 31.16, but they contribute little to the matter. Finally we may again[23] refer to 32.18–22,
where, for the shepherd's act in 'saving the life' of the lamb, it is
not the word 'save' (*ujeei*) but a causative form (*t^{e}nho*) of 'life'
(*ōn^{e}h*) that is used.

4   Last in this group we may consider a set of words which are
characteristic of both Gospels: light and darkness, day and night.
According to John, Jesus himself is the ἀληθινὸν φῶς (1.9; cf. 8.12),
attested by secondary lights, such as John the Baptist (5.35; cf.
1.8). The darkness which follows daylight limits men's work and
even the work of Jesus himself (9.4). This does not mean that darkness can overpower light (1.5); darkness is not a term for an absolute mode of being, existing in its own right, but a metaphor
describing what life becomes when the Creator is rejected. It follows
that the shining of light is a process of judgement, in which it becomes clear whether men will turn to or from God (3.19ff.). It is
characteristic of John that for him light and darkness are not static
terms but describe God in motion, as it were, towards his world, and
the negative response of the world to this movement. This *is* judge-

ment; but behind the judgement, and giving depth to it, is the thought of salvation, of that which God does for man by coming to him (8.12: . . . ἕξει τὸ φῶς τῆς ζωῆς).

The word group occurs with similar frequency in *EV*. *Waein* (light) occurs in nominal and verbal forms seventeen times; *kekei* (darkness) three times; *hōw* (day) twice; *ūshē* (night) three times. 'Day' and 'night', however, are not such significant and interesting terms in *EV* as in John.

Several passages may first be disposed of in which light and darkness are purely figurative and contribute to the context nothing more than greater vividness:

24.32—25.3

As a person's ignorance, at the moment when he comes to know, disappears of its own accord; as darkness dissolves at the appearance of light; so also deficiency is eliminated by the fact of plenitude.

We may add from the same context:

25.12–19

By means of a *gnosis*, he shall purify himself of diversity with a view to unity, by engulfing the matter within him like a flame, darkness by light and death by life.

In these passages light and darkness are no more than metaphors; it is, however, well to observe the negative view of evil which is implied: it is a void, which may be filled up by God's fullness, as darkness is the absence of light.

The next passage takes us a little further.

28.24–32

What then is it that he desires man to think? This: 'I am as the shadows and phantoms of the night.' When the light of dawn appears, this man understands that the terror he had apprehended was nothing.

Man as a prey to evil is like one who suffers the illusions of bad dreams. This figure is continued through the following pages. 'As long as ignorance inspired them with terror and confusion . . .

there were many illusions by which they were haunted, and empty
fictions, as if they were sunk in sleep, as if they found themselves a
prey to troubled dreams' (29.1–11). The coming of truth and the
consequent dispersal of these fantasies is like the coming of daylight.

30.2–6

They abandon them as they would a dream of the night, and
they esteem the *gnosis* of the Father as they would the light.

Thus darkness (ignorance) *seems* to constitute a real attack upon
man, though in truth it is unreal. Man does not need to be transformed but to perceive the truth, though in fact this perception will
effect a transformation.

Further passages make clearer the relation, already implied,
between illumination and divine revelation. Revelation is given
through the Son of God.

31.13–16

Light spoke through his mouth, and his voice engendered life.

The metaphor is violent, but its violence is significant. It was that
which came out of the Son's mouth, that is, his teaching, that was
light. The Son communicated to men *gnosis*, which is light and life.
It is for men to receive this and turn to God.

30.32—31.1

He appeared, instructing them about the Father, that incom-
prehensible One. He inspired them with that which is in the
Mind (of God), while accomplishing his will. Many received
light and turned towards him.[24]

Compare

18.16–21

Through him he enlightened those who were in darkness because of oblivion. He enlightened them, and indicated a path;
and that path is the truth which he taught them.

Enlightenment is the communication of true knowledge taught by
the Son, Jesus Christ. Cf. 36.10f., 'the light of truth'.

Two further passages may be considered. One has already been quoted (32.22–34; see p. 57). Here there is clear but not close contact with John. The Johannine statement that Jesus is the light of the world (8.12) is related to the Sabbath miracle and Sabbath controversy in John 9; and in the similar miracle and controversy of John 5 the idea of God's continuous beneficence is used; but John never develops the thought of the Sabbath as a day of perfect and unfailing *light*. It is very probable that *EV* represents a more developed stage of thought in which themes previously separate were combined. Note that in *EV* believers *are* the perfect day; light dwells in them.[25]

Finally, towards the close of *EV* we read:

43.9–16

It is they who manifest themselves truly since they are in that true and eternal life and speak of the perfect light filled with the seed of the Father, which is in his heart and in the pleroma . . .

'They' are the 'true brothers over whom is spread the love of the Father' (43.5ff.; see p. 55). They in turn become agents of the generative light which proceeds from the Father; cf. 31.15f., quoted above.

Study of this word group reveals only superficial contacts between John and *EV*. To speak of the Revealer as communicating light to men, and of those who receive revelation as being illuminated by it, is to use metaphors too obvious to be significant. John and *EV* each have a truly significant development of the theme of light, but these are different. In John, light (set over against darkness) means judgement. In *EV*, light suggests the eternal and perfect day of God, the Sabbath whose light never fails. This eternal daylight dwells in God's elect, who *are* God's Sabbath. John's treatment of light, though it shows God in movement towards men, at the same time emphasizes the difference between God and men, who are never anything other than creatures whom God judges.[26] The tendency of *EV* is rather to demonstrate a continuity between men (when freed from the illusions of darkness and error) and God.

These observations may be linked with what was said above (p. 53) about the disappearance of the primitive Christian eschatology from *EV*. This is at once the outcome and the cause of a less radical view of sin, an estimate of man's predicament which emphasizes less his rebellion against the will of the holy and righteous Lord than his misfortune in being attacked by supernatural (even if ultimately unreal) forces of ignorance. This view makes it possible to conceive a measure of continuity between man and God, and this in turn leads to a conception of God's attitude towards man and action on his behalf completely different from that found in John and in the rest of the New Testament. In the New Testament God is under no constraint of kinship to love his sinful creature: his love is a matter of free grace and is expressed most clearly and adequately in the forgiveness of sins. It scarcely exaggerates to say that in *EV*, notwithstanding the emotional appeal which its author undoubtedly found in the cross, God's love is erotic desire for what is ultimately a part of himself.

The belief that the evil situation in which man finds himself is due to ignorance leads also to a constant emphasis upon revelation and the divine work of teaching the truth – in a word (and it is a common word in *EV*), upon gnosis.

3

The material sketched here[27] does not permit a complete answer to the questions raised on page 50. The differences rather than the resemblances between John and *EV* have been brought out. This was intended, not least because most of the verbal contacts have already been shown.[28] It is easy, and true and profitable too, to say that the differences which have been demonstrated show the fundamentally biblical and anti-gnostic content of John. But how is John's gnostic terminology to be accounted for?

Alternatively we may ask, Why does *EV* differ from John in the ways in which it does differ? Does *EV* mark a further stage of development on the road already taken by John, or is it the result of the contamination of John by extraneous elements? If the former alternative is chosen, we must say that the 'development' was accompanied by much misunderstanding; and this in effect means that we are driven to the latter alternative, since misunderstandings must have causes.[29] It is for many reasons unlikely that a non-Christian Gnosticism arose full-grown between the writing of John and the writing of *EV* in such a way as to influence the author of the latter. We must speak (however slight the direct evidence may be) of a pre-Johannine (no doubt also of a pre-Christian) Gnosticism. And since John appears to use its language, we must assume that he was aware of it and took it into account. Was it then simply his intention to camouflage anti-gnostic thought in gnostic language, so as to deceive the deceived and win back captives from the devil's snare (2 Tim. 2.26)? The answer to this question will depend on the depth to which the parallels, the most important of which it has not been possible to mention here, run, and on the seriousness with which John took his theological vocabulary. Even when such words as light, darkness, life and salvation are considered, and still more when study is extended to son, father, word, truth and knowledge, it is difficult to doubt that John detected real theological appropriateness in the words he used, that in fact he was giving a Christianized – though that meant often an inverted – and always a historicized version of a way of thinking that was not simply too popular but also too near to and too far from the truth to be ignored. Gnosticism raised questions that the theologian could not ignore.

NOTES

1 I have given a short popular account of this document in *Expository Times*, 69 (1958), pp. 167–70. The fundamental edition of the text is by M. Malinine, H. C. Puech and G. Quispel (Zürich 1956). For the four pages of text missing from this edition, see W. Till, 'Die Kairener Seiten des Evangeliums der Wahrheit' in *Orientalia*, n.s. 28 (1959), pp. 170–85. I should like here to express my gratitude to my colleague Dr K. H. Kuhn, whom I have consulted on all points of Coptic scholarship. He is not, however, responsible for any views expressed in this essay.

2 See note 27. Henceforth, the Gospel of Truth (*Evangelium Veritatis*) is referred to as *EV*. References are by page and line.

3 See, for example, 17.18; 20.21.

4 Following the edition of Malinine, Puech and Quispel (see note 1).

5 Cf. pp. 52ff. below on judgement.

6 Cf. Matt. 11.25; Luke 10.21; and other synoptic passages.

7 In John, only God and Christ are glorified.

8 Error became angry with him, persecuted him, oppressed him, annihilated him. He was nailed to a tree.

9 John never uses πλάνη, and the verb πλανᾶν only at 7.12, 47, in a different sense.

10 Cf. Heb. 4.12.

11 Cf. John 9.39ff.

12 See further the discussion of light, etc., on pp. 58–62.

13 The Coptic is obscure, but this rendering is probably better than that of Malinine, Puech and Quispel. See Till, ZNW, 50 (1959), p. 170.

14 Malinine, Puech and Quispel, op. cit.

15 Cf. John 4.23, where, however, the sense is different – 'this is how God requires men to worship him.'

16 See p. 52.

17 For example, 18.4ff.: 'That which comes into existence in him is the gnosis, which appeared in order that oblivion should be abolished.'

18 Cf. Rev. 5.1.

19 I may refer here to my commentary on John (London 1955), pp. 67, 78–81, 182, 303f., 358f.; 2nd edn, pp. 80, 92–5, 218, 365f., 429f.; also *Essays*, pp. 62–5; also in this volume pp. 113f.

20 It is worth noting that though both John and *EV* use the figure of the shepherd, they use it quite differently.

21 Cf. Heb. 4.9.

22 Cf. p. 56.

23 Cf. p. 57.

24 Note that those who do *not* receive light are men of matter (*hulē*), 31.4. This is not a Johannine distinction.

25 Cf. 34.5ff. and 35.28 quoted on p. 52.

26 John 12.36 is no exception to this, since in John 'light' is not the nature of God.

27 It was my original intention to include in this essay discussion of the words 'son', 'word', 'truth', 'know' ('knowledge'), but the material collected could not be brought within the necessary limits of space.

28 See the notes in Malinine, Puech and Quispel, op. cit.; also W. C. van Unnik, *Het kortgeleden Entdekte 'Evangelie der Waarheid' en het Nieuwe Testament* (Amsterdam 1954), pp. 23–7.

29 It would not be incorrect to ascribe the kind of 'misunderstanding' in question simply to original sin, which always leads men to place themselves on the same level with God. But original sin is not peculiar to the author of *EV*, and the particular (gnostic) form of original sin that he displays was characteristic of his age.

5

SYMBOLISM

The longer one studies the Johannine literature the clearer it becomes that these books raise theological questions of great – one might say, of universal – importance, questions significant not only in the first and second centuries but whenever and wherever theology is discussed in Christian terms. I am not so foolish as to think that four such topics can be adequately dealt with in four lectures; that could not be done by a far abler theologian than I am. I hope, however, that we may be able to hear, without too much distortion, a little of what John has to say about them. I have given as titles for my lectures four significant words: Symbolism, Sacraments, Paradox, History. Behind each stands at least one great theological theme.

I begin at once with the first – Symbolism. Arising out of this word there is the whole question (and it is well that we should see it at once) of the nature of theological language. In what forms of language can theological truth be conveyed? Does theology have a language of its own which alone is suitable for theological purposes? All language is symbolic; is there a special set of symbols which alone are suitable for the kind of statement theologians have to make? Can theology only be expressed, or best expressed, as Plato seems to have thought, in myth? If it is expressed in myth, can the myth be demythologized, or does it in the process of demythologizing lose something essential to itself? If it cannot be demythologized can it be legitimately deemed rational? If it is not fully rational can it be communicated from one mind to another? In other words, is talk about God possible? If it is, on what terms and by what means? Of course, I shall not attempt to answer all these questions, either on the exegetical level or, still less, on the philosophical. But it is well that we should have some idea of what we are talking about, if only that we may approach it in a suitably humble frame of mind. We are talking about theological truth and the ways in which it may be communicated, and especially about John's use of symbols to express truth. It will be useful first of all to gather some information about the word symbol (though John does not use it), so that we may have on hand, provisionally at least, an objective definition of the thing we are to seek in the Gospel.

Symbolism originates in the Greek word σύμβολον. This hardly occurs in the LXX. At Hosea 4.12, without direct Hebrew equivalent, it presumably refers to idolatrous images, false pictures of false gods. A similar but more respectable meaning must be given to it (assuming the reading to be correct) at Wisdom 16.6 (σύμβολον σωτηρίας), where it must refer to the brazen serpent, an image of the destroying serpents which brought healing to those who looked at it (Num. 21.9), a story used also by John (3.14). At Wisdom 2.9 the meaning of σύμβολον is disputed. The simplest meaning is probably the best: it refers to the signs of merriment left behind by the merrymakers. It makes little difference if, instead, the word is taken to refer to a ring or other token left as a pledge by a reveller who lacked the ready cash to pay for his drinks. The word means a visible token of something other than itself – the good time that was had, or the credit that purchased it. The LXX has no more to offer; the word is a Greek word. It may be useful to bear in mind that the word John prefers, σημεῖον, has a substantial Old Testament background.

In Greek literature σύμβολον is used in a variety of senses. At the root of them all is the tally, that is, each of two halves or corresponding pieces of some object which two contracting parties broke between them, each party keeping one piece, in order to have proof of the identity of the presenter of the other. Hence the word came to mean any kind of token, a clue, a sign, an omen, a portent or a secret code; in a literary context, allegory. This lecture would be a long one if I were to provide examples of all these uses (and of the important later Christian use of the word for a creed). The term came to be used of quite arbitrarily chosen representations, whose value, for example in a code, might lie precisely in their arbitrariness. But I believe it to be right to retain in one's understanding of symbolism some idea of a necessary relation between the two elements concerned. They are not identical; if they were we should not have symbolism. But they fit together. There must be appropriateness in the representation if we are to have symbolism and not a mere cypher.

I shall keep this feature of symbolism in mind, but it would hardly be legitimate to expect to find it everywhere. We must not approach ancient literature, and John in particular, with *a priori* assumptions but observe them as they are to see how symbolism is used. It may take two forms, a simple and a more complex. We may distinguish the simple image, of which we find an example in the fourth Hermetic tractate, and the more elaborate myth, for which we may turn to the first. In the former a great basin is sent down from heaven to earth, and the hearts of men are summoned to baptize themselves in it. Those who do this and thus receive the baptism of the mind become perfect men and themselves possess mind (νοῦς). They ascend to him who sent the basin down to earth. The image is used but not developed. When Tat declares (6) κἀγὼ βαπτισθῆναι βούλομαι, the reply makes no further use of the symbol of the basin; he is told that he must hate his body in order that he may truly love himself and so become νοῦς. In the latter tractate a complete story of the alluring of the heavenly man by material φύσις is told in order to account for the mixture in man as we know him, partly spiritual and immortal, partly material and mortal. It is clear that the author believed that Ἄνθρωπος and φύσις really existed, at least as personifications of that which really existed, and that the symbolism consists in the story, or myth, of man's looking out of heaven and falling in love with his own reflection which he saw as in a looking-glass. Symbolism has now taken narrative form, the form of myth.

Image and myth: these are the basic forms of literary symbolism. Wider observation confirms this, but makes it difficult to draw a sharp line between the two forms. Thus (to take one of the most familiar of all passages), Daniel 7 presents us with a sequence of images: four beasts (who represent four kingdoms) and a human figure. But the animal and human figures are not still and silent; each acts, and their actions represent the history – past, present and future – of a people. The images become a myth – and incidentally illustrate very clearly the ambiguity of the word myth, for part of the mythologically presented story had actually happened and part was yet to happen – and never did happen in the way the author expected. I have spoken of literary symbolism, and this is what we are most concerned with, for Johannine thought is known to us through a literature. Symbolism occurs also in art; here too the distinction between image and myth occurs. Coins often bore symbolical pictures; with John in our minds we may think, for example, of the radiate crowns worn by divine or semi-divine

Hellenistic rulers on the coins they circulated, and of the menorah or sacred lampstand that appears on Jewish coins, recalling both the sacred furniture of the temple and the theological affirmation, 'The Lord is my light'. Myth is harder to find, especially in the Jewish world, but there is a magnificent piece of narrative symbolism in the wall paintings in the Dura synagogue,[1] where the Old Testament story is portrayed, probably with the intention of encouraging the interpretation and practice of Judaism as something like a mystery religion, in which a saving myth was re-enacted for the benefit of the worshipper. This in turn will lead on to symbolism in action, or ritual, but this we must reserve for another occasion.

Behind the various forms that religious symbolism may take, various motives and interests lie, but all come to rest ultimately in the disclosure of a god believed to be ordinarily and in himself invisible. He cannot be perceived by the senses, but the symbols can, and image may point to the nature of his being, myth to the manner and purpose of his action. The use of symbolism is thus connected with the theme of revelation, but in such a way as to make clear (what is indeed implicit in the word) that revelation itself presupposes concealment, indeed that concealment is the normal condition, varied only by the special kind of disclosure that symbolism makes possible. It is at this point that we should recall, with a view to raising but not at present attempting to answer an important question, the fact that symbol, strictly understood, suggests the dividing of a unit into two matching pieces which fit together. Symbolism cannot, or should not, be arbitrary; there must be some congruity between the symbol and the reality. This means that it is not every image that can be used in speech about God, unless symbolism is to degenerate into the use of codes and cyphers. Of course there could be a place for this; it might make theology possible in an atheistic state that forbade all reference to God. But these would not be ordinary circumstances and this would not be symbolism, as we may perhaps claim that it is when John declares, God is light, and in him is no darkness at all. But already we are embarking on Johannine material and must do this system- atically and not at random. I am concerned not so much with the particular symbols John used as with the way in which he used them, the way in which he spoke of God, the way in which he under- stood and answered the question about the appropriate forms of theological discourse. Direct speech about God is impossible, if only for the reason that, by definition, God is an entity of which no second specimen exists. If I am describing to you a man you do not know I can picture him for you in terms of a man whom you do know: A is taller than B, darker, thinner in the face, broader in the shoulders, and so on. God I cannot describe in this way. I can speak of him only in terms of things that belong to an order of being different from his own. He, the Creator, I may say, is like the light he has created. It is not very satisfactory, but some such symbolical language is necessary. John does not theorize about the necessity, as I have been doing; he proceeds immediately to the business of symbolic description. How?

We can easily recognize in the Johannine writings the various kinds of symbolism that I have noted elsewhere. There is, for example, symbolism in the form of the single great image; and the most superficial reader of the Gospel is aware of the great christological images that form so striking a feature of the book. Jesus is the bread of life, the light of the world, the good shepherd, and so on. All these designations are introduced by the formula ἐγώ εἰμι, 'I am the bread of life' (6.35), for example. There is another smaller group of passages which contain the same verbal formula without any predicate (6.20; 8.24, 28, 58; 13.19f.; 18.5, 8); Jesus simply declares ἐγώ εἰμι.[2] These are impossible to translate in a literal way, and the English versions normally turn them into 'I am He', supplying an unexplained predicate which does nothing to illuminate the meaning. These 'I am' without predicate sayings are often given particular prominence as containing a direct and explicit claim to divinity. Jesus' words (so it is often claimed) are based on Old Testament models, notably Exodus 3.14, where God answers the question about his name אהיה אשר אהיה, 'I am what I am', and continues, 'Thus shall you speak to the children of Israel, אהיה has sent me to you.' This is not convincing. אהיה was not taken as a name (see for example Shebuoth 35a), and the LXX changed both wording and sense in rendering ἐγώ εἰμι ὁ ὤν, and ὁ ὤν 'has sent me to you'. More important, but still not decisive, are a number of passages in Isaiah, where God declares, 'I am He', אני הוא (especially 41.4; 43.10; 46.4; 48.12). Of these the first three are translated ἐγώ εἰμι in the LXX. It must, however, be noted that ἐγώ εἰμι is not here used as a name or even a designation of God. In each case the speaker is identified with someone described in the context as carrying out a particular action. Thus in

Isaiah 41 the question is asked, 'Who hath raised up one from the east, whom he calleth in righteousness to his foot?' That is, Who is it who has set Cyrus upon his victorious course which will result in the liberation of the Jews from Babylon? Who hath wrought and done it, calling the generations from the beginning? The prophet answers in the name of God, 'I am He'; that is, I, God, am the one who has called Cyrus, and so on. The name of God is different; this is supplied in 42.8, אֲנִי יְהוָה הוּא שְׁמִי, ἐγὼ κύριος ὁ θεός, τοῦτό μού ἐστιν τὸ ὄνομα; 'I am YHWH, that is my name.'

Even more important than this Old Testament material are the contexts in which John has placed the words ἐγώ εἰμι. We need not linger over 6.20; 18.5, 8. Here too (as in Isaiah) the speaker identifies himself with reference to the context: If it is Jesus of Nazareth you are looking for, I am the man. This is particularly clear if we compare 9.9: If you are talking about a blind man who used to sit here begging, I am the man. John 8.58 is theologically more significant, but its significance arises out of the contrast between the aorist verb in πρὶν Ἀβραὰμ γενέσθαι and the continuous εἰμί. Unlike even such notable figures as Abraham, who, great as they are, appear on the world's scene and having played their parts disappear, Jesus the Son of God eternally is. The remaining passages are more important. Do they mean, 'Jesus says that men must believe that he bears the divine name "I AM" '3? I think they do not, and that this appears clearly from the context. At 8.28 Jesus declares, 'when you have lifted up the Son of man, then you shall know that ἐγώ εἰμι, and I do nothing of myself, but as my Father taught me, so I speak.' He goes on immediately with a reference to 'Him that sent me'. Is it conceivable that this sentence should mean, At a point in the future, when the Son of man has been exalted in suffering and glory, then you shall know that I am God almighty, and that being God I always do and say exactly what I am told to do and say by the one who sent me on my errand? The verse as a whole expresses Jesus' dependence on, and obedience to, one other than himself; it cannot identify him with the one God of the Old Testament. John 8.24 is only slightly less clear; its main function is to lead up to verse 28, for when the Jews hear ἐγώ εἰμι without a predicate they immediately ask for one: σὺ τίς εἶ; To this there is no direct answer, but Jesus goes on in verse 26 to say, 'He who sent me is true, and, as for me, it is the things I heard from him that I speak in the world.' Again, mission, dependence and obedience are emphasized. In 13.19f. there is a similar connection of thought. Jesus is announcing in advance his betrayal by one of his disciples in order that, when it happens, 'you may believe that ἐγώ εἰμι'. He immediately continues, 'He who receives anyone I send receives me, and he who receives me receives him who sent me.' The two parallel clauses interpret each other. Those whom Jesus sends are not identical with him, though they bear his commission, speak his word and do his bidding. Similarly, Jesus is not identical with the Father, but was sent by him, spoke his word and did his bidding. This thought is in fact central in the Gospel. Where much might be quoted, let us be content with 17.25: 'Righteous Father, the world did not know thee, but I knew thee, and these men have come to know that thou didst send me.' Jesus' ἐγώ εἰμι is not a claim to divinity; John has other ways, both more explicit and more guarded, of making this claim. These words point to Jesus as the authorized envoy. He does not declare his own name, whether this be thought of as κύριος or as ἐγώ εἰμι; he declares his Father's name (17.26). I am the one, he says, look at me; this is where you will see that which otherwise is invisible. In fact, what he says is the opposite of those words in the Passover Haggadah which are sometimes quoted to illustrate his ἐγώ εἰμι: אני הוא ולא אחר, I am He and not another. Jesus says: I am the one who reveals the Other. He is a symbol of the Other; and we must remember that symbol and reality belong together, are the two halves of the one broken stick.

Since we are considering the Johannine use of symbolism rather than the meaning of particular symbols, we need not spend long on the more numerous sayings in which ἐγώ εἰμι is provided with a noun predicate. When the reader's attention has been drawn to the figure of Jesus, a particular focus is given to his gaze. This is done by means of images used previously in a variety of ways but now drawn into the service of Christology. The Christology in turn, however, is, as we have seen, itself an image. 'He that hath seen me hath seen the Father' (14.9); Jesus is the visible image of the invisible Father (1.18). Jesus himself is to be understood by means of a special series of symbols, but he is the symbol by means of which God is known. Almost the only symbol applied directly to God is Father, and in Johannine usage the significant thing about God as Father is not that he is the father of all mankind but that he is the Father of Jesus; that is to say, the symbol used of God points back by way of the unique Father–Son relationship to Jesus as the one in

whom God is known. The same is true of the image of God used in
15.1: 'I am the true vine, and my Father is the husbandman.' Not
only is the term Father present and determinative; the relation of
husbandman to vine is itself analogous to the relation of Father
and Son.

Thus Jesus says ἐγώ εἰμι, and so far from calling himself God
points away from himself to the one whom he reveals; the question
of the proper being of the one in whom God is uniquely made known
is hinted at here and there in the Gospel but comes to light explicitly only in the theological framework that John is careful to
provide for his story. 'In the beginning was the Word, and the
Word was with God, and the Word was God' (1.1). The setting of
this proposition, the Prologue, will remind us of another vital fact.
The images of Jesus, and Jesus as the symbol of God, fail to make
their point. The Word was in the world, the world was made by
him, yet the world did not recognize him. He came to his own, and
his own people did not receive him (1.10f.). Even images which for
John were hallowed by their use in the earlier tradition, and in their
use in that tradition had been hallowed by their use in the Old
Testament, failed to achieve their purpose; they failed to set up
communication with those to whom they were addressed. It was
necessary to use images; suitable images – especially suitable in
that they arose out of the initiative of the person symbolized, who
was himself the perfect symbol – were employed; but they were
not accepted, or, if they were accepted, were accepted only by the
elect (1.12f., etc.). This is an important observation to which we
shall return at point after point.

So much for the great static images, especially as represented by
the 'I am' sayings. Next to be considered are the moving images, or
myths. Merely to use the word myth is to raise the well-worn
question of the relation of John to the gnostic myth of the descending
and ascending Redeemer. Did John use this myth? Did he know it?
Was it there for him to know? – for, as everyone is aware, the non-
Christian evidence for the existence of the myth is later than John.
I do not intend to take up this question in its familiar form. No
really firm and incontrovertible answer can be given on the basis of
the evidence at present available, for inference from the Gospel
itself cannot *prove* the existence of a pre-Christian myth, nor can
lack of evidence, which may be purely fortuitous, *disprove* it. What
we may say beyond any possibility of contradiction is that the

Gospel as it stands contains the outline of the story. The divine Logos did come into the world from outside it: 'He came to his own, and his own people did not receive him' (1.11). Curiously the Prologue contains no direct reference (though it does contain an allusion) to the return of the Logos to the heavenly world, but the main body of the Gospel, which constantly reiterates the theme that Jesus has come into the world to do the will of the Father who sent him, also repeats again and again that he is returning to the glory that he had with the Father before the world was. His departure is a departure in death, his exaltation a lifting up on the cross, but when the moment comes, when he has accomplished his work, go he will. The movement is summed up in 3.13: 'No one has ascended into heaven except the one who came down from heaven.' In this context the person concerned is given a special designation: he is the Son of man. This is important, for the usage of this term points out of Gnosticism into a different but related realm of mythology and imagery, the realm of eschatology. It may seem at first that all that eschatology and Gnosticism have in common is that there is no established definition of either. Everyone defines them as he will, with resultant confusion. In fact, I believe this to be too gloomy a picture, and that some clarification is emerging. I hope it may increase rather than decrease this clarification if I say that eschatology is essentially the myth of time. The gnostic and the eschatological myths are not so far apart as might seem, though of course they differ in regard to the timing of the descent and ascent of the heavenly Revealer and Redeemer. Especially in John the two approximate to each other. The symbolism of time as it is used in standard Jewish eschatology means that the past belongs to God, as Creator; the present is disputed, since the powers of evil dispute it with God; the future belongs to God, as Judge and Deliverer. Primitive Christian eschatology modified this by claiming that the decisive action in the conflict between God and evil had taken place in the life, death and resurrection of Jesus, who, having now been vindicated, reigns until all his enemies, including death, have been finally placed beneath his feet (1 Cor. 15.25). John develops the symbolism of time still further by seeing an actual penetration of the future into the present, of the third act into the second. 'The hour is coming, and now is' (4.23; 5.25). That is, the story of Jesus is a playing out in advance of the final and finally decisive events. His ministry means simultaneously the judgement and the deliverance to which I have referred: 'For judgement I came into this world, that those who see not might see, and that those who see might become blind' (9.39). It is apparent that belief in the incarnation made possible a blending, a harmonization, of the two myths, the two sets of images, the gnostic (or astrological) and the eschatological. In fact, John is not so much the heir of pre-Christian Gnosticism as one of the agents in the production of post-Christian Gnosticism. The gnostic movement extends on both sides of the Johannine movement, or rather, since it is not John only who is concerned, of the Christian movement. John plays a part in the complex, and still inadequately analysed, movement in which various kinds of speculation, including apocalyptic speculation, combined to produce what we can recognize, even if we cannot define, as Gnosticism. All this, however, cannot be considered in detail in this lecture.

It is hard to see how serious theology could have been written at the end of the first century without some reference to these two sets of symbols, the gnostic and the eschatological. But what I have already said about the great images is enough to hint at what the outcome in John would be. The end of the Revealer is rejection. 'This is the judgement, that the light has come into the world, and men loved darkness rather than light, because their deeds were evil' (3.19). The effect of the entry into the world of the gnostic Revealer is apocalyptic judgement. Gnostic and apocalyptic myths usually have happy endings. True, the ὑλικοί have no share in the happy ending, and the wicked are consigned to the torments of hell, but the atmosphere and presuppositions of Gnosticism and apocalyptic are such that no one worries about this; the tragedy would be if particles of light were left mingled with darkness, if the righteous failed to receive their due reward. Tragedy of this kind is always avoided. There is no automatic conclusion to the work of Jesus. This does indeed divide men into two classes. To continue the previous quotation (3.20f.): 'Every one who does evil things hates the light, and does not come to the light, lest his works should be exposed. But he who does the truth comes to the light, that it may be made clear that his works have been worked in God.' The mission of Jesus is directed to the world; God loved the world (3.16). The Word came into the world (1.10). The whole world was made by him, not simply a restricted number of spiritual beings, the material being excluded. Yet (and this is the point that has to be made here) the declaration of the truth and the act of deliverance are not automatically and universally effective.

We have now considered John's use of the great static symbols, or images, and of the moving images, or myths. Image and myth are normally expressed in language, but some kinds of language, of literary form, are in a special sense symbolic, and we should consider next John's use of the παροιμία – parable, proverb, allegory; it is hard to find a satisfactory rendering. The word occurs at 10.6, with reference to what Jesus says about the shepherd, the sheep, and the fold; at 16.25, where Jesus says that up to that point he has spoken to his disciples ἐν παροιμίαις, but that a time is coming when he will do so no longer, but will speak to them about the Father plainly, παρρησίᾳ; and at 16.29, where the disciples take up the word and exclaim with satisfaction, Now you are speaking plainly and speaking no παροιμία; now we know that you know all things.

From all these references one thing is clear. No one understands παροιμίαι. In the first passage it is explicitly stated that the hearers did not know what Jesus was saying to them. In chapter 16 Jesus recognizes that what he has hitherto said has not been said plainly; he has had to cover it up. And when at the end of the chapter the disciples rejoice in the belief that they do now understand, Jesus deflates their confidence with, 'Do you now believe? Behold, an hour is coming, and has now come, when you shall be scattered each one to his home and shall leave me alone.' So much for the gnostic élite, so much for the apocalyptically predestined! The παροιμίαι of the last discourse will presumably include the allegory of the vine, which in some formal respects resembles that of the shepherd, but they can hardly be confined to this, or to this and the image, which immediately precedes the saying of 16.25, of the woman in childbirth. The whole discourse, about Father, Son and Spirit, and their relation to the body of believers, is παροιμία; and it is not understood. Nothing could underline more forcibly the two-fold attitude of John to symbolism, which we have already begun to observe. Speech about God is necessary to Jesus because he is himself the Word of God, and speech about God must needs be symbolic. In this age he can only speak to his disciples ἐν παροιμίαις; plain, open speech will become possible in the future, but not at once, and if the disciples think they can anticipate the time of open speech they delude themselves and invite the disaster that is sure to follow.

Even the symbols chosen by him who himself is the symbol of God
fail to illuminate.

Symbolism in speech suggests παροιμία; symbolism in action suggests σημεῖον. This is an important word in the Johannine vocabulary, but it has often, I think, been wrongly assessed. It occurs in the
Gospel seventeen times; of these twelve (eleven) are in the plural
and refer generally to the actions, especially the miraculous actions,
of Jesus, rather than to specific acts. Thus: 'No one can do these
signs that you do, unless God is with him' (3.2); 'Unless you see
signs and portents, you will not believe' (4.48); 'Although he had
done so many signs they did not believe' (12.37). One of the occurrences in the singular applies to John the Baptist: John did no sign
(10.41) – and it is worth noting that the sentence does not continue
with 'But Jesus has done many'; it continues, 'But all that he said
about this man was true'. This leaves five (six) occurrences in the
singular, of which 2.18 is the question, 'What sign do you show?'
and 6.30 the almost identical, 'What sign do you do?' In each case,
the crowd, or opponents, are challenging Jesus to prove the truth of
the claims he is understood to be making for himself. This leaves
only 4.54; 12.18; and possibly 6.14 (where the reading is in doubt)
to refer to specific miracles; cf. 2.11. But none of these occurs
within the miracle narratives themselves. These simple observations
seem to me to make nonsense of the theory that John used a special
source consisting of miracles, describing them by the term σημεῖον,
and giving them a special evaluation – which, as some hold, John
proceeded to correct. It is possible that there may have been a
special Cana source which related, and described as signs, the
wedding feast and the healing of the nobleman's son; anything
beyond that is fantasy.

This observation does not reduce the importance of the word
σημεῖον; if anything, it increases it, since it means that the word is
John's own choice for the actions of Jesus and was not simply
borrowed from a source. It is John's general interpretative term for
the actions of Jesus, especially his miraculous actions, actions on
which faith ought not to depend, though they may be expected to
evoke faith, and sometimes do so. Merely to be the fortunate
recipient of an act of compassion is not in itself to witness a sign.
This important conclusion rests on 6.26; the crowds seek Jesus not
because they saw signs but because they had a satisfying meal from
the loaves he broke and distributed. And it becomes evident, as the

ensuing discussion proceeds, that this crowd does not in fact believe; only a few verses later (6.30) they are seeking a sign, apparently unaware that a sign has already been demonstrated. John uses so many double-edged expressions that it can hardly be doubted that he does so intentionally, and this is so in regard to signs. The intention of signs is to lead to faith: 'These (signs) are written that you may believe that Jesus is the Christ, the Son of God' (20.30f.). Yet the signs, thus hopefully recorded, had, on John's own showing, not led to faith even those who observed them at first hand (12.37). If they had done so, it would have been a second-rate kind of faith (4.48); it is implied that men ought to believe without signs.

This double attitude to miraculous signs has been explained in terms of John's use of sources; this, in at least one form, we have already seen to be an improbable view. The only alternative is to suppose that John means both propositions, and has thought them through for himself. This is very characteristic of John's theology and an important point to observe in our quest for his understanding of symbolism. There is no automatic transfer from symbol or sign to reality, and that even though there is manifest appropriateness in most of the miraculous symbolism that the Gospel employs – feeding the hungry, giving sight to the blind, raising the dead, are precisely the acts that should make clear the substance of Jesus' message. It becomes even clearer that John is aware both of the necessity and validity of symbolism and of its ineffectiveness; that is, there is nothing in the ministry of Jesus that enables one simply to read off the truth about God from observed phenomena. Nor does a symbolic discourse designed to accompany the symbolic action clear up the difficulty. The miracles are provided with such discourses, but so far from bringing home the meaning, and leading to the acceptance, of the signs they cause further secessions among the disciples (6.60, 66).

To sum up: Jesus draws attention to himself under great pictorial images; he lives out the historicized myth of the Revealer and Redeemer who descends in love; he speaks in parables and he enacts signs. Yet unbelief remains. What is the significance of this for the question with which this lecture began? What does John contribute to the problem of theological language?

At first sight the observations we have made may seem to have no great theological significance, but closer examination will show how John stands under the great theme of secrecy and disclosure which dominates the New Testament as a whole. There is no time to discuss this fully, and I must be content to make a few remarks without either substantiating or elaborating them. We use the term 'Messianic Secret', especially when discussing Mark. There were two messianic secrets. There was a messianic secret in the time of Jesus, and another, similar but not identical, in the time of Mark; it is the interplay of these in the Gospel that causes so many exegetical problems, notably in the interpretation of Mark 4.10–12. It is true, as Dodd argues, that the formulation of these verses owes something to the experience and thought of Paul; but it is not true that they have nothing to do with the experience and thought of Jesus. It was (in Mark's words) οἱ περὶ αὐτόν to whom the secret of the Kingdom of God was entrusted; they had it not on the ground of intelligence or any other human qualification or achievement but because they were united to Jesus in loyalty and faith. Fundamentally the same truth is taken up by Paul in the theme of *sola fide*. By works of the law no flesh can be justified before God, and the mark of a true apostle is not his display of outward authority but the fact that he carries about the dying of Jesus, proclaiming Jesus as Lord and himself as a slave. It is by faith in Christ only that the truth is known.

We turn to John and find the clue that we need in the Prologue. Word is revelation, the thought of God uttered, the mighty דבר יהוה if you speak Hebrew and read the Old Testament, the λόγος προφορικός if you speak Greek and read the philosophers; the Revealer, if you are sufficiently up to date to be a Gnostic. The Word was the source of creation: δι᾽ αὐτοῦ τὰ πάντα ἐγένετο. It is true of human beings, and surely true of divine beings too, that they are known by their creative works. The Word of God, and thus God himself, since the Word is God, will surely be known in the world that he has made. But it is not so. 'He was in the world, and the world was made by him, and the world knew him not' (1.10). The Logos, the truth of God, the mind of God, is not known in creation; there is no natural theology. The fact that John assumes but does not express is that the world as it is is not the world as the Word made it; it has fallen from its pristine state. The Word, and through him God, is known not in creation but in his incarnate saving mission (1.14). And even there he is not known necessarily by a simple process of self-manifestation. He himself had no means of expressing himself that could ensure universal acceptance. Symbolic language, freely ascribed to him in this Gospel (and in different ways in the other three Gospels also), did not in itself clarify the matter. The difficulty lay in the fact that symbolic speech and symbolic action can all too easily be separated from the speaker and the actor; and this means incomprehension. He who speaks and acts is in the end more important than what he says and does. The way in which the Prologue describes the mission of Jesus is suggestive. 'He came to his own, and his own did not receive him' (αὐτὸν οὐ παρέλαβον). But παραλαμβάνειν is the word for receiving a tradition, traditional teaching, though it is applied here not to teaching but to a person. It was those who received him (in 1.12 John drops the compound and writes ἔλαβον, in accordance with Greek idiom) who were given power to become children of God. It is Mark's περὶ αὐτόν, Paul's πίστις Ἰησοῦ Χριστοῦ, again. Coming to Jesus, hearing his word, abiding in him and having him abiding in oneself: it is these that matter, and since he is the symbol, the 'other piece' that requires and demonstrates the existence of its partner, who is the Father, to know and to abide in him is to know and to abide in God. Symbolism, even theological language, can be dispensed with, though it may help; faith cannot be dispensed with. 'Because you have seen me, you have believed; blessed are those who have not seen, yet have believed' (20.29).

NOTES

1 See M. I. Rostovtzeff, *Dura-Europos and its Art.* 1938.
2 This matter is treated in the essay 'Christocentric or Theocentric?' in this volume, pp. 12f.
3 R. E. Brown, *The Gospel according to John*, vol. i (1966), p. 350.

6

SACRAMENTS

When I spoke about symbolism I was able to point out that the single word raises a major theological topic, indeed one might say the supreme theological topic; the question whether theology can exist at all, the question whether there is any kind of human language that is suitable for theological purposes. There is no need for a similar argument in this lecture. The word sacrament is in itself sufficient to denote an important, and controversial, theological topic. It is controversial in itself, and it is controversial in regard to John. It is well known that Bultmann believed sacramentalism to be completely alien to Johannine thought, which, in his view, moved on completely different, non-sacramental lines. From this conviction it will follow that if here and there in the Gospel there are found what appear to be allusions to baptism or the Lord's Supper they cannot have been put there by John himself; they must have been introduced by a process of ecclesiastical redaction, in which an editor, not satisfied with a gospel that contained no allusion to the sacraments, wrote such allusions into the text, not noticing or perhaps not caring that the interpolations contradicted the framework of thought into which they were interpolated. At the other end of the scale stands Cullmann, who finds allusions to sacraments at every end and turn; any reference to water, or to eating and drinking, seems to be sufficient to justify a sacramental allusion.

In discussing this subject we can and must make use of the work we have done on symbolism. Symbolism, somewhat narrowly defined, suggests contact with God on the level of epistemology: by what means can man know God, in the sense of knowing the truth about God, who he is and what he does? Sacraments, in contrast and analogy, may be described as acted, ritual symbolism and the means by which man has ontological contact with God; it is not simply a matter of knowing about God, understanding the truth about God, but of personal, ontological, relation with him. By what means can such contact, or union, be effected? This is perhaps too sharp a distinction, and we shall have occasion to criticize it; it will

be recalled that symbolism itself requires, if it is to be effective, a personal relationship; but this will do to start with.

What is a sacrament? In considering symbolism we were able to make a beginning by going back to the Greek word σύμβολον, which is the origin of our word. This we cannot do in the study of sacraments. It is a fact which seems to me not sufficiently observed that the New Testament does not contain the word sacrament. It would be wrong to make too much of this fact; it goes without saying that a thing may be present even when no technical terminology has been evolved in order to represent it, just as we may say that there is Christology in the New Testament. But sacramental theology could not get very far without terminology, without at least a word to cover the genus of things in question, and it would be foolish to expect a developed theory of sacraments where the word sacrament is not to be found. At least, the word Christ does occur in the New Testament. Where sacraments are concerned we cannot even do much by tracing back etymologies. There is the Latin *sacramentum*, but the ancient non-Christian use of this word, whether in legal or military contexts, has little to do with sacraments as Christians have traditionally understood them, though we may in the end find the Latin word in its non-Christian settings somewhat more significant than is commonly allowed. Originally a sum of money deposited with the *tresviri capitales* by the parties to a suit, it came to be used for the suit itself; then for, first, the initial engagement entered into by newly enlisted troops, and then the *iusiurandum*, the military oath of allegiance. Hence it came to be used of any solemn undertaking, interestingly enough by Pliny in his description of the Christians he encountered in Bithynia-Pontus (*Epistles* 10.96). The Christians were accustomed, so they told him, 'se sacramento non in scelus aliquod obstringere, sed ne furta, ne latrocinia, ne adulteria committerent, ne fidem fallerent, ne depositum appellati abnegarent'. This was a solemn undertaking, not, it seems, what we should call a sacrament, for it was not an initiation, and, having made this vow 'ante lucem', the Christians departed and then returned (presumably having done their day's work) 'ad capiendum cibum'. The making of a pledge of loyalty may, as I say, turn out to be more relevant than is sometimes thought, but there is also truth in the view that the Christian use of *sacramentum* arose out of a direct return to the notion of *sacer*, the sacred, or holy.

The word *sacramentum* appears in Christian use as the translation of the Greek μυστήριον, in both its paradoxically related senses. It can mean simply a secret. 'Sacramentum regis abscondere bonum est' (Tobit 12.7). It can mean specifically a divine secret: 'Sacramentum septem stellarum quas vidisti in dextera mea' (Rev. 1.20). This points onward to the second meaning: a secret in process of revelation, thus, 'Secundum revelationem notum mihi factum est sacramentum' (Eph. 3.3). The word does not in the Bible mean sacrament. Thus at Ephesians 5.32, where the Vulgate has 'Sacramentum hoc magnum est', there is no suggestion that marriage is a sacrament, though the notion that marriage is a symbolic representation of the relation between Christ and the Church is suggested, and *sacramentum* will mean such a symbolic representation. In the place (1 Cor. 4.1) where some have, quite mistakenly, supposed that μυστήρια referred to sacraments, the Vulgate does not use *sacramentum*: 'dispensatores mysteriorum Dei'. In fact, it is not easy to know why μυστήριον is sometimes transliterated as *mysterium* and sometimes translated *sacramentum*; but it is the later, sacramental, sense of μυστήριον that determined the eventual Christian meaning of *sacramentum*. μυστήριον, beginning with the simple sense of secret, opens to us a wide range of meanings; in particular it was used – at first, outside Christian circles – for secret religious rites. It is their secretness, and hence their sacredness, that the word emphasizes, and the connection between μυστήρια and sacraments, which is not made in the New Testament, was a most unfortunate one. It has led Christians to a secretive and exclusive treatment of their rites which has had and continues to have regrettable consequences, and is in truth pagan rather than Christian. Most of the secret rites of antiquity were kept secret because they were believed to convey benefits that were not to be offered to all and sundry – illumination, knowledge, immortality, deification. You will think, and rightly, of the mystery religions, which there is no space now to describe in detail. *Opera operata*, witnessed, participated in, conveyed great blessings to those who by appropriate qualification and payment were allowed to approach; this was a very different matter from the free offer of the Gospel to a world which could never deserve or pay for it. Things were done in the mysteries which necessarily and indispensably effected the desired results. There was an acted symbol, and the acted symbol conveyed what it represented. When the light shone in the Mithraic cell the initiate was illuminated. The psychological effect was no doubt in most cases such that he also *felt* illuminated; but to the Mithraist the feeling was not all.

In this sense the Hellenistic world had its sacraments. Whether the world of Judaism also possessed sacraments is a disputed question, which turns to some extent on the meaning given to the word. Proselyte baptism undoubtedly admitted the convert not only to a new religion but also to a new set of family relations, and to this extent he could be compared to a newborn babe and thus be said to have been born a second time. This, however, was not a regeneration, a new life conferred by the rite of baptism itself. And though Philo occasionally employs the language of the mystery cults he does not turn Jewish rites into mysteries. Indeed, Philo (who hated and despised the mysteries as the pagan rites they were) came nearer to doing what the Hermetic and other gnostic writers did when they adapted the language of sacramentalism and used it to produce non-sacramental images. In the lecture on Symbolism I quoted the fourth Hermetic tractate (on the Basin), in which the rite of baptism (and baptismal rites were common) is spiritualized into illumination, the communication, that is, of the knowledge (γνῶσις) of God. This is a process that must be borne in mind as we study John. In sum, there was a good deal of sacramentalism of one kind and another in John's environment, though not on the strictly Jewish side. Where it existed, it existed sometimes in the crudest form, in a rite that was spiritually effective provided only that it was carried through in a mechanically correct way; sometimes it was recognized that the physically correct action had to be accompanied by a spiritually correct attitude; sometimes sacramental action was used as no more than an image of a non-sacramental event or truth – that is, the sacrament became a symbol, an image and nothing more. How far these attitudes had entered into pre-Johannine Christianity is a difficult and complex question; and it must not be assumed that any of them must be in any way determinative of John's handling – or, it may be, rejection – of the theme. For this we turn to the Gospel itself.

It is a familiar fact that the Gospel (and the same is true of the Epistles) contains no explicit reference to either Christian baptism or the Lord's Supper. This fact is capable of various interpretations; it is possible on the one hand that John thought these things so unimportant that there was no need to mention them, on the other that he thought them so sacred that they would be profaned by mention in a book that might fall into the hands of the uninitiated. It is not hard to think of other possibilities. Given that there are no explicit references, one asks whether there are allusions. The answer to this question is that, assuming the text of the Gospel as it has been transmitted to us, there are such allusions. Not many would deny some kind of allusion to baptism in the words, 'Unless a man is born of water and the Spirit, he cannot enter the kingdom of God' (3.5); probably most would acknowledge an allusion in the account of the washing of the disciples' feet by Jesus (13.1–17). And it is, I believe, almost universally agreed that in 6.53–8 there are at least allusions to the Lord's Supper. After a long discourse on the importance of eating the bread of life we learn first (v. 51) that this bread not merely is Jesus but is his flesh, and then (v. 53) that eating flesh must be accompanied by drinking blood. The pair, eating flesh and drinking blood, is repeated several times over. 'Unless you eat the flesh of the Son of man and drink his blood, you have no life in yourselves; he who eats my flesh and drinks my blood has eternal life ... my flesh is true food and my blood is true drink. He who eats my flesh and drinks my blood abides in me, and I in him' (6.53–6). It is true that we have here flesh and blood rather than the familiar body and blood of the synoptic and Pauline tradition, but, even if we do not follow Jeremias in thinking that flesh rather than body is the primitive term, there is no barrier here to a eucharistic allusion. It would be hard to find any other way of accounting for the introduction of blood.

I propose to begin with a consideration of this passage in chapter 6.[1] It is Bultmann's opinion that the eucharistic passage (he reckons it as running from 6.51c to 6.58) is an interpolation into the original Johannine text, distinguishable from John's own writing not stylistically, for the ecclesiastical redactor imitated John's style, not unsuccessfully, but by the fact that it differs doctrinally from John. The literary and historical judgement that the Gospel has been subjected to interpolation is thus dependent on the interpretation of the passage in question. Bultmann's interpretation is clear. The passage is analogous in its understanding of the Last Supper with the famous passage of Ignatius (*Ephesians* 20) in which the Eucharist is described as a φάρμακον ἀθανασίας, ἀντίδοτος τοῦ μὴ ἀποθανεῖν, a medicine of immortality, an antidote against death. If these words are taken literally, they mean that Ignatius held a purely magical view of the Eucharist. Simply to eat the broken bread was to

achieve immortality. Whether such a belief may be attributed to
Ignatius is not quite certain. Lightfoot refers to Irenaeus (iv. 18.5;
v. 2.3), 'who argues that our fleshly bodies must inherit eternal life,
because they partake of the eucharistic bread'. Lightfoot continues,
'We need not, however, suppose that Ignatius had this very material
conception in view.' This may or may not be a valid qualification.
Lightfoot gives no reason for it. It is clear from the context that, for
Ignatius, the efficacy of the Eucharist was dependent upon a number
of spiritual conditions, including a right belief in Jesus Christ as Son
of man and Son of God, and wholehearted obedience to the bishop
and presbyterate. These things, however, are not important in the
present discussion; what matters to us is whether this more or less
mechanical conception of the Eucharist (and no amount of qualification can completely free Ignatius from this charge) was shared by
John. There is something to be said for this view of Bultmann's; I
have already quoted the words, 'He who eats my flesh and drinks
my blood has eternal life' (6.54a). This seems to imply that the
food and drink in themselves convey life. But a brief preliminary
consideration will show that Bultmann's interpretation of John is at
least unsatisfactory. First, it must be remembered that John is not
explicitly writing about the Eucharist at all. He is not even describing the Last Supper. Had he wished to represent the sacred meal as a
lifegiving drug, he could have made his point much clearer by
putting his teaching in the traditional place. Secondly, in verse 58
he goes out of his way to distinguish between the eating he is
speaking of and the eating, that is, the physical eating, by the fathers
in the wilderness, who ate the manna, which, though given miracul-
ously by God, was nevertheless material food: οὐ καθὼς ἔφαγον οἱ
πατέρες. Not as the fathers ate are men now invited to eat. Theirs
was a literal eating, this is not; at least, it is not only a literal,
physical eating. Thirdly, we should note the last clause in verse 54,
κἀγὼ ἀναστήσω αὐτὸν τῇ ἐσχάτῃ ἡμέρᾳ. When this clause occurs in
verses 39, 40, 44, Bultmann treats it as an ecclesiastical interpolation, designed to introduce conventional eschatology into a work
that lacked it; as I have said, he regards the whole of verses 51c–58
as such an interpolation, designed to introduce conventional sacramentalism into a work that lacked it. What we must note is that,
whether the material be interpolated or not, the same person who
was dealing with eschatology and the Eucharist qualified the latter
by the former. Eucharistic communion does not confer immortality

in such a way as to make the recipient himself immortal. If he is to live at the last day it will be because he is raised up. True, in the eating and drinking he is given (in some sense) life. This is a constant theme of the Gospel, expressed in one image after another. But he is never the source of his own life, and never ceases to be utterly dependent upon God.

So we may approach the interpretation of John 6.51–8 with clear minds, noting incidentally Bultmann's too little observed qualification of his own position: 'If the Evangelist did come to terms with the sacraments, he can only have understood them in the sense that in them the word is made present in a special way.'[2] This could be regarded as another way of saying that Johannine sacraments are a special case of the symbolic language we have already studied. And this may not be far wrong.

This observation suggests the essential starting-point. John 6.53–8 must not be studied on its own but in the context of the whole sequence of events of which it is part (John 6). The story begins with a miracle, the feeding of the five thousand, which supplies the language and imagery of the discourse. Both story and discourse are about the bread by which men live, without which they will die, and Jesus' provision for the multitude who depend on him. This is the essential image, but it is supported by a number of minor points: the helplessness even of the disciples when they are left to their own resources; their failure to understand what is happening in contrast with the statement that Jesus himself knew what he was going to do; the use of eucharistic words, ἔλαβεν, εὐχαριστήσας, διέδωκεν; the gathering together of the fragments of bread, that nothing might be lost. There can be little doubt that the miracle provides the basis for the chapter as a whole. Bread is the lifegiving gift of Jesus.

It is not surprising that such a miracle, of such power, and so vital to the well-being of those who experienced it, should create a powerful impression on them. Saved from starvation, they naturally thought highly of their benefactor; perhaps they also recognized the specific work of the Prophet-King, and thus had a double reason for seizing Jesus with a view to making him king (6.15).

Was the miracle a sign? This question raises again the difficulties in the use of the word σημεῖον that were discussed in the lecture on Symbolism. They are complicated by a textual problem. In 6.14 the great majority of manuscripts have: The men, when they saw the sign that he had done (ὃ ἐποίησεν σημεῖον), said, This is truly the prophet who is coming into the world. Here the word *sign* (in the singular) must refer specifically to the incident which immediately precedes, the feeding of the five thousand. But the important Bodmer Papyrus P⁷⁵, with B a and a few other authorities, has the plural, the signs that he had done (ἃ ἐποίησεν σημεῖα). There would be a natural inclination on the part of copyists to make a reference to the miracle they had just written down; this speaks in favour of the plural as the original reading. The plural, however, might be due to assimilation to verse 26 (cf. 2.23). It is difficult to reach a decision on this question; it is in any case less important than those that are to come. Verse 14 asserts that the people saw (ἰδόντες) the sign, or signs, that Jesus had done. In verse 26, however, Jesus says to the people, 'You seek me not because you saw (εἴδετε, the same verb) signs, but because you ate some of the loaves and were satisfied.' This is ambiguous. It may mean: It is true that you saw signs (including no doubt the miraculous feeding), but that is not the reason why you are seeking me; you are seeking me because you enjoyed an unexpected meal. But it may be taken differently: You did not see signs; that is not why you are seeking me; you are seeking me because you enjoyed an unexpected meal. The latter seems to be the more probable way of taking verse 26 since it is in harmony with verse 30, where the same people, in response to the claim implicit in 'This is the work of God, that you believe in him whom he sent', challenge Jesus with, What sign do you do, that we may see (ἴδωμεν) (it) and believe you? This surely means that they have not seen a sign – at least, that they have not seen anything that they recognize as a sign. This brings out the difficulty that leads to the obscurity in John's writing. All that was to be seen, they had seen. They had seen that they themselves, all five thousand of them, were in a desert place without food. They had seen that Jesus had distributed among them five loaves and two fish, and that they had all had enough to eat. They had seen that this was a very marvellous thing. But they had not seen that it was a significant thing, or at least they had not seen what it was significant of. Had they done so they could not have asked now (v. 30) for a sign.

We thus return to our discussion of symbolism. In the sign, acted symbolism is presented, but it is not accepted. Acceptance remains on the physical level – ἐχορτάσθητε (6.26). The meaning of the acted symbolism, as of other kinds of symbolism, is rejected. This provides the background for the rest of chapter 6, which proceeds with the discourse on the bread of life, a discourse punctuated by objections on the part of the hearers and divided by these interruptions into sections.

The discourse begins, as we have seen, with the negative statement of verse 26 (All you are interested in is physical food), which is given its positive counterpart in verse 27. This is in fact a summary of the discourse as a whole. Man's concern should be with food that lasts into, or produces, eternal life; this the Son of man will give him in virtue of his authenticated commission from God. This leads naturally to the question what authentication Jesus can actually produce: τί οὖν ποιεῖς σὺ σημεῖον; and thus to the reference to the Old Testament story of the manna, not as narrated in Numbers but as alluded to in Psalm 78, He gave them bread from heaven to eat. Jesus takes up the Old Testament phrase and expounds it in a thoroughly Jewish manner which has been demonstrated most convincingly by Peder Borgen.[3] All that we are to notice here are the divisions and breaks in the discourse.

In the first few verses the basic proposition is stated: 'I am the bread of life' (v. 35). Immediately after this there follows the first break, which is made not by complainers in the crowd but by Jesus himself. 'You have seen and yet you do not believe' (v. 36). In this verse too there is a textual variant: most manuscripts have, You have seen me (ἑωράκατέ με); but this assimilates to verse 40, and the με should be omitted. We have here the explanation of verse 26. You have seen: that is, you have beheld the observable actions of the miracle, yet you do not believe (v. 29). Merely to behold with one's eyes the external events does not constitute seeing a sign. For this, faith is necessary. And faith is the gift of God. The Father gives, and the Son, whose will is only to do the Father's will, receives. At this the Jews interject their first complaint. Jesus of Nazareth is a familiar person. We know his father and mother, they say. It is absurd for him to claim that he has come down from heaven as the bread of life. Jesus replies by reiterating that faith is God's gift. There is no point in trying to prove that he, the boy from Nazareth, is the Son of God, the bread from heaven. No one will believe this unless God grants the power to do so: No one can come to me unless the Father draws him. All is dependent on the Father's will, yet it is the Father's will that what he does for men and gives to them should be done and given through his Son; hence at the end of this part of the speech comes the weighty repetition of the main proposition: 'I am the bread of life' (v. 48); 'I am the living bread which came down out of heaven' (v. 51). This verse goes on to emphasize the two points (a) that the gift of God is eternal life (ζήσει εἰς τὸν αἰῶνα) and (b) that the source of life is the human Jesus, who will give himself for the benefit of others (ἡ σάρξ μου ὑπὲρ τῆς τοῦ κόσμου ζωῆς). The word *flesh*, which undoubtedly points to the full humanity of Jesus but might be taken in a grosser way, provokes fiercer complaint (ἐμάχοντο) than before. How can this man give us flesh to eat? (v. 52). It is here, not at verse 51c, that a new paragraph begins, and here (in verse 53) that the introduction of blood points beyond the mere image of bread to the sacrament (if that is the right word – it is not John's) of the Lord's Supper. This part of the discourse ends where the discourse began. 'He who eats me shall live because of me' (v. 57). 'He who eats this bread shall live for ever' (v. 58). The discourse appears to have come to an end (v. 59), but it is not so. Many not of the crowd but of the disciples now complain. 'This is a hard saying; who can listen to it?' (v. 60). Jesus replies, reaffirming that man's response hangs upon the predestination of God (vv. 64f.). He refers again to the Son of man (v. 62) and surprisingly declares that the flesh is of no avail, since it is the Spirit that gives life, and his words are Spirit and life (v. 63). All the eucharistic allusions must be understood in the light of this principle. This is the moment for the final division among his hearers. Some even of his disciples withdraw; others, represented by Peter, make a double confession, relating both to who Jesus is and to what they have received from him: Thou hast the words (cf. v. 63) of eternal life; thou art the Holy One of God. But the last word of the chapter is that one of you is a devil.

The form of the discourse alone is sufficient to underline the point of the previous lecture. No symbol, however clear, is sufficient to effect understanding. The image of the bread of life is intelligible and acceptable only to those who exercise the faith which God himself gives. But this is not all. The discourse does, as has often been noted, fall into two parts. From verse 35 to verse 51 (or thereabouts) Jesus declares that he is the bread of life; that men must come to him, and can do so if the Father draws them. From verse 53 (or thereabouts) he asserts that men must eat his flesh and drink his blood; by doing so they will have eternal life. It is reasonable to call these two parts (as R. E. Brown does) sapiential and sacramental respectively. The figure used in the former is related to Jewish

Wisdom speculation, and, as we have already seen, the latter makes a hardly doubtful allusion to the Lord's Supper. The question is, how these two parts are related to each other. Bultmann, as I have said, considers only the former to be Johannine; the latter is a supplement by the ecclesiastical redactor. Brown regards the two as alternative treatments of the image of the bread of life. Neither of these views is satisfactory.

Bultmann takes the interpolated passage to extend from verse 51c to verse 58. This is consistent in that it includes all the references to flesh, from the first in verse 51c: 'The bread which I will give for the life of the world is my flesh.' This view, however, does violence to the structure of the discourse, which, as we have seen, is divided by Jewish objections. There is an objection in verse 52, after the first reference to flesh, so that the final unit is verse 52: Jewish objection; verses 53–8: answer to the objection. The consequence of this is that the reference to flesh in verse 51c belongs to the earlier part of the discourse. That is, the earlier part is not purely 'sapiential' but contains a reference to (eucharistic) flesh. This is confirmed by the opening verse, 35, which after speaking of Jesus as the bread which is the answer to human hunger (οὐ μὴ πεινάσῃ) goes on to add – quite unnecessarily if we are thinking simply in terms of the bread image – that he is also the answer to human thirst (οὐ μὴ διψήσει πώποτε). Conversely, the last two verses (57, 58) drop the sacramental language of flesh and blood and return simply to the eating of bread. Thus if we are to think of an interpolation it will not include verse 51c, and this means that to dispose of the supposed interpolation is not to dispose entirely of the sacramental features of the discourse. The same argument, of course, shows that Brown is not strictly correct in speaking of a sapiential discourse and a sacramental discourse, though it is undoubtedly true that the earlier part looks emphatically in a sapiential, the later in a sacramental direction, and it is, as I have said, reasonable to accept Brown's terms as an approximation.

Moreover, as I have already pointed out, Bultmann's rejection of verses 51(52)–8 is based primarily on theological considerations, and thus is dependent on the correctness or otherwise of his interpretation of the eucharistic doctrine contained in these verses. And whatever else they may teach, they do not teach a quasi-magical doctrine of food which automatically confers eternal life upon him who eats it. Word and Spirit are in the end the decisive factors.

The fact is – and perhaps I should apologize for taking so long to reach so simple a conclusion – that the discourse must be read and understood as a whole. Brown comes near to saying this when he says that we may think of verses 35–51 as 'word', 53–8 as 'sacrament', but he fails to recognize that word and sacrament belong together. We must go back to the miracle of the five thousand. This was a sign; it contained within itself a valid, if partial, representation of the truth about Jesus, who does bring food where there is hunger and thus – taking the scene to the limit – life where there is death. This he does out of pure unmerited goodness for those who have no claim upon him. He acts as only the Creator can act, turning five loaves into an adequate supply for five thousand. This is a true picture of the Word, by whom all things were made, in whom was life, who came that men might have life and have it abundantly. Here was the truth; but men lacked the ability to see it. They understood Jesus so little that they sought to make him king. Their enthusiasm was based not on seeing and understanding a sign but on the satisfaction of their physical hunger. The misunderstanding runs right through the chapter, and the sacramental material is used to bring it to a head, precisely because eating human flesh and drinking human blood is the most revolting symbol conceivable, and challenges faith and unbelief in the most radical way possible. If the sapiential part of the discourse stood alone, it would be open to misunderstanding on purely intellectual lines. If the sacramental part stood alone, it would be, on the lines of the miracle, open to two kinds of materialist misunderstanding. It could be understood as a mystic rite which, duly performed, would convey to anyone the blessing of immortality; it could be understood as sheer cannibalism. The sacramental passage prevents the sapiential from volatilizing in gnostic speculation by attaching it firmly to the flesh and blood of the historical Son of man, Jesus. The sapiential passage prevents the sacramental from deteriorating into ritualism, and attaches it not (as the synoptic and Pauline accounts do) merely to one solemn moment in the life of Jesus but to the total act of his descent from heaven and ministry on earth. But the sapiential passage does not contain a rational argument such as must convince all men of reason and good will that Jesus is the lifegiving Word, and the sacramental passage does not offer an *opus operatum* that makes any participant immortal. It is clear from material I have already quoted that there are those who will reject both, and, lacking the faith that God alone gives, not being drawn to Jesus by the Father, will make nothing of either word or sacrament. The offer of flesh and blood calls for proclamation to make it intelligible and supply the necessary understanding of God's action; for faith on the part of the recipient; and (since without this there will be no hearing of the word and no faith) the predestinating prevenient action of God.

I said that we should begin the exegetical part of our study with the bread of life discourse in John 6. I move on now to the two passages that seem to allude to baptism. The first is the statement in 3.5 that 'unless one is born of water and the Spirit, he cannot enter the kingdom of God'. It has been fairly widely supposed that 'of water', ἐξ ὕδατος, is a reference to baptism, but as in chapter 6 there has been controversy over the question whether the words belong to John's own text or are a supplement inconsistent with it. Thus Bultmann[4] writes:

> 'The originality of the words ὕδατος καί, which link the re-birth with the sacrament of baptism, is at the least very doubtful . . . they are, in my opinion, an insertion of the ecclesiastical redaction, which in 6.51b–58 has also forged the link with the Last Supper. The meaning of baptism is not only not mentioned in the following passage, but if mentioned could only confuse the ideas in verse 6 and verse 8 . . . The Evangelist consciously rejects the sacramentalism of ecclesiastical piety.'

Cullmann[5] on the other hand writes, 'ni les données des manuscrits ni le contexte n'autorisent cette suppression [de ὕδατος καί]. Car ici, comme dans l'évangile tout entier, l'auteur tient à l'affirmation de la présence de l'Esprit *dans* l'objet matériel conformément au fait que le Logos éternel s'est fait chair.' The discussion of chapter 6 which we have already conducted will lead us to ask a question that by-passes both Bultmann and Cullmann. Is it possible that ὕδατος was written by the Evangelist, was a reference to baptism, but was intended by him in a sense different from that of contemporary church piety – which, as Bultmann's footnote shows, was tending more and more to see in the baptismal water an agency that effected regeneration *ex opere operato*?

It is worthwhile here to bear in mind Odeberg's suggestion that 'of water and the Spirit' is to be understood as a hendiadys – water in the sense of generative seed, and the noun Spirit as standing for an adjective, so that the whole phrase means 'spiritual (not material) seed'. There is something to be said for this. It recalls 1 Peter 1.23, 'born again, not of corruptible seed but of incorruptible, by the word of God', and it is not far distant from John 1.13 ('born, not of blood nor of the will of the flesh nor of the will of man, but of God'). If we could allow that water, ὕδωρ, would quite naturally suggest seminal fluid, this would be a very attractive suggestion indeed, and would remove baptism from the context completely. But, notwithstanding Odeberg's parallels, it is not likely that ὕδωρ would readily convey this suggestion. There is also something to be said for the view that water does indeed suggest baptism, but John the Baptist's baptism. John appears in the context in chapter 3, and is contrasted with Jesus. Jesus is the bridegroom, John the bridegroom's friend – only a secondary figure at the wedding. This comparison would be parallel to the contrast between water and the Spirit. Moreover, the earlier tradition made precisely the same contrast: 'I indeed baptize you with water, but he shall baptize you with the Holy Spirit' (Mark 1.8). It is in fact very probable that there is an allusion here to John's baptism; but there is probably a reference to Christian water baptism also. It seems that Justin (1 Apology 61) so understood our passage, and the allusion was probably already in the Evangelist's mind. If, however, John did have baptism in mind, how did he understand it?

As with the eucharistic allusion in chapter 6, it is necessary to bear the whole context in mind. The two chapters, though the incidents they describe are completely different, are in fact remarkably similar in structure. In each case the framework is provided by a reference to signs; in each, discourse material is punctuated by objections. Nicodemus's opening gambit is a reference to signs: 'No one can do these signs that you are doing unless God is with him' (3.2). Nicodemus speaks like a theologian, not like the militant nationalists of 6.15, but he has understood the signs no better than they, and is in verse 10 roundly rebuked for his ignorance: 'Are you the teacher of Israel, and do you not understand these things?' He has failed to see that earthly things have heavenly counterparts (v. 12). John does not find it necessary to put a question on Nicodemus's lips in order to set the conversation on the line that it follows; it is enough that Nicodemus is a Jew, a Pharisee, a teacher, a leader of the Jewish people. We may, if we wish, imagine his asking such a question as that of Luke 17.20: 'When will the kingdom

of God come?' But the mere existence, the presence, of such a man
has the effect of raising this question, for it was for the manifestation
of God's reign that Israel existed. The question may remain implicit;
the reply to it is that merely to wait, with the Qaddish prayer on
one's lips ('May he establish his kingdom ... speedily ...'), was
not enough. There could be no kingdom without a new birth,
ἄνωθεν. This proposition Nicodemus fails to understand. Just as the
men in chapter 6 say, Lord, evermore give us this bread; as the
Samaritan woman says, Give me this water, that I may not thirst,
and may not come here to draw; so Nicodemus supposes that he is
being invited to return into his mother's womb so that his earthly
existence may begin ἄνωθεν, all over again. But he has missed the
full meaning of ἄνωθεν: all over again, yes, but also, from above. The
rest of the discourse is an exposition of the aspect of ἄνωθεν that
Nicodemus has missed. This follows two lines. One takes up the
word *Spirit* from verse 5. With a familiar play on the word πνεῦμα,
which means breath, wind and spirit, Jesus goes on to declare that
the wind, the πνεῦμα, blows where it wills. Man cannot control it, he
cannot see it; he can only hear its sound, or voice (φωνή). It stands
for that which is beyond, which is other. The other line takes up the
word ἄνωθεν, and asks how man may have contact with that which
is above him. The answer is that he himself is incapable of it. No
one has ascended into heaven (v. 13). The new birth is not achieved
by a process of religious ascent; hope lies only in the Son of man who
descended from heaven. The parallel with chapter 6 is here particularly close in both respects and extends not only to broad outline
but to detail. Chapter 6 asserts that it is the Spirit that gives life,
whereas flesh in itself is of no profit (6.63); Jesus claims that he is the
bread of life that came down from heaven (6.51), and makes this
claim as the Son of man, for he adds, 'Unless you eat the flesh of the
Son of man and drink his blood, you do not have life in yourselves'
(6.53). John 3.13 implies also that the Son of man, having descended, also ascends; 6.62 asks, 'What if you see the Son of man
ascending where he was before?'

Thus 3.1–21 presents (though in different proportions) the same
constituents as chapter 6, where after a reference to signs there was
a discourse on the bread of life, divided, broadly speaking, into a
sapiential section and a sacramental section. The three elements
belong together and illuminate one another. Chapter 3 also begins
with a reference to signs, which, as in chapter 6, are found im-

pressive but are not understood in their proper sense. The theme of new birth is discussed, and the discussion consists mainly of an account of the way in which the Spirit originates a new life on a higher level than that of ordinary human existence, together with a reference to the opening of intercourse between heaven and earth by the descent and ascent of the Son of man. Along with the account there is what may probably be taken to be an allusion to baptism – the water which plays its part in the new birth. The inference to be drawn from this is clear. Baptism is not to be thought of as a quasi-magical transaction in which a washing in water automatically confers regeneration upon the participant. Quite the reverse: the chapter contains the sharpest possible criticism of such an opinion. There is no new birth without the Spirit and the Spirit is not to be controlled by any liturgical or other device. The Spirit breathes where he wills (ὅπου θέλει), and is not constrained; man can perceive the result of its operation, but does not know whence it comes or whither it goes (3.8). And the same may be said of those who are born of the Spirit. Where the Spirit of the Lord is, there is liberty (2 Cor. 3.17). If we are to speak of interpolation in this chapter it would be better to say that in 3.5 John has interpolated into his source the words καὶ πνεύματος; others might assert that washing in water regenerates, but John insists that there is no regeneration apart from the Spirit – and that means (again we recall chapter 6) God's preventing will and action. I do not in fact suggest that interpolation of a *literary* kind has taken place; John wrote out the Nicodemus dialogue as he thought fit, not in rigid dependence on a written source into which from time to time a word might be inserted. But water was there, in current thought, for there can be no doubt that in John's time the regular Christian practice was to baptize converts, just as the Christian Supper was there and equally open to misinterpretation. It would be unfair to suggest that all John's contemporaries were unmindful of the role of the Spirit; but there is no mistaking John's insistence upon it. And if others left it out, he would put it in.

There is another probable allusion to baptism in Jesus' washing of his disciples' feet; and in this too there recur the same pattern and some of the same features that we have seen in the allusion to baptism in chapter 3 and in the allusion to the Lord's Supper in chapter 6.

John 13 begins with a symbolic action. It is not described as a σημεῖον; it is not important to ask whether John would have accepted the term as appropriate. Unlike the feeding of the five thousand the action is not miraculous. It is nevertheless even more clearly and completely misunderstood. When confronted with Jesus in the guise of a servant, Peter refuses pointblank to be washed. 'Lord, are you washing my feet? . . . You shall never wash my feet' (13.6, 8). When it is pointed out to him that the washing is indispensable to his participation in Jesus, he goes to the other extreme, and desires as much washing as possible: 'Lord, not my feet only but also my hands and my head' (13.9). He is wrong both times. He who is too proud to accept the humble service of the love of Jesus, which may be represented as the servant's act of footwashing but is in truth his dying for men, stands outside the whole divine operation. But he who identifies this process with an ordinary bath, in which the more soap and water the better, shows that he is attaching himself to material things and has not begun to understand what Jesus does for men, in the sacraments or otherwise. Equally he has failed to understand what Jesus does if he does not see that the operation is pointless if it fails to lead to like action on his part. 'You call me Teacher and Lord; and you say well, for that is what I am. So if I, your Lord and Teacher, have washed your feet, you also ought to wash one another's feet. For I have given you an example, that you also should do as I have done to you' (13.13–15). Just as Brown distinguished in chapter 6 between a sapiential discourse and a sacramental discourse, so here Boismard[6] finds a moralizing and a sacramental account of the washing of the disciples' feet. Certainly no one can deny the possibility that there may have been two accounts of the one event. It is equally certain that this cannot be proved, and it is in fact improbable, since what is beyond question, since it lies on paper before us, is that John wishes the one event, and that which it symbolized, to be understood in both ways: what Jesus does for men – whether we think of this historically as his dying for us, or sacramentally, as our baptism into his death, or as the non-sacramental religious experience of bearing about in the body the dying of Jesus – is both effective and exemplary.

There is little to be said for attempts to find in John 13 hidden references to details of sacramental practice; quite a good deal to be said for the belief that when he represented as feet-washing the effective love of Jesus for his own he had baptism at least in the back of his mind. If he had, the chapter contains the ultimate *reductio ad absurdum* of any purely *ex opere operato* theory of sacraments. For among those whose feet were washed was Judas Iscariot; and at the end of the story Judas went out, and it was night.

Before we leave this subject we must return to the point at which we started and ask the question, Where does John stand in the development of Christian thought about the sacraments? The short answer surely is that he represents neither an Ignatian sacramentarianism nor a complete denial of the right of sacraments to exist – though I think he is nearer the latter than the former. He was prepared to accept the existence of baptism and the Lord's Supper; there is no polemic against them. But his acceptance of them was a critical acceptance. In this he follows in Paul's footsteps. Paul was confronted with wild and exaggerated sacramentarianism at Corinth, if not elsewhere. He answered it not by negation but by critical theological analysis, and by dreadful warnings (1 Cor. 10 and 11). John, who must write in a different form because he is composing a gospel, performs the same task in a more developed situation. There is no sacrament without the word, no benefit in the sacrament without faith, and nothing at all apart from the descent and ascent of the Son of man, who once for all in history gave his flesh and blood for the life of the world.

NOTES

1 This matter is treated in the essay 'The Flesh of the Son of Man' in this volume, pp. 37–49.
2 R. Bultmann, *The Gospel of John*, Eng. trans. (1971), p. 472.
3 P. Borgen, *Bread from Heaven*. 1965.
4 Bultmann, op. cit., p. 138, note 3. I suspect, however, that in this quotation the German *Abendmahl* refers not to the Last Supper but the Lord's Supper.
5 O. Cullmann, *Les Sacrements dans l'Évangile Johannique* (1951), p. 46.
6 M. E. Boismard, *Revue Biblique* 71 (1964), pp. 5–24.

7
PARADOX AND DUALISM

Paradox is one of those words that come to us from the past but are used in modern languages – at least, in English – in a sense slightly different from that of their ancestors. παράδοξον is not one of the commonest of Greek words; it usually denotes the surprising, sometimes that which is surprising enough to be incredible. It is not common in the LXX, and occurs only once in translation οι Hebrew. At Sirach 43.25 it translates פלא and refers to fishermen's tales – what incredible monsters are to be found in the sea! When Judith, after her adventure with Holofernes, comes back with his head in her bag the people find it unbelievable that she should return to them (Judith 13.13). Somewhat nearer to our own theme is Wisdom 5.2. The author has described the way in which the wicked set upon the wise good man. Of course, in the first act of the story they have their way, and the righteous man suffers; 'they will see, and will have contempt for him, but the Lord will laugh them to scorn' (4.18). For the Lord knows what he is doing, and in the second act the roles will be reversed, and 'they will be astonished at the unexpectedness, the wonder, of his salvation, or rescue' (ἐπὶ τῷ παραδόξῳ τῆς σωτηρίας). This is all worth noting, but it is not quite what paradox has come to mean in modern usage. For this I can hardly do better than cite the *Oxford English Dictionary*. Paradox is 'a statement seemingly self-contradictory or absurd, though possibly well-founded or essentially true . . . Often applied to a proposition that is actually self-contradictory, and so essentially absurd or false . . . A phenomenon that exhibits some conflict with preconceived notions of what is reasonable or possible; a person of perplexingly inconsistent life or behaviour.'

This is not quite how the Greeks used their word παράδοξον, but the thought contained in the definition is not foreign to the ancient world. Socratic irony is a form of paradox, a paradox both logical and, in its own way, religious. What do people say about Socrates, what is the charge brought against him, not only by specific accusers but by public opinion? 'Socrates is an evil-doer, and a curious person, who searches into things under the earth and in heaven, and he makes the worse appear the better cause; and he teaches the aforesaid doctrines to others' (Plato, *Apology* 19B). This will recall to you, as it did to Socrates himself, the famous scene in Aristophanes' *Clouds* in which the two reasons, or logics, the δίκαιος λόγος and the ἄδικος λόγος, appear and argue with each other, and the later point in the play at which the son, Pheidippides, offers to prove to his father, Strepsiades, that it is right for a son to beat his father (*Clouds*, 1334ff.). I have taken a crude example, though it is the one you can hardly miss in the *Clouds*. To continue, more seriously, with the argument of the *Apology*. Socrates goes on to prove that (as the Delphic oracle declared) he, Socrates, is the wisest of men precisely because he is aware of his ignorance (as other men are not).

There is a somewhat different kind of paradox, a moral paradox, in Stoicism, which it may be simplest to illustrate in the classical form in which it appeared in Hellenistic Judaism. I refer to Philo's tract – probably an early one, a study in the Hellenistic philosophy in which he had been educated, and undertaken before he embarked upon his serious long-term task of expounding the law – *That every upright man is free*, with its matching partner, unfortunately lost, *That every bad man is a slave*. The content of the tract will not, perhaps, today strike anyone as particularly novel or paradoxical, since it represents the kind of moralism in which we have been brought up (though how long that proposition will remain true is a fair question – not to be pursued here). But it does represent the point that the Stoics, when they got away from physics, were concerned to make. 'The wise man only is free, because he alone uses his own will and controls himself; alone beautiful, because only virtue is beautiful and attractive; alone rich and happy, because goods of the soul are the most valuable, and true riches consist in being independent of wants.'[1] Epictetus and Marcus Aurelius will of course supply abundant illustrations.[2] The moral paradox is an accusation against the standards of judgement that men commonly employ. You would think the rich man happy, the poor man unfortunate; you would think the man in high office happy, the slave unfortunate; but you are employing the wrong criteria. The truth is other than you think – indeed, a paradox.

This moral paradox occurs and is developed in the New Testament. 'Let the brother who is brought low rejoice in his exaltation, and the wealthy man in his being brought low' (Jas. 1.9f.). 'Did not

God choose the poor in this world to be rich in faith and heirs of the
kingdom which he promised to those who love him?' (Jas. 2.5). The
moral paradox of poverty and wealth – the fact that it may, contrary to popular notions, turn out to be better to be poor than to be
rich – is reflected in the teaching of Jesus, where it becomes explicitly, as it is not in James, an eschatological paradox; that is, an
apparently absurd remark whose truth will be proved not in this
age but in the age to come. 'Sell all you have, and give to the poor,
and you shall have treasure in heaven' (Mark 10.21). More generally, 'Many that are first shall be last, and the last first' (Mark
10.31). The moral paradox of wealth and poverty shades off into
other kinds. It is perhaps better to be foolish than wise. 'I thank
thee, Father, Lord of heaven and earth, that thou didst hide these
things from the wise and intelligent and reveal them to infants'
(Matt. 11.25). In this sense the whole ministry of Jesus, who is the
friend of the friendless, and in the end, so far from enjoying a
triumph, is crucified, dead and buried, is a paradox. This is taken
up in more theological terms. 'You know the grace of our Lord
Jesus, that though he was rich, for your sake he became poor, that
you through his poverty might become rich' (2 Cor. 8.9). The same
Epistle puts a comparable paradox in a different setting at 5.21:
'Him who knew no sin he made sin on our behalf, that we might
become God's righteousness in him.' Primitive Christology in
general is pervaded with this kind of paradox; we shall be considering at a later point whether this is true also of Johannine theology.
Before, however, we can discuss this question we must introduce
another term into the discussion; this too can be expressed in a
single word, but it is another word that calls for careful definition,
and when carefully defined it is not so easy to locate as is often
supposed. If *dualism* is 'the doctrine that there are two independent
principles, one good and the other evil' (I quote the *Oxford English
Dictionary* once more), and if the word *independent* is to be taken
seriously, there are not many really dualistic systems, systems that
have not only a truly independent God but also a truly independent
devil, eternal and unchanging as God himself. Plato's teaching is
often, and understandably, described as dualistic. Yet if there is a
dualistic distinction between the ideal forms and the empirical
objects of sense, surely there is also a positive relation between them,
since the objects of sense come into being on the basis of the ideal
forms; time may be no more than the moving image of eternity, yet

it is the image of eternity, and is therefore not unrelated to it, not in the strict sense independent.

Gnosis comes nearer to absolute dualism; it is significant that it always finds its chief problem not in the doctrine of salvation but in the doctrine of creation. Salvation means the separation of matter from spirit, of darkness from light, as when for example, month by month, the moon fills up with particles of light, discharges them into heaven and immediately comes back for another load. But how did light and darkness come to be mixed up in the first instance? This is more of a problem, and is usually answered in terms either of an unhappy cosmic accident or of an infinite regress – neither of which expedients can be logically satisfying. There is, however, a real measure of independence in the two principles, which is not compromised by their uneasy contiguity in the make-up of man as he finds himself in the present world. 'For this reason, alone among all the living beings upon earth, man is twofold (διπλοῦς); he is mortal on account of his body (διὰ τὸ σῶμα), immortal on account of the essential man (διὰ τὸν οὐσιώδη ἄνθρωπον). For though he is immortal and has authority over all things, he suffers mortal circumstances (τὰ θνητὰ πάσχει) being subject to fate (τῇ εἱμαρμένῃ)' (Corpus Hermeticum 1.15).

Where else is dualism to be found in the ancient world? We must keep clearly in mind what it is that we are looking for. The mere use of images in pairs, such as light and darkness, or even matter and spirit, is not in itself dualistic. Philo, who shares some of the features of Gnosticism, trembles on the brink of dualism and sometimes seems to go over the edge. The fact is that he is too little of an independent thinker, too much under the control of the line of thought he happens to be following – or borrowing – at the moment, to be consistent. His Platonism and his dependence on the Old Testament meet each other and find some measure of reconciliation in Quis Rerum Divinarum Heres 160. After quoting Genesis 1.31 ('God saw all the things which he had made, and behold, they were very good') he continues, 'Now God praised not the material (ὕλη) which he had used for his work, material soulless, discordant and dissoluble, and indeed in itself perishable, irregular, unequal, but he praised the works of his own art.' To say that matter (ὕλη) is not to be praised is not the same thing as to describe it as essentially evil, and though at first it might seem to be allowed an uncaused origin over against God this is contradicted by its description as perishable

($\phi\theta\alpha\rho\tau\acute{\eta}$); it is therefore not eternal. Philo thus avoids true dualism. The Old Testament itself, though well aware of the existence of evil, is not dualistic, since (though it teaches different ideas about the origin of evil) it never supposes that evil can get beyond God's control; the good God is sure to win in the end. A great deal has been written about the dualism of the Qumran sect, but there is no need to pursue the matter at this point. The sect was far too strongly influenced by the Old Testament to entertain anything more than what is often called a qualified dualism; and this on any strict definition is no dualism at all. For the rabbis, God is always the creator of all things, even of the יֵצֶר, which, evil as it is, has some soul of goodness in it, for without it men would not marry, have children or build cities.

There are thus narrow limits to the area in which true dualism is to be found, and this must be remembered when we study the Fourth Gospel. It is nevertheless true that paradox and dualism form part of the background in the light of which the Gospel must be read. This means that if we are to seek paradox and dualism in the Gospel itself, we shall be unable to avoid questions that go beyond the simple occurrence of literary or philosophical phenomena. Clearly the much discussed question of the relation of John to Gnosticism is one that cannot be altogether avoided, though I shall try not simply to repeat familiar points about familiar controversies. More important and more far-reaching, and perhaps the best way to approach the gnostic issue, is the question how John understood salvation; and we shall begin the examination of the Gospel at this point.

Not that a direct approach by way of the word $\sigma\dot{\omega}\zeta\epsilon\iota\nu$ and its cognates will take us far. They are not common, and their meaning is assumed rather than supplied. The ordinary, unspecialized, use of $\sigma\dot{\omega}\zeta\epsilon\iota\nu$ appears from time to time. This is, for example, the superficial sense of 11.12: If Lazarus has fallen asleep he will get well ($\sigma\omega\theta\acute{\eta}\sigma\epsilon\tau\alpha\iota$). Of course, the Christian reader will sense overtones here, and the Evangelist certainly intended him to do so, but they arise out of the basic sense of restored physical well-being. The same, more or less, is true of 12.27, the prayer that Jesus contemplates: Father, save me from this hour, that is, Rescue me from the terrible fate that threatens me. The reader knows that Jesus' acceptance of this fate means salvation for him. The other occurrences of the verb seem to be technical in the Christian sense. John 10.9 might in the first instance suggest: I am the door of the sheepfold; the sheep that enters through this door shall find safety (σωθήσεται), that is, it will not need to fear the depredations of wolves, thieves and robbers, but will be safely guarded and pastured; but no one will ever have read this verse without seeing in it a reference to whatever it is that Christians mean by salvation. John 3.17 and 12.47 are similar but unambiguous: God did not send his Son into the world to judge it, but that the world might be saved through him; 'I did not come to judge the world but to save the world.' It is to be noted that in each case it is the world that is to be saved. This chimes with the one occurrence of the noun σωτήρ: the Samaritans, having encountered Jesus for themselves, declare that he is truly the Saviour of the world (4.42); 5.34 narrows the immediate reference of salvation. Jesus refers to the testimony of John the Baptist not because he himself is in need of such human testimony but for the good of his hearers, who may perhaps accept it: 'I say these things that you may be saved' (ἵνα ὑμεῖς σωθῆτε) – for unless they believe Jesus they will die in their sins (8.24). This leaves us with only one reference, 4.22: in contrast with the ignorant Samaritans, Jews worship what they know, ὅτι ἡ σωτηρία ἐκ τῶν Ἰουδαίων ἐστίν; salvation is of the Jews.

All this, as I have said, does not take us far. Salvation emerges on Jewish soil; this means only that the salvation John is talking about had been foretold in the Old Testament, which is a Jewish book, and therefore stood a good chance of being understood and received by Jews. But this was no automatic process; Jesus must use whatever means he can find to persuade the Jews that he is the bearer of salvation, and he is not very successful in the task. The salvation that they, on the whole, reject, is in fact designed for the world, that is, for mankind apart from God but not abandoned by him. So much is clear, but what God means to do for the world and how he means to do it, is so far not clear, except in that it involves the sending into the world of his Son.

God and the world; the mission into the world of the Son of God. This leads us back to the questions which it is my intention to discuss. Are we entitled to speak of dualism in the Fourth Gospel, and, if so, in what sense? And is paradox a term that can appropriately be used, especially in Johannine Christology? We may sharpen this question by a reference to one of the most provocative books on Johannine theology to appear in our generation, E. Käsemann's *The Testament of Jesus*.[3] For Käsemann makes the double assertion that John's picture of Jesus is docetic, and that paradox, so often used in the past for the Word become flesh, is a term inappropriate to describe John's Christology. Jesus in John may superficially appear to be human, but, according to Käsemann, he is not really so. Such features of the narrative as his weariness, his thirst, his human ignorance, are precisely the kind of cover that the docetist makes; after all, a docetic Christ has to appear – δοκεῖν – to be something, and the point of docetism is that he appears to be human. But he is not really so. The weariness is apparent; the truth of the Johannine Christ is that he walks across the sea, passes through locked doors, fells his enemies by the simple pronouncement, ἐγώ εἰμι. He is not a man, but a god striding over the earth in the guise of man. Dazzled by the picture of the God-Christ, the Church overlooked the docetism involved and included the Fourth Gospel in the canon – errore hominum, providentia Dei. This conclusion is not to be avoided, Käsemann says, by speaking of a paradoxical combination of the divine and human in one person. One may speak of paradox in the figure of the synoptic Son of man, in whom the heavenly figure appears on earth in a lonely, rejected, despised, mortal human being exposed and vulnerable to fightings without and fears within. But the Johannine Christ changes only his location when he comes from heaven to earth; he remains in control of every situation, and knows that he is about to return to the glory he enjoyed before the world was.

Now this view of Johannine theology and soteriology is entirely coherent. The docetism which Käsemann finds in John implies, or is, a species of dualism. It is because matter is essentially opposed to spirit that the Logos cannot truly become man. It is true that the Prologue (1.14) declares, ὁ λόγος σὰρξ ἐγένετο, the Word became flesh, but this means only that the Logos found a convenient stage on which to display his glory. The radical opposition between matter and spirit is brought out elsewhere in the Gospel: 'That which is born of the flesh is flesh, and that which is born of the Spirit is spirit' (3.6). In other terms, 'You are from below, I am from above; you are of this world, I am not of this world' (8.23). The docetism of the Gospel thus means dualism: and dualism of this kind makes paradox impossible, for paradox, as we have seen, is something other than plain contradiction; it involves some kind of relation between two contrasting propositions. It is for this reason that there is a marked absence of paradox in gnosis. Contradiction indeed there is, and mixture: man as we know him is a mixture of matter and spirit, evil and good. But he is, if one may borrow an analogy, a physical mixture, of which the elements may be separated out, not a chemical compound, where the compounding elements have combined to form a new substance. This latter is paradox – the paradox of the Son of man, who, notwithstanding the prophecy that all peoples, nations and languages should serve him (Dan. 7.14), came not to be served but to serve (Mark 10.45). In comparison with this there is no paradox in the gnostic Redeemer-Revealer. He comes from heaven and sojourns on earth, to do what he has to do and to communicate what he has to communicate, and thence returns whence he came; in order to fulfil his task and make himself known to men, he adopts certain human means of communication; but that is all.

Käsemann's understanding of John is thus coherent, and an important challenge to a number of opinions widely accepted by both conservative and radical scholars. It raises in a particularly acute way the questions that I am discussing in this lecture, and criticism of it will lead to a positive account of paradox and dualism. Perhaps the most vulnerable point in Käsemann's exposition is the one that lies on any showing at the heart of the whole matter. It seems to me doubtful whether in his analysis of the Prologue Käsemann has done justice to the proposition of 1.14, ὁ λόγος σὰρξ ἐγένετο, the Word became flesh. It may, and I think should, be allowed that John's keenest interest lies in the second half of the verse: the result of the process was that we beheld his glory. But the process itself was that in which God (for that is what the Logos is – 1.1) became man (for that is what flesh means), and the glory that we beheld is defined not in terms of miracle (though that will come later – 2.11) but in terms of grace and truth, the grace and truth that did not come by Moses, but only through Jesus Christ. Thus it is right to say that the fundamental assertion is: We beheld his glory. But it is a paradoxical glory that we see, since it consists not in God's self-assertive might but in his faithfulness and self-giving, and in order that it might become visible the Logos adopted a paradoxical, unexpected role – a role that might at first seem inconsistent with his deity. This is prepared for in earlier verses of the Prologue, which does not suddenly become anti-gnostic with verse 14. Since the Word is God and served as the agent of creation, one might expect there to be a revelation of God in creation: God should be known (like any other creative artist) in his works. But clearly there has been a perversion of creation, since when the Logos came into the world, the world which was made by him did not know him. When he came to his own inheritance his own people did not recognize him. Even the Logos thus fails to mediate knowledge of God except in his incarnation, except, that is, in the situation in which God is denied, rejected and veiled from ordinary apprehension. Another observation that can be put with this (though I shall not develop it) is the existence side by side of what may be called 'subordinationist passages' (such as 'The Father is greater than I', 14.28) and 'equality passages' (such as 'I and the Father are one', 10.30). I have discussed these elsewhere[4] and must not linger over them now.

The upshot of these observations is that there is dualism in John, a dualism that is related to gnostic dualism though not identical with it. I am not thinking merely of the fact that John's dualism is not absolute but qualified. This property it shares with Qumran dualism, and indeed with most other dualistic systems. As I have said, there are very few absolute dualisms, for most religious men are apt to claim that however bad things may be at the moment, God will win in the end. The distinguishing feature of John's dualism is its mobility; it is dualism in motion, in becoming. For the keyword is the ἐγένετο of 1.14. The Greek fathers rightly noted the contrast between this word and the continuous tenses that describe the Logos in his relation to God. In the beginning the Word was (ἦν), the Word was (ἦν) with God, the Word was (ἦν) God (1.1). It is not surprising that the word ἐγένετο should be used of the universe (πάντα, κόσμος); it is not to be expected that it should be used of the Word.

It is here, in the fact that John's dualism is dualism in becoming, in motion, that we may find the clue to the problem of paradox in Johannine theology. We have seen that straightforward static dualism is alien to paradox; not so John's dualism. For John's dualism is a soteriological before it is a Christological dualism. This appears in the great pairs of concepts (not in themselves necessarily paradoxical) which are used in the Gospel, such as light and darkness. I do not wish to raise here the question of the authorship of the First Epistle; whatever the answer to that question may be, there is a difference between the static proposition of 1 John 1.5, 'God is light and in him is no darkness at all', and what we read in the Gospel. 'The light shines in the darkness' (1.5); 'This is the judgement, that the light has come into the world, and men loved the darkness rather than the light' (3.19); 'I am the light of the world; he that follows me shall not walk in darkness, but shall have the light of life' (8.12); 'While I am in the world, I am the light of the world' (9.5); 'Yet a little while the light is among you. Walk while you have the light, that the darkness may not overtake you ... While you have the light, believe in the light, that you may become children of the light' (12.35f.); 'I have come as light into the world, that everyone who believes in me may not walk in the darkness' (12.46). These passages hardly call for comment. They do not depict a world of light existing in equilibrium over against a world of darkness. As far as John's expressed thought goes, there is no world of light. There is only a world, above and below, of darkness, and in it there explodes at a given point a rocket whose brilliant balls of light move across the sky and for a moment or two light up heaven and earth. In this moment of illumination men must act before night closes in once more – the night when no man can work or walk (9.4; 11.10). Action means not simply looking at the light but accepting it, believing in it; if men do this they become sons of light, and have the light of life. There is no question here of sorting out light and darkness and keeping them separate from each other, of seeking out those men who already have the seeds of light within them; men become what they were not before, and possess what they did not previously have.

Similar observations could be made about the pair life and death. The two nouns occur together only once, in 5.24, where movement is explicit. 'He who hears my words and believes him who sent me, has eternal life; he does not come into judgement, but has moved out of death into life.' Other passages that are relevant, though slightly less explicit, are 12.24: 'Unless a grain of wheat falls into the ground and dies, it remains alone; but if it dies, it bears much fruit'; the unsuspectingly true words of the high priest in 11.50, and their sequel (cf. 18.14): 'It is expedient for you that one man should die for the people, and that the whole nation should not perish'; and the whole narrative, in 11.1–44, of the raising of Lazarus. The themes of life and death are played upon throughout this story in a way that cannot be traced out in detail here, but 11.25f. may be quoted: 'He who believes in me, even if he dies, shall live, and everyone who lives and believes in me shall never die' (οὐ μὴ ἀποθάνῃ εἰς τὸν αἰῶνα). Jesus enters the realm of death and by doing so transfers men out of it into life. Again, the dualism is not static but in motion.

Finally we may consider the world above and the world beneath, possibly the commonest of dualistic schemes and mentioned explicitly at 8.23, which I have already quoted. What we must consider here is that whereas τὰ ἄνω, τὰ κάτω, are mentioned once only, the verbs, ἀναβαίνειν, καταβαίνειν, with certain equivalents, occur frequently – too frequently for me to refer to all the passages here. Jesus as the Son of man descends and ascends: 'No one has ascended into heaven but he that came down from heaven, namely the Son of man' (3.13). That this notion of the descent and ascent of a Redeemer figure (even though in John the Redeemer ascends by way of the cross) is shared by John with Gnosticism, in no way alters the fact that John does not think of the heavenly world and the earthly world as out of contact with each other. True, contact is made in one person only; but it is the contact in and through that one person that John is talking about.

It is John's dualism in motion that makes it possible to speak of paradox – of light in darkness, of life in death, of a person who is found below when he might be expected to be above – though it is true that John has rethought and re-expressed the old paradoxes of the synoptic tradition. Mark's understanding of the paradox of Jesus led to his theory of the Messianic Secret. This was Mark's post-resurrection version of a pre-crucifixion fact, and the shift in time and context led Mark to an occasional exaggerated statement of the theme; secrecy is insisted on in circumstances where it is manifestly impossible and, by Mark's own account, was not achieved. In John this becomes the secret of divinity hidden behind a humanity whose traits are sometimes (as Käsemann has quite correctly observed) artificially exaggerated; hidden also behind the assertion that Jesus must be something less than God since God is greater than he. But again, John's dualism in motion tends to root the paradox in the theme of salvation rather than in that of Christology. It does appear in Johannine Christology precisely because, in virtue of the movement I have described, John's Christology, like that of most other parts of the New Testament, is primarily functional. So far as it tends to become not only functional but essential, the movement comes to a halt, and the truly paradoxical element becomes less visible.

This leads me finally to look at the twin themes of paradox and dualism with reference to three more topics: the Son of man, worship and John's understanding of man.

First, the term Son of man – a christological term, of course, but the centre of gravity of John's usage lies rather in the realm of soteriology. The Son of man is a figure in motion, or at least one upon whom motion tends to focus. This appears perhaps most clearly in the passage in John 3 to which I have already referred: the Son of man is the person who descends from heaven to earth and then ascends back to the place whence he came, but ascends by way of death, like Moses' serpent, the very image of death. A similar observation can be made about the Son of man in 6.53: 'Unless you eat the flesh of the Son of man and drink his blood, you have not life in you.' I have discussed this passage and its origin in another lecture and must not do so now.[5] The paragraph is certainly part of the Gospel as we have it today, and we may be content to read it in its context. The central proposition, that the Son of man is the one who, in death, gives his flesh and blood for the life of the world, is framed by the assertion that Jesus is the bread that came down from heaven (6.41), and the challenge, Does this offend you? What then if you see the Son of man ascending where he was before? The Son of man is a moving figure, whose movement means paradox as far as his person is concerned, and for men salvation, since in his flesh and blood, given in death, men have life.

We may consider one other Son of man passage – the first, which no doubt was intended to set the interpretation of the Son of man figure in the Gospel as a whole. In 1.51 we read: 'You shall see heaven opened, and the angels of God ascending and descending upon the Son of man.' It is usually, and rightly, supposed that there is here an allusion to Jacob's dream described in Genesis 28. I have shown elsewhere how clearly the significance of John's use of this Old Testament passage is brought out when we compare what Philo does with the same passage. I need not go into detail now.[6] Philo, who gives several interpretations by no means consistent with one another, is freely allegorizing a story for whose historicity he has no real concern. In the end the lesson he derives is of the remoteness of God. God is not confined in a place; he is illimitable, and knowable only through mediators, such as the Logos, who is carefully distinguished from God, who himself is ὁ πρὸ τοῦ λόγου θεός (De Somniis 1.65). It is surely clear that John (in contrast with Philo) begins from the historical scene of the ministry of Jesus, and means to

assert that this is the place where heaven is open and access to God
becomes possible. As Schnackenburg[7] says, 'Heaven opens above
the Son of Man, so that what is a vision of the future in the Synoptics
is already present in John . . . the Son of Man on earth is the "gate of
heaven" (cf. Genesis 28.17), the place of the presence of God's
grace on earth, the tent of God among men (cf. 1.14).' But why
'upon the Son of Man' in the place where Genesis says ἐπ' αὐτῆς
(that is, on the ladder)? John is concerned not only to make a
christological point in a straightforward ontological proposition,
but to emphasize movement, traffic, intercourse. Jesus as the Son of
man becomes the means by which men have communion with
God. The image may be crude, but it leads to the heart of John's
thought. The Son of man is the ladder on which the angelic traffic
moves. It is characteristic of làdders that they have two ends; they
connect two points. This is what John has to say of the Son of man;
he connects heaven and earth. Because he belongs to both heaven
and earth he makes possible communication between the two. We
may return here to the central verse that I have already quoted,
3.13: 'No one has ascended into heaven but he who came down from
heaven.' It has been argued, recently and notably by F. J. Moloney,[8]
that this is an incorrect translation; the εἰ μή should be rendered,
'No one has ascended into heaven but there is one who has come
down from heaven.' This rendering would not entirely exclude the
use that I am making of the verse, but it would give it a very
different balance. It would no longer contemplate the complete
work of the Son of man in his return to the heaven whence he came.
I do not, however, think that Moloney's rendering can be defended.
Had it been intended to leave the proposition 'No one has ascended
into heaven' totally unqualified but simply added to by the second
proposition, a different construction, including a second verb,
would have been used: ἔστι δὲ ὁ καταβαίνων, or ὁ καταβάς, or some
such expression. The Son of man descends and ascends: if this
verse does not state the fact, there are others in the Gospel that
speak of the return of the Son to the glory of the Father. But 3.13
contains more than this if we may accept (with Θ lat (cur) pesh 𝕂)
the long text: 'No one has ascended into heaven save he that came
down from heaven, the Son of man, who is in heaven', ὁ ὢν ἐν τῷ
οὐρανῷ. The paradox of the Son of man is that even when on earth
he is in heaven; the mythical – or historical – descent and ascent is
of such a kind that effectively the Son of man is in both places at

ònce: the top and the bottom of the ladder. Even if this bold piece
of demythologizíng is not an original part of the text of the Gospel,
it is faithful to John's thought and it is in this that John's understanding of salvation is to be found.

I turn to the second theme, worship, for a further illustration of
the kind of paradox that arises out of John's peculiar dualism in
motion. We begin from 4.23f.: 'An hour is coming, and now is,
when the true worshippers shall worship the Father in spirit and
truth, for the Father seeks such men as his worshippers.' God is
Spirit, and those who worship must worship in Spirit and truth. In
the mission of his Son, God is seeking those who will worship him as
he desires to be worshipped. Looked at from man's side, the object
at which John aims is that men shall believe and by their believing
have life (20.30f.). Looked at from God's side, the object is that God
shall find men who worship him rightly. This kind of worship is
explicitly contrasted with that offered, in different forms on Mount
Gerizim by the Samaritans and on Mount Zion by the Jews. It is
spiritual worship, not capable of being localized and described in
terms of cultic act. It is a relation in truth between Spirit and spirit.
At the same time, as we have already seen in another connection,
John regards the historical Jesus, the incarnate person, as the link
between heaven and earth, God and man, so that in a new but
quite precise sense, worship, the religious contact between the
Creator and his creature, is tied to a historical event which took
place in a specific locality. How are these propositions held together?

The passage in chapter 4 is particularly notable in that it expresses in combination a double dualism and a double paradox, the
paradox of time and the paradox of what I may call being. (I am
not sure that 'being' is an entirely satisfactory word for what I take
John to mean, but perhaps for the moment it may serve.) I am of
course referring first to the statement that 'An hour is coming, and
now is': this, surely, if it is not to be dismissed as a meaningless
piece of nonsense, is a paradox; and secondly to the proposition,
God is Spirit, πνεῦμα ὁ θεός. This says something about God, and
also leads to criticism of conventional ideas of worship which centre
upon a supposed holy place where men gather in order to do what is
believed to be pleasing to God. The paradox of time does not call
for long discussion; it is a particularly sharp formulation of New
Testament, and in particular of Johannine, eschatology, which is
never exhausted in either present or future tenses. The Kingdom of

God is here, the Kingdom of God will come. The Son of man is here, the Son of man will come. We are at liberty to ask whether these affirmations, taken singly or in combination, make sense; we are hardly at liberty to question whether they are all to be found in the New Testament as it stands. By bringing two tenses, present and future, into one sentence John not only underlines the paradox involved in asserting that the future has already become present, he points to movement from the future into the present: that which is future ἔρχεται, is on its way; it has also arrived. A connecting line is drawn from the future into the present; and for John, as for other New Testament writers, the line is constituted by the person of Jesus.

God is Spirit. The word πνεῦμα is used in the Gospel in two senses.[9] One is that of inspiration. The Spirit rested and abode upon Jesus, so marking him out as the one who would in turn baptize with the Holy Spirit (1.32f.). The Spirit gives life (6.63), and so is naturally pictured as rivers of living water flowing out of the inner life of the believer (7.38f.). The Spirit is the Paraclete, given to believers and leading them into all the truth; not given to the world, yet operating on the world, through the witness that it inspires in believers (14.16f., 26; 15.26; 16.7-11, 13-15). Here the Spirit is not being, but action. There are, however, other passages. 'That which is born of the flesh is flesh, and that which is born of the Spirit is spirit' (3.6). The Spirit stands over against all kinds of created existence which is capable of being observed and described. πνεῦμα (and it is all one, whether we translate it wind, breath or spirit) blows where it wills; it cannot be seen, its movements cannot be known; only its sound, or voice (φωνή), can be heard (3.8). This describes the kind of being that God is; by definition, no man has ever seen him (1.18); only he who is from God, ὁ ὢν παρὰ τοῦ θεοῦ (6.46), has seen him. The unbelieving Jews of 5.37 have not even heard his voice. But this is because they do not listen to Jesus, for in him God is heard, and even in a sense seen. 'He that has seen me has seen the Father' (14.9); the only-begotten has made the Father known (1.18). And since the message of Jesus is brought home to men by the Spirit, the Paraclete (14.26; 16.14), it follows that unknowable Spirit, that is, Spirit as the being of God himself, is made known through given Spirit, the Spirit whose work is to take the things of Christ and make them available. In other words, God is ineffable Spirit, and he is to be worshipped by the inspiration of the Spirit that Jesus gives, in the light of the truth that Jesus is (4.24).

Here are two lines of movement; and they intersect in the person of Jesus. The futurity of God, his perfected plan and completed action, come into the present. The unknowable otherness of God becomes part of the intimate awareness of finite and sinful man. This is not the same paradox as that of Mark, or, if it is, it is quite differently expressed; but there is an inner paradox of apparent contradictions – present and future, the expressed and the unknowable – a paradox of God which, in a further paradox, is lodged in a human being, Jesus of Nazareth. As I have said, the paradox tends to disappear when John begins to move over into a metaphysical expression of Christology; but he never quite loses its historical and functional setting.

Finally we come to John's understanding of man and of his place in God's purpose, though we shall find that we have not finished with God. We may begin from John 17, the so-called high-priestly prayer, which sums up not only the thought but the motion of the Gospel, for in it the descending Son ascends again in communion to the Father. In the course of the prayer (9) he declares that he does not pray for the world; the prayer is for those whom God has given him, who are in the world but not of it. There is the world; there are the elect. Only the latter are theologically significant and a personal concern to the Redeemer. Yet in 3.16 there stands the statement: 'God so loved the world that he gave his only Son, that whoever believes in him should not perish but have eternal life.' We may recall 6.44, with the restrictive statement, 'No one can come to me unless the Father who sent me draws him', together with 6.37, 'Him who comes to me I will not cast out.' I have discussed these passages elsewhere from the angle of predestination.[10] I am concerned with them now in their bearing on the doctrine of man. With this in mind we may also consider 12.37–50, in which John sums up the effect of the public ministry of Jesus. The passage is one of almost intolerable tension; it oscillates, as it were, from one arm of a paradox to the other. Though Jesus had done so many signs, men did not believe; it is plainly implied that as a result of what they had seen they should have believed. Yet their unbelief fulfilled the prophecy of Isaiah, and was therefore presumably willed by God; indeed, they could not believe, because of Isaiah's damning words, He has blinded their eyes and hardened their hearts. So – no one believed. Yet – even of the rulers many did believe in him, though they did not confess him (12.42). Belief in Jesus means belief in the

Father who sent him, seeing Jesus means seeing the Father (44f.). Yet Jesus does not judge, since he came not to judge but to save. It is the word that he has spoken that shall judge.

There is no simple way of unravelling this speech. Jesus did not judge, yet his word judges. Men cannot believe; yet they must. Man in the presence of Jesus stands at once under the judgement and the grace of God. We are reminded of the paradox of the Pauline anthropology of justification, to which John is far nearer than is sometimes thought. I am not sure that either the adjective or the substantive of Théo Preiss's 'juridical mysticism'[11] is precisely right, but the phrase as a whole is not far from the mark. The world is lost, and yet the world is saved; it can be saved only by ceasing to be what it is; yet it remains the world, the context in which believers live. Believers believe; they hear the witness – it may be, of John the Baptist – and detach themselves from their old life to follow Christ, ostensibly reaching a decision and choosing him against all the other possibilities their environment provides. Yet in the end they learn that they have not chosen him; he has chosen them. They declare with satisfaction that at length he speaks plainly so that they understand him, and are told that they do not believe but are about to abandon him to his fate. Even among those whom he chooses, one is a devil. The grain of wheat has no hope of life except in death; and it is a death which forms with life a recurrent paradoxical pattern.

At first sight, there appears to be an absolute dualism in John's understanding of man, as absolute a dualism as can be found anywhere among the Gnostics. There are the saved and the lost (such as the son of perdition, 17.12), because there are the believers and the unbelievers, determined as such by the eternal will of God, disclosed by the prophets, whose word cannot fail of fulfilment. Yet the boundary line is crossed, and not fortuitously; Jesus came 'that those who see not might see, and that those who see might become blind' (9.39). This means that the paradox lies in God himself, who determines men to unbelief yet sends his Son to induce them to change their minds; who is love and justice. If some kinds of paradox have, in John, disappeared from the synoptic Jesus (and Käsemann's arguments are not without some weight), it is because John has seen the profounder paradox of the Godhead, paradox not only in God revealing but in God revealed.

NOTES

1 Quoted from Zeller's *Stoics* by F. H. Colson, *Philo*, Loeb edn, vol. ix, p. 3.
2 See also Cicero, *Paradoxa* 5: 'Solum sapientem esse liberum, et omnem stultum servum.'
3 E. Käsemann, *The Testament of Jesus*, Eng. trans. 1968.
4 'The Father is greater than I'; in this volume, pp. 19–36.
5 See the preceding lecture, 'Sacraments', pp. 80–97.
6 'Christocentric or Theocentric?'; in this volume, pp. 1–18.
7 R. Schnackenburg, *The Gospel according to St John*, vol. i, Eng. trans. (1968), p. 321.
8 F. J. Moloney, *The Johannine Son of Man*. ²1978.
9 For some points in this paragraph see 'Christocentric or Theocentric?' in this volume, pp. 1–18.
10 See 'The Dialectical Theology of St John' in my *New Testament Essays* (1972), pp. 62–5.
11 Théo Preiss, *Life in Christ*, Eng. trans. (1954), pp. 9–31.

8

HISTORY

It is frequently affirmed that the Fourth Gospel is a work at the same time historical and theological. This is an attractive statement; more than that, it is probably true. But before it can be useful, the terms in which it is made call for definition. 'Theological' is relatively unambiguous. It sums up and evaluates belief about God, its grounds and its content. It is human language about God, merging into God's language about himself and his creation. 'Theological', however, is often accompanied by 'religious' and 'mystical'. These are more difficult, but if taken together may help to define each other. Both of them have to do with man's awareness of a world other than that of time and space, flesh and blood, food and drink, work and play, in which he is normally at home. How can he establish and maintain contact with this other world? As I understand the terms, religion denotes the various devices, institutional and cultic, by which man has attempted to secure this end. He joins with others (to the exclusion of those who fail to qualify) to sing hymns, say prayers, participate in sacraments, all of which bring him into contact with the world of spirit. Mysticism, on the other hand, signifies the attainment of the same goal without the use of external means and often, though not always, in solitude. 'Historical' might seem an easy term to define, and for my part I should be prepared to allow that it is. People and corporate institutions do things and enter into relation with one another in changing patterns. It is possible to write down (if one is adequately informed) what each is doing today; tomorrow today will be yesterday and the account will still stand; it will then be chronicle. When all the days and all the persons and all the corporate institutions are so treated it becomes possible to ask how one day is related to another, and one person to another. At this point chronicle becomes history. Of course we do not have all the facts, and especially in ancient history there are no day-to-day and hour-to-hour records; the art of ancient history consists in guessing plausibly how to fill up the gaps. Even when the data are sufficient, the human creature is such that it is often difficult to see by what logical process today's actions and reactions are related to yesterday's – man is simply not logical enough. There is thus a great deal of history that we cannot and never shall be able to do. But the thing itself is simple and the best small-scale illustration of it is a first-class detective story; and, being myself no philosopher, I become more than a little impatient with the attempt to represent history as a philosophical problem rather than a record. If a man says to me, 'Yesterday I did so-and-so', I recognize the stuff of history; he may be a liar and not have done the thing at all; he may be a fool, and have done a thing beyond reason. But there is no need to begin at once to speculate on the meaning of history; it is enough that it exists.

It may well seem that I have now defined the terms I have used out of the area of the Fourth Gospel. Mysticism may perhaps be allowed to remain, though indeed it must be radically qualified, since though the Gospel speaks of the direct impact of the Spirit of God, the Paraclete, upon the believer, it is the work of the Spirit to bring to the believer's mind things ostensibly said and done by the historical Jesus, so that the mysticism is not pure mysticism but a historical mysticism, or a mystical apprehension of history. Religion seems to have little place in the Gospel if it is defined as I have defined it. Few books can have less to do with institutions and cultus. I must not discuss again the question of the place of sacraments in the Gospel;[1] enough to say that where other Gospels contain commands to baptize, and what we call, not too happily, 'the institution of the Eucharist', John offers at most allusions. And he thinks of the apostles primarily as those through whose word later generations of believers come into being; they are in no sense the primary and normative administrators of an organized community. Perhaps we should at this point observe, as we shall do later in this lecture, that the Johannine Epistles present a somewhat different front. And what of history? I have elsewhere written that the Fourth Gospel is not a historical work; and I should maintain this view, in the sense that it is hardly possible to use the Gospel for a direct reconstruction of the words and deeds of Jesus. Edwyn Hoskyns once used the following analogy: To use the Fourth Gospel as a source for 'instant history' is like arguing that the Poles must be a very active and agile people because that distinguished Pole, Frédéric Chopin, wrote some extremely rapid waltzes. This is true enough; yet it is also true that one can detect Polish folk music in

the work of Chopin, of which it is one constituent, though a constituent that has been absorbed, compounded with others and
re-expressed; and in this sense it is true to say that there is history in
and behind the Fourth Gospel. Had there not been a historical
Jesus there would have been no Fourth Gospel; more, had the
historical Jesus been other than he was, the Gospel must have taken
a different form. Fortunately there is no problem about theology:
the Fourth Gospel is a book about God, and never pretends to be
anything else. It is a book about God rather even than a book about
Jesus, for 'He that hath seen me hath seen the Father'; 'No man has
ever seen God; the only-begotten Son has made him known.' I have
discussed elsewhere the essentially theological character of the
Gospel.[2]

I do not wish at this stage to assert more than that it is possible to
talk about John and his thought in terms of religion or mysticism, of
theology and of history; and that this proposition is one that needs a
good deal of evaluation before we can give it any full and satisfactory sense. The next step is to raise a particular question that
applies, in different forms, to the various categories all of which may
claim a share in the Gospel. This lecture might bear the subtitle, 'The
problem of authority'. There can be few introductions to the Fourth
Gospel that do not contain a section on the authority of the Gospel;
it is not always recognized that authority must take different forms
in different compartments of life. There is, of course, only one sort of
authority of real worth in the realm of history: sound, accurate,
first-hand information. Ideally it will come from the historian's own
observation and recollection, though even here he may find that he
cannot entirely trust his own memory. And even eye-witnesses are
not necessarily to be credited. 'I have found it difficult to remember
the precise words used in the speeches which I listened to myself and
my various informants have experienced the same difficulty . . .
either I was present myself at the events which I have described or
else I heard of them from eye-witnesses whose reports I have
checked with as much thoroughness as possible. Not that, even so,
the truth was easy to discover: different eye-witnesses give different
accounts of the same events, speaking out of partiality for one side
or the other or else from imperfect memories' (Thucydides 1.22).
This is a classical account of the historian's problem; it becomes
more complicated when the possibility of written sources is taken
into account. Tradition makes the Fourth Evangelist an eye-

witness of the events he records, and, as the closest disciple of Jesus, the best of historical authorities. Is there any degree to which this kind of authority can be ascribed to the book today? I shall not attempt a direct answer to this question at this, or indeed at any other, point in my lecture. It is becoming fashionable to rate the historical authority of John more highly than a generation ago, to suppose that the Evangelist possessed sources different from, but as old as, those used by the Synoptic Evangelists. I question whether this is true, but even if it is, the sources have passed through the Evangelist's mind, and it may well be that his concern for history, though perhaps as serious as that of Thucydides, was of a different kind. At present, however, I am not attempting to assess authority but only to consider different kinds of authority.

If religion is understood in the perhaps rather narrow way in which I have defined it, authority must be some form of ecclesiastical authority. This can be expressed in an individual (monarchical), a collegiate, or a universal manner, and we have seen all these expressions of authority in Christian history and in our own time. It is interesting to note that one verse in the Gospel points in the direction of collegiate authority: 21.24, where the authority of the writer is backed up by an undefined group: This is the disciple who bears witness about these things and wrote these things, and we know that his witness is true. Again, the theme is not one that I shall pursue at this stage, though it is impossible today to speak about a 'John the Evangelist' without also considering the possibility, or probability, of a 'Johannine school' to which he belonged.

The only authority for the mystical element is the individual, who in the secret core of his own existence knows that he has communion with the divine. No one can give it to him; no one can take it away. No one can validate or invalidate it for him. If the experience does not validate itself it is not true for him, and in this context only that which is true for him is true at all. If the experience does validate itself, no one can take it away or disprove it. Mysticism is the area where subjectivity is not merely allowed but by definition reigns supreme – unless, that is, John finds some way of qualifying it.

Some would say that the same is true of theology: that this is an area in which neither verification nor falsification is possible. This is in a sense true, but it does not mean that theologians are irresponsible creatures, able to say without control anything that comes into their heads. But what is authority in theology? It is not hard to name some of the authorities that are recognized by some theologians today: Scripture; tradition; the living magisterium of the Church in its teaching office. But none of these, certainly not the first, will serve when we are talking about the Fourth Gospel; indeed it cannot but raise some difficulties for us when we speak of the authority of Scripture, for the story and the teaching of Jesus in John are different from those that we read in the Synoptic Gospels. Either John did not know the synoptic but some other tradition; or, knowing the synoptic tradition, he modified it with very considerable freedom. Since this distinction applies to the story and the teaching of Jesus, to say that the theological authority behind John is to be found not in written sources, not in oral tradition, but in the figure of Jesus himself, is not without its difficulties. At this point historical authority and theological authority overlap, for John clearly does not intend to make statements about God simply on the basis of reason and natural revelation. He claims that God is known by special revelation in Jesus. 'He that has seen me has seen the Father'; but seeing Jesus, and so receiving an authoritative understanding of God, depends on the historical authority of the account of Jesus supplied. Since precisely this historical authority is in question, we note for the present that history, religion, mysticism and theology seem at least to point us in different directions when we inquire into the authority on which they rest; and that there is no evident relation between the different kinds of authority involved. Let us note this, and go on to take account of a related but different kind of problem. Up to this point, when I have spoken of historical questions, the question in mind has been essentially, What does John tell us about the Jesus of history? And, Is what he tells us about the Jesus of history historically correct? But the book suggests another set of historical questions, which are closely related to the question about its own authority in matters of religion and theology. In what historical circumstances was it written? I have in mind more than the old-fashioned questions about date and authorship, though these of course remain fundamental. Whoever the author was, in what setting, under what pressures, did he write? I have in mind the sort of question that Käsemann raised in his lecture, 'Ketzer und Zeuge'[3] – what sort of role did the Evangelist play in the ecclesiastical cross-currents of his day?; the search for a Johannine school out of which Gospel and Epistles emerged; J. L. Martyn's fascinating attempt[4] to reconstruct out of material in the Gospel the groups to whose debates the Gospel itself was a contribution. The Gospel must be considered as conditioned by the religious, ecclesiastical and theological convictions and disputes of its environment. With what sort of authority did it make its voice heard?

This question can be approached from the other side – from outside the Gospel. What sort of authority can it be shown to have had in the early Church? It is well known that the answer to this question is that it seems, in the earliest period, to have carried very little weight in orthodox Christian circles. If we exclude Ignatius, who probably bears witness to common traditions rather than to knowledge of the Gospel itself, its first users and interpreters were Gnostics – and Ignatius himself was partly gnostic. The Muratorian Canon shows awareness of the problems caused by the divergent tradition represented by John, and it was only Irenaeus, who discovered how to use the Gospel in an anti-gnostic sense and thus to turn the Gnostics' weapon against them, who really established its position among the orthodox. Irenaeus did this by his insistence on the view that the book was written by John the son of Zebedee, the intimate disciple of the Lord. From this point onwards even such groups as the Alogi became unimportant; but what of the earlier period? Then, it seems, both the history and the theology of the book were anything but authoritative; that is, there was no external authority that guaranteed the accuracy of the history and the orthodoxy of the theology. If the Gospel was written by an eyewitness apostle, who must be supposed to have known both what happened and what this meant, the fact was not generally known or generally accepted. It had to make its way and establish itself by its contents and such intrinsic authority as these carried with them; and, as I have said, these commended themselves to the Gnostics before they commended themselves to the orthodox.

It may well be questioned whether this judgement is expressed in the right terms. What, if anything, did the terms 'orthodoxy' and 'heresy' mean at the time when John was written? This question was raised long ago by Walter Bauer.[5] Orthodoxy and heresy are meaningful only when set against some accepted standard of right belief. And what sort of norm may be said to have existed in the New Testament period? Was Paul aware of one? It is true that he argues vehemently on theological subjects, but he never, Bauer points out, suggests that anyone should be excluded from the Church, or excludes himself from salvation, by reason of his mistaken opinions. He requires in 1 Corinthians 5 the exclusion of an offender, but this is in order that his spirit may be saved in the day of Christ, and the offence in question is the moral one of incest, not doctrinal; and at the end of the same Epistle he invokes an anathema, but solely on the man who does not love the Lord – his theology is not called in question, only his personal loyalty. What we see in the New Testament is the rising of a number of springs, close enough in their origins but destined to flow out in different directions and empty themselves in different seas. The New Testament is a book of variety, not of uniform consistency. The concepts of orthodoxy and heresy belong to a later stage of development, and we must recognize that, essentially, orthodoxy denotes the side that won, heresy the side that lost.

Now I am not sure that Bauer (to whom I have certainly not done justice in this scrappy sketch) has adequately evaluated the early history of Christian thought. There were some issues on which Paul was prepared to stand firmly and even aggressively. He was not (it seems) greatly concerned about the formulation of Christian belief, but if the purity of the gospel as he understood it was touched, he reacted at once. There was only one gospel, only one Jesus, only one Spirit, and those who attempted to deflect his churches to a different gospel – which could not really be another gospel since it was not a gospel at all – received short shrift. In fact we see fundamental conceptions such as the freedom of God to act in grace struggling into and out of formulations – into formulations lest they be corrupted, then out of formulations again lest they become ossified through identification with the formula, and a new legalism result.

The upshot of this is that, in dealing with Christian thought up to and including the time of John, we are dealing with a fluid situation, perhaps better, with a sequence of fluid situations, and when one takes a section out of this moving current to examine it one runs the risk of petrifying the mobile and alive. We are concerned with the development and interaction of the historical tradition and the theological tradition; if we are to retain the image of a stream, we might perhaps describe the banks between which the two streams jointly flow as the religious framework of the early Christian Church. If one is to look for a place in the picture for something that can be labelled mysticism this will perhaps best be found in the motion itself, the impetus of the joint historical – theological stream. This can be thought of as an entity in itself, though of course it cannot exist apart from actual water particles in motion.

Enough of metaphor and generalization. The way to proceed in this matter is to consider the interaction of the historical and religious traditions in the Johannine environment. If one representative of those who have attempted to explore this field is to be mentioned, I should choose J. L. Martyn,[6] both for his ingenuity and his moderation. He has made a much strongre case than any of his predecessors for locating John in the diasporasynagogue. It will be recalled that he argues that the Gospel was written on two levels, one of which he describes by the German adjective *einmalig* – it relates to what happened on a particular occasion in the past, in the life of Jesus. The other level relates to the Evangelist's own time and religious environment. His best illustration of this two-dimensional kind of writing is the story (John 9) of the man born blind, which, as many commentators have suggested, seems to contain an allusion to the exclusion of Jewish Christians from the synagogue by the *birkath hamminim* of *c.* AD 85. He is, inevitably, I think, less successful in making his case elsewhere, but he is all the more convincing in that he does not try to prove too much.

John was neither playing a kind of code-game, nor trying to instruct members of his church about points of correspondence between the Jewish hierarchy of Jesus' day and that of their own day. One may be confident that he did not intend his readers to analyze the dramatis personae in the way in which we have done it. Indeed, I doubt that he was himself *analytically conscious* of what I have termed the two-level drama, for his major concern in this regard was to bear witness to the essential *integrity* of the *einmalig* drama of Jesus' earthly life and the contemporary drama in which the Risen Lord acts through his servants (op cit., p. 77).

Yet the impression of patchiness remains. There are aspects of the Gospel which the book leaves out of account. Martyn himself acknowledges (p. xii) that the major thesis of Bultmann's commentary, that John's work must be understood in the context of gnostic thought, still seems to him to be 'partly correct'. Does not this sum up the core of the problem that confronts us when we study John? One writer expounds the Gospel in terms of the Evangelist's 'love–hate' relation with Judaism, and it seems to us partly correct. Another expounds the same work in terms of a similar relation with Gnosticism, and this too seems to us partly correct. Under these main headings minor sub-headings can be found. John is related to Judaism: some will say to diaspora Judaism, others to rabbinic Judaism, others to the Hellenistic Judaism of Philo, others to Qumran Judaism. John is related to Gnosticism: some will say to the gnosis of the Mandaean texts, others to the Corpus Hermeticum, and others again will pick up Philo on his non-Jewish side. It is no desire to keep on good terms with all my colleagues (for I shall probably succeed in offending all of them) but a simple attempt to do justice to the evidence they have unearthed that leads me to conclude that the background of the Gospel must have been exceedingly diverse, and its relation through its own history to the history of Jesus extremely complicated.

I have discussed some aspects of the matter in detail elsewhere and do not wish to repeat myself here. In any case a lecture does not permit detailed study of so vast a field. Let me, however, return to Ignatius. I do not raise the old and familiar (and important) questions whether Ignatius had read, and quoted, the Fourth Gospel; and why, when writing to the church at Ephesus, he fails to refer to John, who, according to the Irenaean tradition, lived in Asia until not many years before the date of Ignatius' letter. In some ways Ignatius is a better witness if he had never heard of the Gospel. For, unless we are to embark upon a somewhat improbable analysis, Ignatius bears witness to the existence of people who are Jewish, gnostic and (though Ignatius himself would have denied it) Christian. It is another significant part of the picture that he himself may be qualified by the same three adjectives: Christian, of course; gnostic, though not docetic, in that he knows the Gospel as a mystery and sets forth the descent and ascent of the Redeemer; and Jewish, in that he claims the prophets as his – that he is uncircumcised is no barrier, since some of his Jewish adversaries were uncircumcised too. We need not stop to inquire whether his, or their, Judaism owed something to Qumran. In Ignatius, as in John, Christianity, Judaism and gnosis exist side by side, and each owes something to the others, even while each reacts violently against the others. Thus John can treat the Jews, οἱ Ἰουδαῖοι, in general terms, as the enemy; yet he also affirms that salvation, Christian salvation, springs out of Judaism (4.22). He avoids the noun γνῶσις – surely this is no accident; but the verbs γινώσκειν and εἰδέναι are very common, and he can sum up his message in the proposition –

which, with any necessary change of names, any Gnostic would have affirmed – 'This is life eternal, to know thee, the only true God, and Jesus Christ whom thou didst send' (17.3). It would be proper, but evidently is quite impossible, to examine the debt of gnosis to Christianity and Judaism, and of Judaism to gnosis – hardly to Christianity, for some Jews at least were clearsighted enough to perceive that Christianity was so like Judaism as to constitute its greatest danger, and for this reason to keep it at arm's length: even apparently wise remarks, and miraculous power, if connected in some way with the deceiver, were to be eschewed.

All this was happening at a time when the boundary-lines between heresy and orthodoxy had not yet been firmly and finally drawn upon the doctrinal map, though, as we shall see, tendencies in the direction of precision were at work. John's was a comprehensive mind, and it is characteristic of him that he was able to see the interrelationship of strands of thought which might at first seem diverse. I have claimed, in these lectures and elsewhere, that John did not abandon eschatology, that, for example, the clauses in 6.39, 40, 44, 54 which refer to raising up at the last day are not to be ascribed to an ecclesiastical redactor but should be seen as the work of the Evangelist himself. To say this, however, is not to say that his eschatology was the same as that of Paul, or of Mark or of Enoch. It was much closer (if a parallel is to be drawn) to the eschatology of Johanan b. Zakkai, who, when national hopes were dashed by the defeat of the state and corporate religion lost its focal point in the sack of the Temple, re-established Judaism on a more individual basis. The individual Jew, frequenting the synagogue indeed so far as the times permitted, observed those parts of the law that an individual could observe, keeping the Sabbath and circumcising his children, for example, and looked forward not so much to a cataclysmic overthrow of the existing world rulers as to his own reward in heaven. John's eschatology too moved in an individual direction, and by putting the individual into close and hopeful contact with a higher world served the same purpose as gnosis. Thus chapter 14 begins with a somewhat personalized version of futurist eschatology. 'In my Father's house are many dwellings (μοναί) . . . I am going to prepare a place for you. And if I go and prepare a place for you, I come again, and I will take you to myself, that where I am you may be also.' Later in the chapter, however (and I omit the Paraclete passage as a complicating factor), the direction of motion is changed.

The disciple does not go to enjoy the μονή in heaven; there will be a μονή on earth. 'He who has my commandments and keeps them, he it is who loves me; and he who loves me shall be loved by my Father, and I will love him and will manifest myself to him ... If any one loves me he will keep my word, and my Father will love him, and we will come to him and will make our dwelling (μονή) with him.' Eschatology becomes something very much like mysticism; it becomes a way of describing the pressure of the divine otherness upon this world, and this time. John's mind was large enough to comprehend both, and to relate both to the story that he was telling.

It is perhaps this comprehensiveness of John's mind and method that, more than anything else, makes it difficult to remain content with even the most persuasive attempts to locate his historical situation in some precise region, such as the diaspora synagogue. John belongs to the whole world of Hellenistic syncretism; but in that world he takes his place as a Christian, and it is ultimately in this role that he has to be considered.[7]

There is a historical question here, also a theological question; perhaps they will prove ultimately to be one, but we may begin on the historical side and with a reference to another notable study of the Johannine literature; I have in mind Ernst Käsemann's[8] *The Testament of Jesus* and his earlier lecture 'Ketzer und Zeuge'. Briefly, the point that Käsemann brings out in the lecture is this. Especially in the Second and Third Epistles, explicitly in the Third, we find the unnamed Presbyter standing over against one Diotrephes. 'Rein und ein Glaubender ist man für den Presbyter eben nicht schon auf Grund der Taufe oder der eigenen Rechtschaffenheit oder der Zugehörigkeit zur katholischen Kirche. Rein wird man nur durch die immer neue und unmittelbare Begegnung mit dem Christus praesens, die keine Tradition ersetzen kann, weil nur der Christus selbst der Weg, die Wahrheit und das Leben ist. Es muss so aussehen, als sei der Presbyter ein Enthusiast gewesen, der jegliche Tradition abgelehnt und damit die Kontinuität der Kirche geleugnet, ja die Existenz von Kirche illusorisch gemacht hatte' ('Ketzer und Zeuge', p. 185). 'Die johanneischen Schriften müssen aus der Antithese zum beginnenden Frühkatholizismus verstanden werden' (p. 182). It is this 'Frühkatholizismus' that Diotrephes represents. He 'war nicht nur machthungrig und auf seine eigene Autorität bedacht, obgleich der Presbyter es so darstellt. Er war in

Wahrheit Repräsentant der frühkatholischen Kirchenordnung und handelte aus gesamtkirchlicher Verantwortung heraus. Er wäre nicht echter Bischof gewesen, wenn er anders gehandelt hätte' (p. 186). There is a problem here, for in the Gospel and First Epistle the Presbyter shows himself concerned about tradition and testimony to Jesus. The answer to this problem is that the relation of the Presbyter to tradition was a dialectical one. 'Er hat die Tradition nicht den Geist ersetzen und die praesentia Christi überflüssig machen lassen ... Alle Tradition hat Sinn nur als Aufruf, die Stimme des gegenwärtigen Christus zu hören' (p. 185).

Already we see how easily and swiftly historical analysis moves over into theology and demands theological treatment. The historical issues are theological issues too. It may well be that Käsemann made things unnecessarily difficult for himself by assuming common authorship for the Gospel and all the Epistles. There is in truth no reason why a number of authors should not be involved: one for John 1–20, another for John 21, a third for the First Epistle and a fourth for 2 and 3 John. Those who venture upon a more extensive analysis of the Gospel may of course find a larger number of distinct authors and editors. In addition it would probably not be wrong to find a place for the Apocalypse in the same Johannine school of theology, though the apocalyptist certainly stands a little apart. The Presbyter (the author of 2 and 3 John) was more 'catholic', and the Evangelist less heretical, than Käsemann allows. There is little to choose between the Presbyter and Diotrephes in their understanding of the Church. Diotrephes, it is true, does not 'receive us', and does not receive the brothers; and those who wish to do so he casts out of the Church (3 John 9f.). But the Presbyter writes to the Elect Lady about those of whose teaching he does not approve: 'If anyone comes to you and does not bring with him this (sound) doctrine, do not accept him into the house, and do not so much as give him a greeting, for he who gives him a greeting shares in his wicked works' (2 John 10f.). Here is a state of mutual excommunication, and though we may approve of the Presbyter's anti-docetic Christology this is hardly a valid defence of his ecclesiastical methods.

I do not wish to lay much stress on what must inevitably be a problematical and hypothetical distinction in authorship – though it must be remembered that all the Johannine works, except Revelation, are anonymous, and authorship must therefore be an open question. It does seem, however, that a difference, a progression, in attitude can be traced in the several books. Let us start with 2 and 3 John, since I have already quoted from them. Here, at least on the Presbyter's side, the decisive issue is between true and false doctrine. The Church and its teaching must be kept pure, and for this reason the man who teaches error must not be allowed into the house. Is the Presbyter unfair to Diotrephes when he puts his similar action down to a different motive and describes him as φιλοπρωτεύων, loving to have the first place? We could answer this question only if we knew all the facts, and we know practically none of them. We do know, however, that the Presbyter insisted that Jesus Christ had come in the flesh (if this is indeed the right way to take the surprising present participle in 2 John 7) and described those who asserted the contrary as Anti-Christ. This means that there was a doctrinal difference between the two groups, and Diotrephes may have been sincerely concerned for his own belief (even if it was mistaken) as well as for his personal status. In 1 John the doctrinal position is the same. The decisive issue is the coming of Jesus Christ in the flesh, and those who hold a docetic view are described as Anti-Christ (1 John 2.18; 4.3). There are, however, three differences. In the first place, no disciplinary rules are laid down. The false teachers are described not as having been, or as to be, ejected; they have gone out from us (2.19). It may be that, if they were available for consultation, they would put the matter differently, would say that conditions had been made intolerable for them, or perhaps that they were mixing with the world in the endeavour to win the world for the Gospel; but at least the author of 1 John does not instruct his reader to pass them by in the street. Secondly, the difference between the two parties is a matter of inspiration. Those who teach error profess to be inspired, and inspired in some sort they are, though by a spirit of error (4.1f.), which makes them false prophets. Thirdly, as such false prophets they are a mark of the end, a sign that the last hour has already arrived (2.18). Precisely because God himself is about to execute judgement there is no need for men to anticipate his work. 1 John represents a stage somewhat earlier than that of 2 and 3 John, but even so it is one at which dispute has become congealed in party slogans – 'Ιησοῦς Χριστὸς ἐν σαρκὶ ἐληλυθώς, Jesus Christ come in the flesh – and parties are separating out from one another.

What of the Gospel? Would it be wrong to say that the Evangelist feels the pull of the various strains of doctrine in his own person?

Such a proposition might at least account for the fact that though most students of the Gospel have seen in him the great opponent of docetism, Käsemann finds in his book a naïve docetism. And it is true that he depicts a Christ who walks over the water (as of course he does in the Synoptic Gospels too) and passes through shut doors, a Christ whose weariness and thirst can be described as hasty, exaggerated and unconvincing counter-measures. Let it be so: this means that the Evangelist is both a naïve docetist and a still more naïve anti-docetist. He represents both tendencies in his own person. What of other doctrinal issues? Some of them I have already referred to. John is Jewish and anti-Jewish. Unlike the earlier writers he seldom names the Jewish parties and groups – Pharisees, Sadducees, Scribes. The Jews as such are the enemy: they have a law, and by that law Jesus ought to die, since he made himself the Son of God. Yet salvation comes from the Jews; Moses the law-giver wrote of Christ, Abraham the father of the race rejoiced to see his day, Nathanael the believer, who confesses Jesus as the Son of God, the King of Israel, is praised as the true Israelite. Perhaps then we must describe John as a naïve anti-Judaist and a naïve pro-Judaist. Again, we have looked at the eschatology of the Gospel, and the supposed inconsistency of the scattered remarks, 'I will raise him up at the last day'. Someone, and I see no reason why it should not have been the person we call John, believed both that believers have already passed from death into life so that they now enjoy eternal life, and that they would be candidates for resurrection at the last day – dead until Christ raised them up. He can describe the work of the Son of man as a descent and an ascent, in that order: a descent accomplished in the incarnation, an ascent accomplished in crucifixion and resurrection. Yet he also represents Jesus as promising his disciples that he will come again, and not only, it seems, in resurrection appearances. Apparently then, he accepted (in our modern jargon) both realized and futurist eschatology. His attitude to sacraments could be described in a similar way. It was neither unquestioning acceptance nor outright rejection, but critical acceptance. In some ways the most important issue is that of John's relation to tradition, and on this the essential observation has already been made by Käsemann himself, whom I quoted, all too briefly, at an earlier point. John's attitude to tradition is, as Käsemann says, dialectical: he uses, that is, traditional material and traditional interpretations not in order to set up a historical image, safely remote in a respectable antiquity, but in order to confront his readers with the living and ever-present Jesus. What Käsemann has failed to see is that John's work as a whole, his various theological attitudes, have this dialectical quality. This is true of his treatment of the sacraments: the material, the flesh, is of value just so far as it represents the Spirit; the historical memorial of the Jesus of the past is of value just so far as it constitutes an encounter with the living Jesus of the present. Eating a bit of bread is a valueless act; coming to Jesus, who is and always will be the bread of life, is of eternal significance. Eschatology means that I am confronted with the merciful Judge, Jesus Christ, today, and will be confronted with him every day up to and including that mythical concept 'the last day', which means nothing if it does not mean every day in eternity. The relation of John to Judaism is the purest dialectic, since it consist of a running conversation; though in this we sense the tragedy that the Jews are breaking off the debate. Perhaps it was John's fault; perhaps he was as keen to put them out of the church as they to put him out of the synagogue. And John's Christology is a dialectical one, not in the simple sense of a contiguity of the (apparent) opposites, Logos and flesh, but in the sense of a contrapuntal development of the relation between the essential Jesus and the various aspects of his existence. We see Jesus in relation to God, Jesus in relation to his own humanity, Jesus in relation to Jews, Jesus in relation to disciples, Jesus in relation to life, Jesus in relation to death; and the whole constitutes a kaleidoscopic variety of theological and christological insight. And I can only say that if this is naïveté, I wish I were half as naïve as John!

I have in this lecture allowed myself scope enough to look somewhat broadly at John's aims and methods, but it is time to gather the loose ends together. The universality and comprehensiveness of John's mind, and of the theology that he conceived, may lead us back to the proper topic of the lecture. We have travelled so far that I fear you may have forgotten it. We are dealing with the theme of history, inseparable as it is in John from theological and other interests, and with the kind of authority that may be ascribed not simply to the historical statements in the Gospel but to the book as a whole. How does John regard history? It is not a matter of indifference to him, or he would have written a work more like the Gospel of Truth. We may approach the question thus. When we study the Synoptic Gospels we repeatedly find paragraphs which almost certainly rest upon things really done or spoken by Jesus, but where this primitive material has been placed and viewed by the Evangelist in a new setting – not altogether different, not contradictory, yet not the same. To generalize: Jesus engaged in controversy with his Jewish contemporaries; we know this because he was in the end cast out by them. The bearers of the tradition, culminating in Mark, also engaged in controversy with their Jewish contemporaries. The controversies were not unrelated, for in one way or another Jesus was at the heart of both, yet they were not identical, for the latter were formalized and focused on the question whether or not it was legitimate to apply to Jesus titles which for the most part he had not used. This sort of tension presents the student of the Synoptic Gospels with most of his problems, and it is his task to show how the same material, in modified forms, was used to deal with both situations. When we turn from this study of the Synoptic Gospels to John, we may occasionally find that John has adapted traditional material to yet another historical setting; but much oftener we find that John has liberated his material from particular settings to give it universal applicability. It is characteristic of him to see the part in relation to the whole, and the whole in each part. One may think here, for example, of his treatment of the bread of life, and of the washing of the disciples' feet.

This means inevitably a record that is impressionistic rather than photographic, and any authority that it may have is not the authority of the trained eye-witness reporter. It is, rather, in Hoskyns' phrase, the 'non-historical that makes sense of history'. If the claims of the Christian faith are true, the history of Jesus of Nazareth was pregnant with universal meaning, a significance that can be personally apprehended in a process that bears some relation to mysticism, is rationally worked out in theology, and has not yet been killed even by the institutions of the professionally religious. John's achievement was to liberate the universal significance of Jesus; in this way we can make Hoskyns' insight more precise. The many-sidedness of his Gospel, which may expose him to the charge of naïveté and contradiction, bears witness both to the breadth of his mind and to the fact that the Jesus of history really did transcend the limitations of space and time.

NOTES

1 See 'Sacraments'; in this volume, pp. 80–97.
2 See 'Christocentric or Theocentric?'; in this volume, pp. 1–18.
3 E. Käsemann, *Exegetische Versuche und Besinnungen*, i (1960), pp. 168–87.
4 J. L. Martyn, *History and Theology in the Fourth Gospel*. 1968.
5 W. Bauer, *Rechtgläubigkeit und Ketzerei im ältesten Christentum*. 1934.
6 See note 4.
7 On Hoskyns and Bultmann in this respect see my *The Gospel of John and Judaism*, pp. 3–7.
8 See note 3 above and 'Paradox and Dualism', note 3.

9
JEWS AND JUDAIZERS IN THE EPISTLES OF IGNATIUS

Ignatius, travelling from Antioch in Syria to his martyrdom in Rome, showed no concern for his own safety and life. Rather, he looked forward, with an almost pathological eagerness, to his destruction by the wild beasts. Only when, as God's bread, he had been ground between their teeth would he truly be a disciple (*Rom.* 4.1f.). For him, death would mean not so much a release, though travelling in the charge of 'ten leopards' (*Rom.* 5.1) can have been no holiday, as the consummation of his unity with Christ crucified. He was, however, deeply concerned for the well-being, security and purity of the churches – his own church in Syria, left with no bishop but God and Jesus Christ (*Rom.* 9.1), and the churches of Asia with which his journey brought him into contact, whether because he visited them (Philadelphia and Smyrna) or because they sent delegates to greet him (Ephesus, Magnesia and Tralles). He exhorted them to maintain faith, unity and love, and warned them against false teaching.

Several times in the epistles he refers to *Judaism*, to those who *judaize* and *sabbatize*, to those who are *circumcized*, and to the prophets and priests of the Old Testament. Here, one might suppose, is fruitful ground for those who would study the interrelation of Judaism with Christianity in and just after the New Testament period, and indeed with the Hellenistic world in general.[1] Examination of this material is, however, immediately complicated by one of the most familiar, and most disputed, questions in the study of Ignatius. Was the false teaching to which he was opposed single though complex, and maintained by one group of teachers, or did it comprise at least two distinct heresies, maintained by different groups?

Undoubtedly, Ignatius was opposed to docetism. To deny the physical, fleshly reality of Jesus, and especially to assert that his death and resurrection happened only in appearance, was to cut away the ground from under the Christian faith and to turn the whole into illusion. It would be not only doctrinally but practically ruinous, since it would take the reality out of the Eucharist, for if Christ had not been physically present in history he could hardly be present in the sacrament. Furthermore, it would empty Ignatius's own passion of significance, for it was the fact of Christ's suffering that gave meaning to his. But, for Ignatius, Judaism was equally destructive of Christianity. 'If we live according to Judaism, we confess that we have not received grace' (*Magn.* 8.1). 'If anyone expounds Judaism to you, do not listen to him' (*Phld.* 6.1). 'It is out of the question to speak of Jesus Christ and to judaize' (*Magn.* 10.3); Christianity has now replaced Judaism. If we are to ask what Ignatius meant by Judaism, why he opposed it, and whether, notwithstanding his opposition, it had any influence upon him, we must consider whether the Judaizers were also docetists, the docetists Judaizers, or whether the two groups were separate. We must not assume that, for Ignatius, 'to judaize' meant exactly what it did for Paul.

The question of the unity, or otherwise, of Ignatius's opponents, the question, that is, of the relation between Judaism and docetism, has been discussed for many years, and it will be useful to begin with a sketch of a few of the views that have been expressed.

The briefest sketch of an Ignatian question can hardly omit J. B. Lightfoot,[2] though Lightfoot himself is brief on this matter. He expresses his opinion in his note on *Magnesians* 8 (ii. 124f.). 'It [the heresy] belongs to the same category with the heresy of the Colossian Church . . ., of the Pastoral Epistles, of the Apocalypse, of the Catholic Epistles, and of the Corinthians. It is Judaism crossed with Gnosticism . . . In attacking this foe, [Ignatius] condemns two things: first ([*Magn.*] Sections 8–10), *Judaizing practices*, i.e., the doctrine of the permanent obligation of the Mosaic ritual, more especially the observance of sabbaths (section 9); and secondly, *Docetic views* . . . The foe in question therefore was Doceto-judaism.' Much in this judgement may have to be questioned, such as the assumption that 'sabbatizing' means an insistence upon the rigid observance of the seventh day of the week, but the parallels Lightfoot draws, with, for example, the Pastorals and the Apocalypse, are of great importance.

In his Commentary on Ignatius Walter Bauer argues similarly, though he notices that the epistles are not uniform in their description of heresy, and expresses himself with some reserve:

Zwar die Ausführungen von Eph., Trall. und Smyrn. würden nicht darauf führen, dass sich mit der doketischen Christologie auch noch judaisierende Neigungen verbunden hätten, wohl aber verknüpft Magn. mit der Bestreitung der Judaisten deutlich antidoketische Polemik, die offenbar die gleiche Adresse hat (*Magn.* 9.2; 11). Zeigte jedoch in Magnesia die Häresie ein doppeltes Gesicht, so wird es in den übrigen von Ignatius mit Briefen bedachten kleinasiatischen Gemeinden bei der nahen Nachbarschaft kaum anders gewesen sein.[3]

In a later book, however, Bauer took a different view:

Ich möchte also das Nebeneinander von Gnosis und Juden-christentum im Bilde der von Ignatius in jenen beiden Städten [Magnesia and Philadelphia] bekämpften Ketzer weniger auf die Kompliziertheit der Irrlehre zurückführen, als aus der zusam-mengesetzten Persönlichkeit des Ignatius erklären, der als Kirchenmann die Gnosis zurückweist und als syrischer Heiden-christ jüdischer Verfälschung des Evangeliums, wo immer er sie anzutreffen meint, entgegentritt.[4]

That is, out of two errors, both of which, for different reasons, Ignatius felt he must resist, he made one error, combining the properties of both. This must remain a possibility, and it is indeed more than possible that a man of Ignatius' temperament would tend to combine the characteristics of all his opponents and attack them in one sweeping assault. At the same time, Ignatius evidently knew at first hand the errors and the heretics he had to deal with, and a grossly inaccurate account of them would have done him and his readers little service.

Moving back a little from Bauer we find a different kind of attempt to deal with the heretics made by Johannes Weiss, who thought that Ignatius was describing not a phenomenon he had first encountered in Asia, but one with which he had long been familiar in Syria, and accordingly placed his discussion of the Judaeo-docetic error in the context of his account of the syncretistic Samari-tan gnosis.[5] It was unthinkable, said Weiss, rightly, that a Judaism that affirmed the permanent validity of the law should have been assimilated to the teaching of the Samaritans, according to which the law belonged to the angelic world which was subordinate, and inimical, to God, or that Saturninus, who was notoriously anti-

Judaic, should have absorbed Judaistic elements into his gnosis. But Ignatius's Judaism did not insist on the law.

According to the manner of thought and expression of Ignatius, 'Jewish life' means nothing other than sharing in the ideas of those who were not persuaded of the true nature of Christ either 'by the prophecies or by the Law of Moses or the Gospel or the martyrdoms' (*Smyrn.* 5) (p. 764).

To this corresponds the fact that Judaism is designated not as a way of life (perhaps a πολίτευμα or a θρησκεία), but as 'heterodoxies' and 'useless old myths' (*Magn.* 8); one must not listen to one who 'expounds Judaism' (*Philad.* 6), i.e., who pleads for Jewish ideas by reference to Scriptural texts . . . Ignatius gives their doctrine this name [judaizing] because they sought to support their docetic ideas by 'old fables', i.e., by cosmological myths, which they verified from the Scriptures. They are thus Gnostics of non-Jewish origin, but with a Jewish secret wisdom – just as, for example, Saturninus developed his doctrine of man from Gen. 1.25 (p. 765).

Weiss thinks this error characteristically Syrian. It is doubtful whether he does justice to the Asian context to which Ignatius addressed himself,[6] or to the genuinely Jewish element in the Judaism Ignatius complains of.

A new stage in the study of Ignatius was opened by H. W. Bartsch,[7] whose handling of the question of Judaism is incidental to his main concern with Ignatius's understanding of God. Earlier study of Ignatius, he complains, was too eager to make historical identifications of the heresies attacked by Ignatius; one might add, though Dr Bartsch does not himself say this, I think, explicitly, too ready also to regard Ignatius himself as impeccably orthodox. We must think of heresy not so much as something that attacked the Church from without, as of something that grew up within it. 'Von daher ist also ein Zusammenhang zwischen den beiden Strömungen auf Grund ihrer verschiedenen Herkunft abzulehnen' (p. 35). As the title of his book suggests, Dr Bartsch sees in the Ignatian epistles a community tradition of common Christian doctrine into which Ignatius himself has infused gnostic material; in addition, Ignatius's main concern was with the unity of the Church, which he understood mainly in sacramental, that is, in eucharistic terms. These fundamental observations provide the basis for Dr Bartsch's understanding of the Ignatian Judaism and its relation with docetism.

It is in *Philadelphians* and *Magnesians* (if anywhere) that we see the combination of Judaism and docetism; but it is just here that the new approach to Ignatius makes a difference. *Philadelphians* 3.3; 4.1 point to those who take part in a 'different Eucharist'; this, however, as other evidence will suggest, Judaizers might do. In addition only *Philadelphians* 8.2 could suggest a combination of Judaism and docetism, and this passage is in fact not anti-docetic; all that Ignatius asserts here is that it is the new saving Christian facts (*Heilstatsachen*) that are normative, not the Old Testament.

What then of Magnesians? Here 'tatsächlich antidoketische Polemik neben der Bekämpfung des Judaismus vorhanden ist' (Bartsch, p. 37), notably in *Magnesians* 11. It was, however, the mistake of the older investigation to conclude that this meant the existence of a docetic party; the danger is one that Ignatius sees always threatening from within. *Magnesians* 9.1 (cf. *Phld.* 8.2) does not imply docetism: the Jews prefer Sabbath to Sunday, and *thereby* deny the Lord's resurrection.

Es war mit dem Judaismus also eine Abwertung der Person Jesu Christi verbunden. Der Doketismus ist aber gerade von der entgegengesetzten Tendenz geleitet. Sein Interesse ist die Bewahrung der Gottheit Jesu Christi (an diesem Punkt steht also Ignatius den Doketen näher als den Judaisten), darum verneint er das wahre Leiden und Sterben, weil es ihm ein Anstoss ist. Das Interesse des Judaismus liegt aber in der entgegengesetzten Richtung (Bartsch, pp. 38f.).

From this we can go back to and explain the dispute referred to in *Philadelphians*. The division of the community found expression in two separate Eucharists, held respectively on Sabbath and Sunday, as the cultic terms used in 7.1, 2; 8.2 confirm.[8] The concluding words of 8.2 (ἐν οἷς θέλω ἐν τῇ προσευχῇ ὑμῶν δικαιωθῆναι), which Dr Bartsch interprets by means of *Romans* 5.1, prove the relation of the whole dispute to the cultus.

So können wir abschliessend sagen, dass in dem Streit um die ἀρχεῖα um den rechten Vollzug der Eucharistie geht, und aus dem Wesen der im ganzen Brief bekämpften häretischen Strömung

erschliessen wir, dass es um den Termin der Eucharistiefeier
Sabbat oder Herrentag geht (Bartsch, p. 42).

The same theme is in mind when in *Philadelphians* 9 Ignatius goes
on to speak of the superiority of Christ as of the High Priest to the
priests. That Christ was High Priest was common belief (see, in
addition to Hebrews, 1 *Clem.* 61.3; 64). But Ignatius himself develops
this in the observation that Christ as High Priest is ὁ πεπιστευμένος
τὰ ἅγια τῶν ἁγίων, which refers to the Eucharist;[9] and the next clause
may well point in a gnostic direction.

Nun könnten die Judaisten in Philadelphia behauptet haben, dass
τὰ κρυπτὰ τοῦ θεοῦ allein im Alten Testament verborgen liege. Dann
würde der Begriff esoterisches Wissen bezeichnen. Wir hätten
dann einen gnostischen Begriff bei den Judaisten der philadel-
phischen Gemeinde festzustellen. In der Gnosis wurde dieser
Begriff geradezu technisch (Bartsch, p. 47).

But this does not identify the Judaizers with the docetists! There is
a similar gnostic interpretation of the traditional[10] image of the door
(*Phld.* 9.1), which Ignatius, using a christological interpretation of
Psalm 117.20 (LXX), uses as a further expression of unity, whereas it
was formerly eschatological.

There is much that is instructive in Dr Bartsch's handling of the
errors that Ignatius attacks; some points also that will find implicit
criticism in our detailed discussion of the texts.[11] Here two general
observations may be made. In the first place, the observation that
error is not so much a force that attacks from without an inwardly
orthodox Church as a tendency for ever springing up within is both
true and valuable,[12] but it must be accompanied by the recognition
that error (like truth) cannot exist, or at least can never find expression, apart from people. Error, or indeed any sort of opinion,
can only arise within the Church so far as it is held by members of
the Church. There may always exist a tendency to view the person
of Jesus in a docetic way, but what this means is that there are always
people who are disposed to hold docetic views, even if they consider
only to reject them. If Ignatius attacks docetism, this may be because he is aware of a tendency to docetism in himself, but more
probably because docetism was visible as a tendency in the churches,
that is, was maintained by some who belonged to them. In the
second place, it does not seem likely that any of Ignatius's contro-

versies simply resolved itself into a dispute on the question whether the Eucharist should be observed on Saturday or Sunday. Ignatius was a sacramentarian and ecclesiastic, and it is quite possible that he held strong views on such questions.[13] It may, however, be questioned whether his convictions in such matters were so strong that he was prepared to die for them alone. Yet for him the eucharistic aspect of docetism touched the question whether his martyrdom made sense or nonsense. The flesh and blood of Christ were real, as his own flesh and blood, shortly to be broken and shed in Rome, were real. To deny the reality of the flesh and blood of Christ in the Eucharist was to deny their reality in the incarnation, and to make a mere show, a mere appearance, of the flesh and blood of Christ in the incarnation was to make his own martyrdom a sham and a show. To change the date of the Eucharist would not in itself have done this, and Ignatius would have staked his life on the one issue, but not on the other.

A further step in the investigation was taken by V. Corwin. According to her, the Docetists and the Judaizers were real, and distinct, groups:

> At least three parties seem to have been present . . . On the right was the group deeply influenced by the Old Testament, who wished to see the Christian pattern become more strongly Jewish. On the left stood the Docetists, who were the chief 'teachers of strange doctrine'. In the middle, we may suppose, was a center party of which Ignatius was the spokesman, agreeing in part with both of the more extreme groups but in other respects sharply distinguishing the median position from what seemed perverse in the right and left.[14]

These divisions existed in the church at Antioch; the parties of right and left were minorities; the divisions were not irreparable (*Phld.* 10.1; *Smyrn.* 11.2; *Pol.* 7.1).

The Judaizers were not orthodox Jews, since they did not practise circumcision (*Phld.* 6.1). Their slogan was: 'Christianity bases its faith on Judaism' (*Magn.* 10.3). They probably observed the Sabbath (*Magn.* 9.1), and held distinctive and separate meals (*Phld.* 4.1; and cf. Ignatius's insistence that there should be *one* Eucharist). They held theories of their own about the priests (*Phld.* 9.1), and accepted the authority of certain written documents, ἀρχεῖα (*Phld.* 8.2), which surely included the law and the prophets. But they and Ignatius are evidently reading the prophets differently. They see a contradiction between the ἀρχεῖα and the Gospel. Ignatius maintains there is none because the prophets bear witness of Christ. The Judaizers reply, as Ignatius quotes them: 'That is the question at stake' (*Phld.* 8.2). They and Ignatius accept the prophets, but the Judaizers probably insist that Christian truths must be consistent with the prophets as they interpret them (Corwin, p. 59).

One may surmise that to them Christ was primarily a teacher, and perhaps not the only one, for Ignatius insists that he is our only teacher – and was so even for the prophets (*Magn.* 9.2). This proves also that the judaizing and docetic groups must have been distinct: they had different Christologies.[15]

Here then in Antioch was a group of Christian (in Ignatius's opinion, imperfectly Christianized) Jews. Where did they come from? It is Dr Corwin's suggestion that they came from Qumran. This, she thinks, would account for several features of the Ignatian epistles. Ignatius's Judaizers 'sabbatize' (*Magn.* 9.1); *Jubilees* and the *Damascus Document* emphasize Sabbath observance. The *Manual of Discipline* (6.5; cf. Josephus, *Bell.* II. 130ff.) tells of common meals; were these continued to become the invalid Eucharists of which Ignatius complains? Priests were important to the sect (1 *QS* 1.21; 2.2, 11, 20; 5.9; 6.5, 8; 8.1; *CD* 6.1–3), as they hardly were to Pharisaic Judaism. The patriarchs (cf. *Phld.* 8.1) dominate *Jubilees*, and were regarded as the forerunners of the sect (*CD* 4.2f.), which also had its Teacher of Righteousness, who was the interpreter of the prophets (1 *QpHab.* 2.10). True, the Ignatian Judaizers did not practise circumcision; but we must remember that they were Essenes who had been converted to Christianity. 'What we know of the Judaizing group in Antioch accords in important respects with a Judaism of an Essene character and certainly better with it than with a Pharisaic form of Judaism' (Corwin, p. 64).

Dr Corwin goes on to trace Ignatius's contacts in other directions. He knew Matthew, written perhaps in Antioch 'to demonstrate to Jews and to Essene-Christians that the teachings of Jesus, grouped as we find them in the Sermon on the Mount, constituted a new Law which took the place of the Torah, and perhaps also of the regulations of the *Manual of Discipline*' (Corwin, p. 68).[16] Ignatius probably knew the Fourth Evangelist and the outlines of his work in its preliminary, Antiochene, stage; the presence of Essene-Christians in Antioch, deduced from Ignatius, helps to explain the background from which the Gospel emerged. Further, Ignatius probably knew the *Odes of Solomon*; there are parallels in *Trallians* 6.2 (*Ode* 38); *Romans* 7.2 (*Ode* 11); *Ephesians* 19.3 (*Ode* 7.21). And 'in Ignatius, the *Odes* and the Fourth Gospel there is unmistakable resemblance to the rich imagery of the Essene psalms and the earlier Pseudepigraphs' (Corwin, p. 77). She notes the following images: Odour (*Eph.* 17; *Ode* 11.15; John 12.3; *Test. Sim.* 6.2; 1 *Enoch* 24.5; 25.6; 32.3); the fruitful earth (*Trall.* 11.1f.; *Phld.* 3.1; *Ode* 1.5; 11.12; 38.20; John 15.1ff.; 1 *QS* 8.5; 11.8 (Isa. 60.21; 61.3)); music (*Eph.* 4.1f.; *Rom.* 2.1; *Phld.* 1.2; *Ode* 6.1f.; 7.17; 8.4; 14.8; 24.1f.; 26.3; 1 *QS* 10.9); crown (*Magn.* 13.1; *Ode* 1.1–4; 5.12; 9.8; 17.1; 20.7); fountain (*Ode* 11.6; 26.13, 30; 1 *Enoch* 22.9; 96.6). These figures, which Reitzenstein and Schlier took to be of gnostic origin, are more probably Essene and pseudepigraphic.

The importance of Dr Corwin's work is evident. Rightly or wrongly she takes us back to the historical localization that Dr Bartsch abjures, and paints a picture of a deviant form of Judaism, existing in Antioch, reflected in its Christian and non-Christian forms in such important literary sources as Matthew, John, Ignatius and the *Odes of Solomon*, and thus a major element in the religious history of Syria. Its value is not greatly affected by the question whether Ignatius could have known the *Odes of Solomon*, which may well have been written somewhat later than his epistles. A community of thought[17] would be significant, wherever the priority might lie. Location raises a more serious question than chronology. It is true that Ignatius's basic acquaintance with Christianity and its fringe sects was formed in Antioch, but we shall see reason to think that his remarks about Judaism relate primarily to Asia, and there it would be much harder to establish a relation involving Matthew, Qumran and the *Odes*.[18] A third question calls for examination of the parallels Dr Corwin finds between Ignatius and the Qumran literature; they are not such as to warrant direct literary dependence, and without literary dependence historical connection must remain at most an unproved hypothesis.[19] Fourthly, it may be asked whether Dr Corwin has not, if her argument stands, proved too much. She distinguishes between the judaizing and the docetic heresies, but relates the judaizing heresy to a brand of Judaism which is widely held to have had gnostic tendencies and thus to be a near ally of docetism. The argument is at least in danger of destroying itself.

Einar Molland's discussion of the heretics is brief, but worthy of serious consideration.[20] There was only one group of heretics; and they were docetists. Yet Ignatius accuses them also of Judaism. Wherein did their Judaism consist? They were not the Judaizers with whom Paul contended; they did not require obedience to the law. But they did (though Christians) maintain, 'If I do not find it in the Old Testament, I do not believe in the Gospel' (*Phld.* 8.2 – other interpretations of this passage are artificial). They recall the Jews of Justin, *Trypho* 90.1, who required Old Testament proofs before they would believe in a suffering Messiah. Dr Molland sums up his conclusion in two propositions:

1   The heretics combatted [*sic*] by Ignatius were docetists claiming to have the support of the Old Testament for their christological doctrine, but they were not Judaizers in any other sense of the word.
2   It is their use of the Old Testament that is branded by Ignatius as Judaism (p. 6).

Dr Molland himself raises the question that must suggest itself to any reader. Could people who claimed to be Christians have said what is quoted in *Philadelphians* 8.2? He answers, Yes – though the words may have been said in the heat of argument, or be Ignatius's (loaded) résumé.

L. W. Barnard's recent contribution to the discussion is also brief, but throws out an important hint.[21] He disagrees with Dr Corwin in thinking that Ignatius was opposed to one complex heresy, not to two, referring to *Magnesians* 8—11; but he agrees with her in appealing to Qumran – the Dead Sea Scrolls bear witness to the invasion of Palestinian Judaism by Hellenistic ideas and terminology. From *Philadelphians* 8.2 it 'follows that these Judaeo-Gnostics had their own interpretation of the Old Testament in which they found support for their Christological position' (Barnard, p. 25). On the other hand, the Nag Hammadi manuscripts show that 'Jewish speculation, particularly concerning the Name of God and of angels, did influence incipient gnostic thought' (Barnard, p. 24). What was really at stake may have been the interpretation of the Old Testament – 'an unbridled interpretation of the Old Testament along gnostic lines' (Barnard, p. 26).

There is much here that remains speculative because it is not worked out in detail; but the two kinds of affiliation suggested – with Nag Hammadi and with Qumran – provide an important hint worthy of further study.

No conclusion appears so clearly from this sketch of work on Ignatius's Judaizers as that the experts are by no means agreed, and that the question is worthy of re-examination, even though a new-comer to the discussion is unlikely to solve all the problems, or any of them, at a stroke. The most important feature of any study of this subject must be an examination, as detailed as space permits, of the relevant texts, but a few observations may be made first.

First, there is a body of Christian literature available for com-parison, not only the *Odes of Solomon* but Revelation, John, Colos-sians, Acts, the Pastoral Epistles. These writings cast different kinds of light on a situation somewhat earlier than that in which Ignatius found himself. All are related, most of them closely, to the province of Asia. In Revelation 2.9 and 3.9 we learn that in Smyrna and Philadelphia, important Ignatian centres, there were groups of those who called themselves Jews but (in the writer's view) were not. They were a synagogue, but a synagogue of Satan. They constituted some kind of threat[22] to the Church and had forfeited their right to regard themselves as the people of God.[23] The Fourth Gospel depicts the same situation in different terms. The synagogue had cast off the Church (9.22; 16.2) and the Jews were children of the devil (8.44). Colossians supplies evidence for the amalgamation of Jud-aism with Gnosticism.[24] The Pastorals may give further evidence of this,[25] and in a different way Acts bears witness to the breach between Church and synagogue. A detailed examination of all this material is highly desirable, but in this essay I can do no more than call attention to its existence.

A second point that should be borne in mind here is that the story of Ignatius's relations with Jews, whether in Antioch or in the cities of Asia, is a small part of a long record of tension and strife, of which some of the earlier evidence is provided by Josephus.[26] Ignatius takes us to a later date, for which we have less information. It is tempting to refer to the martyrdom of Pappus and Julianus under Trajan as illustrative of Jew–Gentile relations in Laodicea, and thus in Asia, but the story is probably worthless. Again, we must be content to recall that judaizing in Ignatius calls for study of a wide background.

The last observation leads to a further point. There can be little doubt that Judaism played a part in the development of Gnosticism from its uncombined constituents into a recognizable system; indeed, it played more parts than one. Philo already shows that mingling of oriental religions with Greek philosophical thought which forms one of the bases of Gnosticism. The period after AD 70 witnessed the breakdown of apocalyptic which contributed a further element to mature Gnosticism;[27] the more remote Jewish sects showed considerable readiness to accommodate themselves to magic[28] and to pagan religion.[29]

With these observations we may turn to the epistles themselves. The crucial passages for our subject occur in *Philadelphians*, and it is with this epistle that we must begin. If we can establish a clear understanding here, other passages will become more intelligible. Not that the texts in *Philadelphians* are easy; their importance lies in the fact that Ignatius had himself been in Philadelphia and narrates (obscurely, it is true) events that had happened within his own experience. Elsewhere it is often difficult to tell whether he is dealing with a concrete situation in Asia, with what he remembers of conditions in Antioch, or with what he conceives in principle to be a permanent and universal danger to the Church and therefore to exist at least potentially in any community to which he writes. It remains possible that he misunderstood the situation in Philadelphia, but at least he had observed it, and wrote of what he had witnessed.

Though there are several references to judaizing, the main theme of *Philadelphians* is unity. It is true that this is a theme that Ignatius never tires of sounding, and possible that he may have overestimated the danger of disunity in Philadelphia; but in this epistle we have not only the general kind of warning that appears in *Philadelphians* 2 (as it does, for example, in *Eph.* 7.1; 8.1) but an account of a particular occasion (7.1f.) when Ignatius spoke in the Christian assembly at Philadelphia in inspired language.[30] He cried out, 'Give heed to the bishop, and to the presbyterate and the deacons'; and again, 'Do nothing apart from the bishop . . . love unity, flee from divisions.' Ignatius disclaims in this passage any prior knowledge of disunity in Philadelphia. Some had, apparently, tried to deceive him about this (7.1), and indeed had succeeded. But they could not deceive the Spirit, and Ignatius could not believe, at the time or subsequently, that the Spirit had mistaken the needs of the Church. Later information, it seems, had confirmed this inference, and led to the warning in *Philadelphians* 2.1f. about specious wolves who took people captive. The epistle as a whole mentions no error but Judaism, and it must be concluded that there existed in Philadelphia a Jewish group which, though not yet separated from the main body of Christians, had at least separatist tendencies. We may recall Revelation 3.9.

What was the Judaizers' view of the matter? This appears at once, for it must have been the Jewish separatists whom Ignatius heard saying,[31] ἐὰν μὴ ἐν τοῖς ἀρχείοις εὕρω ἐν τῷ εὐαγγελίῳ οὐ πιστεύω (8.2). The punctuation and interpretation of these words has been discussed at great length, and I do not intend here to list all the possibilities. Our understanding of them must be determined by Ignatius's reply: γέγραπται. This refers to Scripture;[32] in particular, in Christian usage, to passages of the Old Testament cited because it was believed that they were fulfilled in Jesus Christ. The opponents (as Ignatius evidently regards them), with their πρόκειται, do not altogether dismiss but do not immediately accept Ignatius's assertion. No discussion is reported, but we can infer from the context answers to the fundamental questions: What is supposed to be written? and where? Since Ignatius is denied access to the archives of the Old Testament he turns to what is the heart of his conviction and his message: Ἰησοῦς Χριστός, ... ὁ σταυρὸς αὐτοῦ καὶ ὁ θάνατος καὶ ἡ ἀνάστασις αὐτοῦ καὶ ἡ πίστις ἡ δι' αὐτοῦ. This is the proposition that he wishes to assert and to authenticate. Since his opponents question whether it is authenticated by the Old Testament, he asserts that it is self-authenticating: the saving events are their own archives. It is clear, however, that his desire is to use the Old Testament as further authentication, and within the Old Testament he would undoubtedly have turned to the prophets, who in *Philadelphians* 5 are mentioned along with other witnesses, the apostles and the presbyterate. Their proclamation was directed towards the Gospel;[33] they hoped for Christ, and waited for him. Moreover, they enter into God by the same door as the apostles and the Church, Christ himself (9.1).

Did then the Judaizers deny that the Old Testament pointed forward to a Messiah? This might seem to be suggested by the words, ἐὰν δὲ ἀμφότεροι περὶ Ἰησοῦ Χριστοῦ μὴ λαλῶσιν (6.1), but the possibility is weakened if we note (1) that the subject of the verb is ἀμφότεροι – what Ignatius means is that anyone, Jew or Gentile, who seeks salvation in any other than Jesus Christ lacks true life, and (2) that Ignatius speaks not of 'Christ' but of 'Jesus Christ' – it is not any Messiah but a particular Messiah who is in question, a Messiah who lived and died. Moving back through 6.1 we meet the balanced clause: ἄμεινον γάρ ἐστιν παρὰ ἀνδρὸς περιτομὴν ἔχοντος χριστιανισμὸν ἀκούειν ἢ παρὰ ἀκροβύστου ἰουδαϊσμόν. Taken at its face value, this means that 'Judaism' may be proclaimed by an un-circumcised man; such a Judaism could only be an unorthodox, perhaps a gnostic, syncretistic Judaism. This may well be the right conclusion to draw from Ignatius's words; it would be consistent with the view that the Judaism and docetism combated by Ignatius were different aspects of the same religious phenomenon. It is not, however, certain, for at least two other possibilities exist. The 'un-circumcised man' who preaches Judaism may be an *originally* uncircumcised man, that is, a convert to Judaism. Or Ignatius may be trapped in his own rhetoric: he meant to say that there was no harm in hearing Christianity from a Christian Jew, but having begun the sentence with ἄμεινον he constructed a comparison that he did not really intend.[33a] In any case, what he most wishes to convey is all contained in the opening sentence of 6.1: ἐὰν δέ τις ἰουδαϊσμὸν ἑρμηνεύῃ ὑμῖν, μὴ ἀκούετε αὐτοῦ. After the reference in *Philadelphians* 5 to the prophets, it seems very probable that this refers to an exposition of prophecy that did not reach Christian conclusions.[34]

We conclude that there existed in Philadelphia a Jewish group, almost certainly unorthodox in its Judaism (and therefore perhaps not requiring circumcision) since it existed in some sort of relation to what Ignatius regarded as the orthodox, catholic, Church, and is blamed by him for not being in closer relations with it. It is wise to remember that all sorts of fringe groups must have existed round the first - and second-century Jewish and Christian circles that are familiar to us. We cannot expect to be well informed about them, but there are sufficient hints of their existence. We must now ask what sort of interpretation of the Old Testament such a group can have offered, and how it was related to the main streams of Judaism and Christianity.

A complete answer is beyond our grasp, but it seems probable that the Jews in question were a group intent upon accommodating themselves to their environment, or, to express the matter more favourably, upon presenting Judaism to their pagan neighbours in the most attractive light possible. To this end they dropped circum-cision, which the pagan world, often unable to distinguish it from castration, found particularly revolting, and also abandoned the national messianic expectation, which, from a different point of view, was equally unacceptable. Philo was capable of hellenizing and at the same time of retaining devout faithfulness to Torah Judaism and to the messianic hope; not so all Jews of the dispersion.[35] His 'proto-gnosticism' was to some extent held in check by biblical convictions; he could use the language of the mystery religions but also make it clear that he regarded such religions as abominable.[36] It is, however, easy to imagine (and not wholly *imagine*) the readiness with which others would assimilate themselves to their surroundings, and might at first find themselves attracted to the Christian version of Judaism, only to be disillusioned when they found that the new faith remained essentially historical and included a new form of the messianic hope. Here were men who might possibly be Gnostics, but were truly neither Jews (Rev. 3.9) nor Christians (*Phld.* 6.2). Trying to make the best of both worlds they remained in contact with neither. This means that the question whether Ignatius's opponents were Jews or judaizing Christians has no simple answer – at least, no simple answer can be given on the basis of *Philadelphians*. We must see if the picture thus outlined can be filled in from the other epistles.

Unlike Philadelphia, Magnesia did not lie directly on Ignatius's route, but he received a deputation from the church while he was in Smyrna (*Magn.* 2.1), and wrote a letter in reply. He thus had only second-hand information about Christian affairs in Magnesia, and accordingly makes it clear (perhaps a little late in his letter – 11.1) that his exhortation and admonition are not to be taken to imply knowledge on his part of error and division in the church: he is writing to put the Magnesians on their guard against possible error in the future. He is less than they, and simply wishes them to hold firmly to the historical events that happened 'in the time of the governorship of Pontius Pilate' (11.1). Magnesia, however, was no more than about forty miles from Smyrna, the deputation must have supplied, and Ignatius have taken in, some information, so that we may assume that Ignatius, notwithstanding his protestation, had at least some idea that his warnings might not prove unprofitable. Moreover, in *Magnesians* 4.1 he does not warn but makes a plain statement: there are some who invoke the bishop's name but take no notice of him. This statement gives more precision to *Philadelphians* 7.1f. (see above, pp. 144f.). To 'do everything without the bishop' (χωρὶς αὐτοῦ πάντα ποιοῦσιν) will no doubt include the holding

of a separate Eucharist, even if ποιεῖν[37] is not itself a eucharistic
term; this may well be connected with what Ignatius says a little
later (*Magn.* 9.1) about Jews, or Jewish Christians, in Magnesia who
'sabbatize'. As in Philadelphia, we are dealing with a separatist
sect whose fault (in Ignatius's eyes) reaches a focal point in the fact
that they hold their own Eucharist.

To speak of Jesus Christ and at the same time to 'judaize' is out
of the question: ἄτοπόν ἐστιν Ἰησοῦν Χριστὸν λαλεῖν καὶ ἰουδαΐζειν
(*Magn.* 10.1) – out of the question, but Ignatius writes as he does
because he either knows or fears that it is happening. It is out of the
question because Christianity has supplanted Judaism as the means
by which mankind as a whole (πᾶσα γλῶσσα) is to be brought to God
(10.3). This seems to be the meaning of the proposition that
Christianity did not believe in Judaism, but Judaism in Christianity.
But does this proposition further imply that some Christians were
adopting a form of Judaism? Probably it does; such men could
possibly be among the uncircumcised who preached Judaism (see
p. 146 above). They were, however, joining a body which, as a
whole, was not adopting but continuing Jewish practices; this
seems to be the force of μέχρι νῦν in 8.1: if up to this moment we still
continue to live κατὰ ἰουδαϊσμόν we confess thereby that we have not
(yet) received grace. What living 'according to Judaism' means may
be inferred from other points in the letter. (a) It means following
ancient myths (8.1). (b) It means behaving in old ways (ἐν παλαιοῖς
πράγμασιν ἀναστραφέντες, 9.1), of which observance of the Sabbath
rather than the Lord's Day appears to be one. (c) It means adopting
an interpretation of the prophets which the prophets themselves
would not approve (9.3).

Judaism is associated with mythology in the Pastoral Epistles also
(Titus 1.14; cf. 1 Tim. 1.4; 4.7; 2 Tim 4.4), and neither there nor
in Ignatius is it easy to say precisely what is meant. If either stood
alone it might be possible[38] to draw the conclusion that a Deutero–
Pauline author, aware that in a Pauline context Judaism had to
be treated as an enemy but unable to understand the real substance
of Paul's argument, had associated Judaism with all the evils he
could think of, including gnostic mythology. But the independent
agreement of the two sources must be taken seriously, and, as we
have seen (p. 134), this and other New Testament evidence was regarded by Lightfoot as supplying the clue to the 'Judaism' of
Ignatius: it is Judaism crossed with Gnosticism. This view is prob-

ably in essence correct, but belongs within a situation more complex than Lightfoot was in a position to grasp. Ignatius himself goes on immediately to write in gnostic terms of Jesus as the procession of God's word from his silence (αὐτοῦ λόγος ἀπὸ σιγῆς προελθών).[39] In fact, the context as a whole makes clear how close Ignatius is to both the Judaism and the Gnosticism (docetism) that he attacks, for here as in *Philadelphians* the interpretation of the prophets is at the heart of the dispute. The prophets, Ignatius claimed, lived κατὰ Χριστὸν 'Ιησοῦν (*Magn.* 8.2), and therefore presumably not κατὰ ἰουδαϊσμόν. The Judaizers might claim them, but that they stood on the same side as Ignatius is attested by the further fact that like him they too were persecuted (*Magn.* 8.2). If we may draw on *Philadelphians*, Ignatius held that the prophetic literature of the Old Testament constituted the archives of the Christian faith and bore witness to the life, death and resurrection of Jesus. In his opinion, the Judaizers turned them into mere ancient mythology; this may mean that they took a more historical view of their contents.[40]

The context of σαββατίζοντες in *Magnesians* 9.1 makes it clear that the observance of a day is in mind; the κυριακή with which the Sabbath is contrasted is defined as the day on which our life dawned through Christ and through his death (*Magn.* 9.1) – that is, as Sunday. It is, however, certain too (see above, p. 139) that more than a calendrical dispute is involved; it is one of the less happy features of Ignatius's way of thinking that he sees great issues in terms of relatively superficial points of order and practice, and does not clearly distinguish between them. The real question is whether prophecy finds its fulfilment in the life, death and resurrection of Jesus or not, and we see in Ignatius's dispute with the Judaizers an early stage of a controversy that was to be of considerable importance in the development of Christian doctrine. It is unfortunate that neither Ignatius and Justin (who stand fairly close together) nor Marcion (who develops the attitude of *Phld.* 8 in a way Ignatius would not have countenanced) learned as much as they might have done from a more soundly based historical Jewish exegesis of the Old Testament. In the end it was the Christian allegorists who turned the Old Testament into ancient mythology.

To Smyrna Ignatius wrote two letters, one to the church and one to Polycarp, its bishop. The latter contains nothing to our purpose, the former a good deal. Ignatius had resided in Smyrna (*Eph.* 21.1;

Magn. 15.1; *Trall.* 12.1; 13.1; *Rom.* 10.1), and knew it as well as he knew any Asian town, and there can be no guesswork (though there may be misjudgement) in his assessment of the inroads of heresy. He uses (*Smyrn.* 4.1) the same word, προφυλάσσειν, that he uses in other circumstances (*Magn.* 11.1), but here at least his warning must be based on knowledge. He knows, though he forbears to mention, the names of the heretics (*Smyrn.* 5.3). The danger is serious, and the only way to counter it is to avoid the heretics, or schismatics, completely: οὓς οὐ μόνον δεῖ ὑμᾶς μὴ παραδέχεσθαι, ἀλλ', εἰ δυνατόν, μηδὲ συναντᾶν (4.1); πρέπον ἐστὶν ἀπέχεσθαι τῶν τοιούτων (7.2). It is proper to pray for their repentance, but no more (4.1); and Ignatius's language does not suggest the kind of prayer that believes it already possesses what it seeks. The situation is similar to that of the Johannine Epistles.[41]

Were these heretical and loveless persons (6.2 – perhaps they did not find Ignatius and Polycarp very loving) Jews? They were docetic, in regard to the person of Jesus, and also in regard to the Eucharist, which they did not acknowledge to be the flesh of our Saviour Jesus Christ (6.2); it is not so clear that they were judaizing, but this is a probable inference. They have not so far been convinced by the prophets, the law of Moses, the Gospel or the sufferings which Christians are prepared to endure for their faith (5.1). They seem (5.2) to have thought well of Ignatius personally, but this did not prevent them from blaspheming his Lord (that is, expressing what Ignatius regarded as an inadequate Christology). It is unlikely that Ignatius would blame Gentiles for not having been convinced by the law and the prophets – the Old Testament, probable therefore that his opponents at least included a substantial number of Jews. This would mean that they were in the same position as the heretics Ignatius had to contend with at Philadelphia, who, if they could not find basic Christian affirmations in the archives (in the Old Testament), would not believe in the Gospel. There is some confirmation of this in Revelation 2.9, which deals with the Smyrnaean Jews in the same way that those of Philadelphia are dealt with in Revelation 3.9.

Ignatius's language in *Smyrnaeans* is vigorous, but there are only two respects in which it adds substantially to our picture of the judaizing heretics. It does not, for example, inform us what kind of Christology, if any, they drew from their use of the Old Testament. But the reference in 6.1 to τὰ ἐπουράνια καὶ ἡ δόξα τῶν ἀγγέλων καὶ οἱ ἄρχοντες ὁρατοί τε καὶ ἀόρατοι suggests (though it cannot prove) some kind of gnostic mythologizing – even the mythological powers, says Ignatius, will come under judgement if they do not believe in the blood of Christ, and Ignatius's charge that the heretics fail not only in doctrine but in love and service to the needy (6.2) may have had some substance in it. So far as it does, it points to a very un-Jewish kind of society. Abstinence from the bishop's Eucharist (7.1; 8.1f.) could be linked with a celebration on the Sabbath rather than on Sunday, but Ignatius does not say so.

The epistles to the *Ephesians* and to the *Trallians*, though they contain warnings against and attacks on false doctrine contain nothing that bears unambiguously on Judaism. The epistle to the *Romans* makes no reference to heresy.

This brief examination may lead, not to conclusions, for only a far more detailed study of the epistles in relation to their background could do this, but to a few observations which, if they have any use, may serve as signposts rather than arrival notices.

1 On the whole, Ignatius gives the impression that he is dealing with a situation that he has encountered on his travels in Asia, rather than with one he has long known and recalled from the days of his settled ministry in Antioch. As we have seen, the great importance of *Philadelphians* 8 (which is not inharmonious with the rest of the epistles) is that it shows Ignatius caught up in an actual situation, and himself involved, in Philadelphia, in debate. The church in Antioch may have encountered similar, or even identical, problems in relation to the Jewish tradition, but of this we cannot be sure, and *Philadelphians* 8 (especially when taken with 7) suggests the picture of a man taken by surprise, and unprepared with an answer likely to carry conviction to his opponents. It is a further, but not unreasonable, guess that Ignatius did not fully understand the position that confronted him – this would partly account for his failure to make it clear to his readers, as it would certainly mean that he had not previously dealt with it in Antioch. Conversely, it is possible that if he failed to deal with judaizing Christians in Asia this was because he employed arguments that were appropriate in Syria, but not in the new environment (which, it must be remembered, he was hardly in a position to study at leisure).

2 If this observation is true it is bound to lessen the relevance and importance of the connections found by Dr Corwin between Matthew, John, Qumran, the *Odes of Solomon* and Ignatius. These

are in any case, as we have seen, questionable. The relation with
Matthew seems fairly firm; that with John is much more doubtful,
and though it is plausible to explain the Johannine echoes that are
heard in the epistles as due to Ignatius's contacts with an early,
Antiochene, stage of Johannine theology, it is equally plausible to
explain them as the sort of thing Ignatius might have picked up in
his transit through Asia, if, as tradition asserts, this was the home
of the Johannine literature.

It is doubtful whether Nag Hammadi will provide a more useful
area of comparative study than Qumran – not because Nag Hammadi is itself unimportant, or because Judaism is unrelated to
Gnosticism,[42] but because we simply do not know enough of the
Judaizers' opinions to compare them fruitfully with anything. If
indeed their Christology was docetic so was that of the Gnostics in
general, not only of those known to us from Nag Hammadi; and
traces of Judaism in Nag Hammadi documents could have been
drawn from other Jewish sects.

The Ignatian epistles do, however, provide useful confirmatory
evidence of a Jewish contribution to Gnosticism. 'There are cases in
which the Gnostic myth is little more than a reinterpretation of the
Genesis creation story in Gnostic terms.'[43] Dr Wilson goes on to
indicate the uncertainty whether the gnostics were Gentiles who had
acquired a smattering of Judaism or Jews who had shed many of the
characteristics of Judaism. There can be little doubt that some
gnostic groups belonged to one, others to the other, category; the
Ignatian letters serve as a reminder that some – perhaps many –
gnostic groups contained both hellenized Jews and judaized Gen-
tiles. The Jewish myths ($\mu\upsilon\theta\epsilon\acute{\upsilon}\mu\alpha\tau\alpha$, *Magn.* 8.1) may have been, as
was suggested above (pp. 148f.), a quasi-historical (non-allegorical)
treatment of Old Testament narrative, or possibly creation myths
based on Genesis.

3   It is natural in this book, appropriately devoted to the study
of Judaism and Hellenism, to widen the inquiry to a more general
consideration of the Jews in the Graeco–Roman world. It was in
Asia[44] that the classical encounter between Jew and Greek took
place.[45] It is not necessary to accept the historicity of the incident,
on which different views have been held: the story of Aristotle and
his Jewish companion, even if legendary, bears witness to a relation
that began early and continued at some depth. 'Hellenizing Jews of
this type [who "had abandoned both the Jewish community and

Judaism in order to become assimilated among the Greeks"] were to be found in every locality and we have no means of determining their number.'[46] The existence of Christianity may well have accelerated this process, for Christianity must have presented Hellenism in a form exceptionally attractive to Jews, for it retained features that were central in the old religion: belief in one God, which, even if modified, was modified by the incorporation of a messianic figure by no means unknown in Judaism; worship of a synagogue type, though it included a new sacred meal; a community of brothers, committed to a high ethical ideal and to mutual concern. The exponents of Judaism in the Ignatian epistles present an obscure and confused appearance; this need not be due entirely to Ignatius's failure to understand them. If we may include Revelation 2.9 and 3.9 in the evidence, they claimed to be Jews. They reverenced Jesus as a teacher, but were perhaps not prepared to allow his person to upset the unity of the Godhead. They were unwilling to follow all the new messianic exegesis of the Old Testament. They adopted the sacred meal (not that common religious meals were strange to Judaism), but associated it with the Sabbath rather than with the Lord's Day, and thought of it in terms of fellowship rather than as a sacrament on Ignatian lines. Possibly under some official pressure they dropped the requirement of circumcision.[47] All this is Judaism with its angularities rubbed off; the process of smoothing looks like a social rather than a purely theological one, and theologians have perhaps been too quick to see theological significance in the hellenizing of Judaism.

4   The most important theological issue that arises here is the interpretation of the Old Testament, on which Ignatius evidently found himself in disagreement with those who practised Judaism. The role of Old Testament exegesis in the development of New Testament thought has been brought out in familiar works by, for example, C. H. Dodd[48] and Barnabas Lindars.[49] The centrality of the same theme in the second century is notably attested by the Marcionite controversy, but there is plenty of other evidence, of which the first substantial representative is the dispute between Justin and Trypho. 'When pressed for evidence of the supernatural origin of Christianity, the second-century Church sought an answer principally in the fulfilment by Jesus of Old Testament prophecy and in the visible evidence of the universal diffusion of the faith.'[50] The dispute over the Old Testament was the framework in which

the doctrine of God as Creator of the material universe was held fast, and Christology developed. The importance of this fact in the story of Christian theology is evident enough and need not be developed here.

5   Only one more point remains to be taken up. Earlier in this essay (p. 135) reference was made to a view expressed in W. Bauer's *Rechtgläubigkeit und Ketzerei*. After nearly forty years the influence of this notable book is still increasing, and it may be asked whether the material we have been considering throws any light upon the questions that it raises. Ignatius was one of the most notable representatives of the first age to understand Christianity, and especially Christian controversy, in terms of orthodoxy and heresy, catholicism[51] and schism, and the relation of Ignatius to Jewish Christians is a significant part of this development. The result, notwithstanding one's admiration for Ignatius's personal and sacrificial devotion to truth and to the person of Jesus, and his not inconsiderable grasp of Christian doctrine, is alarming and depressing.

There stands out first Ignatius's refusal to argue. There is no indication that his opponents were in this respect any better. Γέγραπται – Πρόκειται – Ἐμοὶ δέ (*Phld.* 8.2) form a prospectless sequence of assertion and counter-assertion, affording no hope of reconciliation or even of constructive disagreement. Ignatius does not discuss doctrinal matters and is apt to view them personally – If the docetists are right, why am I in bonds? (*Trall.* 10.1; the answer *could* be, Because you have foolishly misunderstood Christian teaching and duty). Still less will Ignatius reason with what he regards as schism; to be out of communion with himself and with his friends is to be outside the holy place of God's dealings with men (*Eph.* 5.2).

A second feature of Ignatius's attitude is his tendency to attach questions of doctrine to matters of order and even of calendar.[52] Of his attachment to the threefold order of bishops, presbyters and deacons this is not the place to speak, though he is clearly not prepared to consider the claim to orthodoxy of those who stand outside this structure. It seems, however, that he regarded a Saturday Eucharist with displeasure, and probably thought it invalid; it is true that lack of the bishop's authorization, and docetic opinions, contributed to its invalidity, but the date seems to have assumed a prominent place in Ignatius's mind.

This would perhaps be justifiable if the holding of a sacred meal on the Sabbath was in fact the mark of a schismatic religion whose roots were in Judaism and not in Christianity; but where the roots of the Jewish Christianity that Ignatius deals with lay is precisely what the evidence does not allow us clearly to see. That Ignatius was clear in his own mind about the lines of demarcation between orthodoxy and heresy, and was prepared to deal energetically with those who stood on the wrong side of them, is evident, and he marks an important step in the development of clarity about such questions. This, however, does not mean that he drew the lines in the right places, or indeed that he had much right to draw them at all. Dr Bartsch and others have pointed out that in Christology Ignatius was nearer to the Gnostics (and docetists) than to the Judaizers;[53] at the same time he shared in the Judaizers' appeal to the Old Testament, even though his interpretation of the prophets was different from theirs. Dr Corwin, as we have seen (p. 139), speaks of an Ignatian centre party, with docetists on the one wing and Judaizers on the other. If there was even a tendency in the direction of docetism on the part of some Jews the picture becomes far more complicated, and a simple analysis in terms of right and left impossible. It is here that Ignatius's insistence upon order becomes (for good or ill) important. The sorting out of Christian groups that took place during the second century was not carried out on a purely doctrinal basis, but was related to categories of organization and power: we have moved a long way from Paul and John. As most more recent students have recognized, Lightfoot was wrong in identifying Ignatius's attack on judaizing with Paul's,[54] and part of the difficulty in defining the Judaizers' beliefs, which the inconclusiveness of this essay will have made clear, is due to the fact that Ignatius himself finds the Judaizers easier to define sociologically than theologically. The Hellenistic world in general had noted the existence of the Jews as an ethnic group with strange sociological characteristics, to be hated and scorned, or, it may be, tolerated; it is one of the tragedies of Jewish–Christian relations that the Church, which had at first, in the person of Paul, dealt with the relationship theologically, so soon fell out of theology and into sociology, adopting the common Hellenistic attitude.

NOTES

1 The theme is therefore, I hope, one that will serve as a suitable greeting to my old and dear friend W. D. Davies – though in working on it I have found that it calls for a book, not an essay.

2 J. B. Lightfoot, *The Apostolic Fathers*, Part ii: *S. Ignatius, S. Polycarp*. London 1885.

3 W. Bauer, *Die apostolischen Väter ii: Die Briefe des Ignatius und der Polykarpbrief, HNT*, Ergänzungsband (Tübingen 1920), p. 240.

4 W. Bauer, *Rechtgläubigkeit und Ketzerei im ältesten Christentum, BHT*, no. 10 (Tübingen 1934) p. 92; a 2nd edn, with supplement by G. Strecker, 1964; Eng. trans., 1972.

5 J. Weiss, *The History of Primitive Christianity* (completed by R. Knopf). New York 1937.

6 See especially pp. 143f., 151.

7 H. W. Bartsch, *Gnostisches Gut und Gemeindetradition bei Ignatius von Antiochien* ('Beiträge zur Förderung christlicher Theologie', 2. Reihe, 44. Band). Gütersloh 1940. The new stage was perhaps rather opened by H. Schlier (*Religionsgeschichtliche Untersuchungen zu den Ignatiusbriefen* [*BZNW*, no. 8], Giessen 1929, but Schlier has little or nothing on our subject. To some extent Bartsch recalls the later view of Bauer (see p. 135).

8 ποιεῖν and πράσσειν. These words are by no means exclusively cultic, and Bartsch's interpretation is probably too narrow.

9 Bartsch cites *Did.* 9.5; Greg. Naz., *Oratio* 18.10.

10 Bartsch cites Herm., *Vis.* iii 9.6; Herm., *Sim.* ix *passim*; 1 Clem., 48.4: John 10.7, 9.

11 See pp. 144–51.

12 Cf. Bauer, *Rechtgläubigkeit*, as referred to in note 4.

13 See pp. 154f.

14 V. Corwin, *S. Ignatius and Christianity in Antioch* (New Haven 1960), p. 52.

15 See p. 137; also pp. 146f.

16 Cf. also p. 108: Matthew and Ignatius 'represent a similar emphasis on Jesus Christ as the ultimate completion of the message of Judaism . . . It is reasonable to suppose that the gospel came into existence in Antioch in earlier years, influenced by some of the circumstances that faced Ignatius and the need to demonstrate to Jews and to Essene-Christians that the teachings of Jesus, grouped as we find them in the Sermon on the Mount, constituted a new law which took the place of Torah.'

17 See also R. Harris and A. Mingana, *The Odes and Psalms of Solomon* (New York 1920), ii, pp. 40–9.

18 See especially pp. 144–7.

19 In fact, the contacts Dr Corwin cites are extremely general and superficial. All observant Jews kept the Sabbath; their meals commonly had a religious character; the priesthood was essential to the cultus; the patriarchs were the ancestors of the whole nation, and *CD* iii 2f. (the passage probably intended) does not claim them exclusively for the sect.

20 E. Molland, 'The Heretics Combatted [*sic*] by Ignatius of Antioch', in *Journal of Ecclesiastical History* v (1954), pp. 1–6.

21 L. W. Barnard, *Studies in the Apostolic Fathers and their Background* (New York 1966).

22 In Revelation 2.9 βλασφημία suggests a war of words rather than persecution; at a later date cf. *Mart. Pol.* 12.2; 13.1; 17.2; 18.1.

23 With συναγωγή τοῦ σατανᾶ (Rev. 2.9; 3.9) cf. the Old Testament συναγωγή κυρίου. Christians regarded themselves as now the Lord's people.

24 See G. Bornkamm, 'Die Häresie des Kolosserbriefes', *Das Ende des Gesetzes* (Munich 1952), pp. 139–56.

25 Cf. J. N. D. Kelly, *The Pastoral Epistles* (London 1963), pp. 10ff.; 'The most obvious characteristic of the heresy is its combination of Jewish and gnostic ingredients' (p. 11).

26 For example, *Bell.* vii 41–62. And see H. Koester, in H. Koester and J. M. Robinson, *Trajectories through Early Christianity* (Philadelphia 1971), p. 148.

27 See especially R. M. Grant, *Gnosticism and Early Christianity*, New York 1959, a book which has the merit of offering an explanation of the incorporation of Jewish and Christian ideas in Gnosticism. Grant deals briefly with Ignatius on pp. 177–81. See also note 42 below.

28 See, for example, W. Bousset and H. Gressmann, *Die Religion des Judentums im späthellenistischen Zeitalter* (Tübingen 1926), pp. 337–41, 487.

29 See M. Hengel, *Judentum und Hellenismus* ('Wissenschaftliche Untersuchungen zum Neuen Testament', no. 10 (Tübingen 1969)), pp. 473–86; also F. Cumont, *Oriental Religions in Roman Paganism* (Chicago 1911), pp. 63ff.; C. Roberts, T. C. Skeat and A. D. Nock, 'The Gild of Zeus Hypsistos', in *HTR* xxix (1936), pp. 39–88.

30 θεοῦ φωνῇ . . . τὸ δὲ πνεῦμα ἐκήρυσσεν. Cf. *Trall.* 5.1.

31 Presumably in some kind of church meeting (like that in which Ignatius prophesied: note 30) – an important point, for it must mean that the persons in question were Christians, even if (in Ignatius's eyes) unsatisfactory Christians. Ignatius is unlikely to have made his way into the synagogue.

32 So, regularly, in the New Testament; in Ignatius, cf. *Eph.* 5.3; *Magn.* 12.1.

33 εἰς τὸ εὐαγγέλιον κατηγγελκέναι. This is not quite the same as saying that they proclaimed the Gospel.

33a Mr A. Sheppard suggests to me that these uncircumcised Jews may have been Godfearers.

34 *Phld.* 9.1, with its reference to priests and patriarchs, suggests interest in the Old Testament as a whole; it was not difficult to provide a predictive interpretation of all parts of it.

35 See p. 144.

36 E.g., *Cher.* 49; and on the other side, *Spec. Leg.* 1.319f.

37 See note 8.

38 But see C. K. Barrett, *The Pastoral Epistles* (Oxford 1963), pp. 12–15.

39 Cf., for example, the Gospel of Truth, 37.4–21.

40 It is fair to say that, in a somewhat later controversy, Trypho took a more historical view of the Old Testament than Justin.

41 See 1 John 5.16; 2 John 10f.; 3 John 9f.; and on the situation E. Käsemann, 'Ketzer und Zeuge', in *Exegetische Versuche und Besinnungen*, i (Göttingen 1960), pp. 168–87.

42 See note 27; for more recent views, R. McL. Wilson, *Gnosis and the New Testament* (Philadelphia 1968), pp. 20ff.; earlier, idem, *The Gnostic Problem* (London 1958), pp. 172–255.

43 Wilson, *Gnosis*, p. 21.

44 Though at (probably) Atarneus, in Mysia, rather than in the more southerly district through which Ignatius passed.

45 Josephus, *C. Ap.* i. 177–82, quoting Clearchus.

46 V. Tcherikover, *Hellenistic Civilization and the Jews* (Philadelphia 1959), p. 297.

47 But Hadrian's general prohibition, if the account of it (Spartian, *Hadrian* 14) is trustworthy, would be too late to be relevant.

48 C. H. Dodd, *According to the Scriptures*. London 1952.

49 B. Lindars, *New Testament Apologetic*. Philadelphia 1961.

50 H. Chadwick, *The Early Church* (Grand Rapids 1967), p. 70.

51 Note the use of ἡ καθολικὴ ἐκκλησία in *Smyrn.* 8.2.

52 A similar charge has been brought against Laud: E. C. Hoskyns, *Cambridge Sermons* (New York 1938), p. xii.

53 See the quotation on p. 137.

54 See p. 134. It does not appear that the Ignatian Judaizers insisted on the permanent obligation of the Mosaic ritual.

10

JOHN 21. 15-25

One who is confronted in his lectionary by that passage of Scripture, and also finds himself in a pulpit whose diverse traditions combine to prevent him on the one hand from dodging academic difficulties and running away from critical problems, and on the other from blunting the sharp edge of the Gospel by wrapping it in a blanket of abstract and abstruse speculation, remote from the real stuff of human life, takes on a fairly considerable load of problems. They may not all appear above the surface, for he can reasonably claim that a sermon is not the place for discussing some of them, but if there is not at least a tip of the iceberg on show, the preacher will lose, and deserve to lose, both the respect and the attention of the congregation.

We will dismiss as much as we can, but it is a dangerous proceeding, because with this Gospel even more than with most parts of the New Testament serious attention to critical problems is apt to lead to important theological and practical results. Indeed, the critical processes are a necessary part of the attempt to discover what meaning, if any, words written late in the first century may have for readers who come to them late in the twentieth. We have before us a passage from John 21; what is the relation of this last chapter in the Gospel to the preceding twenty chapters? It is an old and familiar observation that the last verses of chapter 20 seem to bring the book to a close: Jesus did many other signs in the presence of his disciples which are not written in this book; 'but these are written that you may believe that Jesus is the Christ, the Son of God, and that believing you may have life in his name'. An impressive conclusion; as Loisy wrote, many years ago, 'L'évangile est fini, très bien fini.' What more could follow such an effective end? Nothing, surely; the book has reached its goal: Jesus is dead, and risen; he is confessed as Lord and God; his disciples are commissioned and inspired. But a whole chapter follows, somewhat clumsily, awkwardly attached to what goes before. Did the author of the earlier chapters spoil the artistic shape and balance of the whole by adding this appendix to his own work? Did someone else, unappreciative of literary form, add it? That question indeed is not important, and we may leave it to the lecture rooms where it may be more appropriately discussed. The question that matters is this. Someone, whether the Evangelist or a continuator, thought that, whatever the cost in artistic terms, something had to be added: why? What supplement was needed by this satisfactorily, impressively terminated book? If we were to take the chapter as a whole we might find several answers to this question, and there is no reason why they should not all be true. Taking the few verses of the Gospel lection, the answer – part of the total answer – is clear. It was necessary to say something about the two men who appear in it, to define their roles, their destiny, the relation between them: Peter, and the disciple whom Jesus loved.

That does not end the questioning. Why was it necessary to say something about these men? The Gospel, whether you take that word to apply to a book or to a message, is about Jesus; how is it that these two disciples suddenly become so important that they need a last chapter to set them in the right perspective? There are two main reasons for this; and I ask you to be patient while I set them out. We shall find, I believe, before we are done, that these two themes, remote as they may at first seem, continue to address the reader of the Gospel, and on topics that are as of great concern today as they have ever been. But no short cuts: the spadework must be done first, or we shall have no solid foundation to build on.

First, this: we are dealing here with a particular form of a problem that vexed Christian thinkers from the time of Jesus until the end of the century – indeed, to judge from the books and articles that are labelled 'eschatology', it vexes them still. It is no accident that the New Testament books are full of the future. Any book must deal with the future if it begins, as the New Testament writers do, from the double conviction that God is a being other than man, whom man must nevertheless take as seriously as he takes himself, and that time is real, that man lives in time, and that past, present and future are no delusion. I live in the present; there is nowhere else I can live; all my contemporaries live with me in the present. And I have my roots in the past, my own personal past and the collective past of the race. It is perhaps as one grows older that one comes to see oneself as a sort of layered structure, built up through

time, adolescence resting on childhood, young manhood on adolescence, and so on. The same thing is true, catastrophes and revolu-
tions notwithstanding, of mankind. My present rests upon the past,
and it is always moving forward into what is now future, but
moment by moment it never ceases to be present. But if God is
other than I am, and we are speaking in terms of time, the future
is his, and to take God seriously is to take the future seriously. It is
there in the teaching of Jesus. It is the future harvest that makes
sense of sowing. It is the future plant that gives meaning to the
minute grain of mustard seed. God will set up his Kingdom, and
that soon: that will make sense of the humble present of Jesus. The
Son of man must suffer, but God will vindicate him. Sometimes this
confidence in the future is expressed in terms of resurrection: in a
little while God will raise him from the dead. Sometimes it is
expressed in terms of a splendid heavenly procession: the Son of
man will come with glory on the clouds of heaven. But always the
confidence is there. The future is God's. The ministry of Jesus came
to its close; surely this was the time for the future climax. But time
went on. What could men make of it now? One of the answers they
gave was this: God had in his patience extended the time, giving
men, and not Jews only, the opportunity of repentance and faith.
This extension, however, would be of limited duration; it would
last no more than one generation. 'Truly I tell you, this generation
shall not pass away till all these things be accomplished.' This was a
conviction that served its turn in the thirties and forties. It was no
doubt beginning to wear thin in the fifties, and in the sixties it became a problem. According to old tradition Peter was killed in
Rome, and though we cannot prove it true it is unlikely to be far
wrong. Peter was dead; what of the promise? The generation was
dying out, but it was not yet gone. Again, tradition tells us of an
aged disciple; it calls him John and says that he was the disciple
whom Jesus loved. We may accept the tradition, since it is only its
existence, not its truth, that concerns us, and may even use the
name John (which has at least the merit of brevity). While John still
lived all was not lost; he would survive to greet the returning Son of
man. But he too died; and they were all gone.

There is far more here than the disappointment of a hope, the
failure of a programme, the disclosure of an error, as when modern
apocalyptic sects, overtaken by events, are obliged to check their
calculations and discover that the world was due to end not after

all in 1978 but in 1982. A profound theological issue was opened –
profound, though it can be stated in few and simple words. Jesus
was vanishing into the past and he showed no sign of appearing in
the future. Yet he was the Lord, the foundation, the core, of
Christianity. How can his people exist without him? Hence the
concentration on Peter and John. They are what he left behind –
people, not books or institutions. Somehow their work perpetuates
the work of Jesus, projects it into the continuing current of time.
How, but for such men, can the Church still be related to its
founder? And how, when they are gone, are men still related to
him, to his work, to his achievement, to his hopes?

> Christ is the end, for Christ is the beginning,
> Christ the beginning, for the end is Christ.

But what of those who are in neither at the beginning nor at the end?
Who see neither the historical Jesus nor the eschatological Jesus?
The Gospel, John's Gospel, cannot end without looking firmly at
these men who did see, and believe.

This was a theological reason. There was another of a different
kind. The new paragraph was needed as part of the Christian story.
Not only was it needed; something of the kind, at least as regards
Peter, must be somewhere near the truth. Two things were facts.
One was the shocking denial of Jesus by Peter, a tale too com-
promising and embarrassing to have been made up by Christians
as a pious fiction. The other was the emergence of Peter as a
dominant figure in the earliest years of the Church. Something
must have happened to provide the hinge about which these two
different aspects of Peter turned; and we may well ask whether his
fellow disciples would ever have trusted Peter if there had not from
the beginning been some story that brought him face to face with the
risen Jesus. The essence of such a story is to be found in one of the
earliest Christian documents, 1 Corinthians. The Gospel story makes
the position clear. 'Feed my sheep'; and, 'When you were younger
you clothed yourself and walked where you liked; when you have
grown old, you will stretch out your hands and another will clothe
you and carry you where you do not wish.' He said this, indicating
by what death Peter would glorify God.

It is a different role that the Beloved Disciple fills. Not a pastor,
ruling and guiding the flock, not a martyr in the sense of one who
commends his faith by dying for it, but a martyr in the true sense of

the word: a witness. This is the disciple who bears witness about these things and wrote these things; and we know that his witness is true.

We may trace in the ancient Church a certain rivalry between adherents of the two apostles: between Rome, which looked back to Peter, and Asia, where also great lights, including John the Beloved Disciple, had fallen asleep, a rivalry oddly expressed in the petty dispute about so trivial an issue as the date of Easter. No such rivalry is permitted in the Gospel, which both differentiates and associates the two. The two, the martyr shepherd and the faithful witness, both follow, and neither may question the other's authority.

It has taken a long time, too long perhaps, to work through these exegetical and historical details, but once they are laid bare the essential content of the Gospel is released and can be applied – one might say, applies itself – not merely to topics of current interest but to matters on which Christian existence turns. I am going to deal with three.

First, and perhaps most fundamental of all, there is the question of the Church and the historical Jesus. It is a fact of the year 1979 that not even a General Election quite submerged public interest in the Turin Shroud. Newspaper and magazine articles, at least two paperbacks, television programmes, together bore witness not only to an astonishing nostalgia for relics but also to lingering belief that somehow Jesus of Nazareth may have something to say even to the twentieth-century world that its scientists, philosophers and politicians are not able to say. Perhaps (such is the unexpressed dream) that apparently well-travelled piece of cloth can span for us the imagined gap between ancient and modern cultures and reveal a timeless wisdom. Well, no doubt it is as good a relic as most, but it asks questions rather than answers them. The wounds of which it may perhaps bear traces are, like Caesar's, but in an even more comprehensive sense, dumb mouths. If they are there they cannot speak; and that will hardly do. Must Jesus pass through the twentieth century like a silent ghost? Or is there some more articulate testimony?

It is no coincidence that it is of the witness to history, the man who tells the tale of the past, that Jesus says, 'If I will that he remain until I come, what is that to you?' True, the saying had been given a mechanical, and therefore a misleading, meaning. That did not mean that it was meaningless. The Jesus of the story was also the coming Jesus; if you like the phrases, the historical Jesus was the eschatological Jesus. For John the tradition became, as Käsemann has said, the servant, the instrument of the *Christus praesens*. Whether there is a date in the heavenly calendar when history will come to a full stop we do not know; if there is, we could hardly understand what it means. History did not come to a stop at the point where many first-century Christians thought it would. What the eschatology means to us is that the historical Jesus is eternally present, every day between this day and the last day, and there is perhaps no writer in the New Testament who so presses this truth upon us as does John. Elsewhere it is possible – and again and again in the history of Christian thought the possibility has been realized – on the one hand to absorb oneself in a tradition which conveys more or less of information about the historical Jesus, and on the other to abandon history in an uncontrolled devotion to an eternal Christ who may be no more than the creature of the worshipper's imagination. It is no more than the truth to say that these alternative errors have from the beginning bedevilled both Christian doctrine and Christian devotion, and have often given rise to a misleading notion of what Christian theology means. Theology has both historical and speculative elements in it, yet it is neither history nor metaphysics, and the very existence of Christian theology turns upon John's apprehension of the meaning of history, the meaning of eschatology, and the relation of each to the other.

This is not an inference drawn merely from a few verses in a supplementary chapter of the Gospel; it is a theme that runs throughout, and it no more turns upon a demonstration of the historicity of individual narratives and sayings than it depends upon the authenticity of the famous Shroud. No writer lays so much stress upon the central importance of the historical events of the life of Jesus; no writer makes it so clear that in themselves they carried no conviction. The story is bracketed between these propositions: 'He came to his own home, and his own people did not receive him'; and, 'Though he had done so many signs before them, yet they did not believe him.' The historical Jesus is not enough; yet the historical Jesus must always be there to control preaching and theology. The Spirit does not introduce some new religion. 'He will take what belongs to me and declare it to you.' He too bears witness, pointing in his own inward way, as the Old Testament, as John the Baptist, as the disciples, also point in their own ways to Jesus.

The story is a myth, of course, if myth is defined as the truth of God in the form of a narrative. But – and these are the fundamental terms for understanding the Gospel – the Word was God, and the Word became flesh. That is, the story is truly about God, and the story truly is history.

It is time to take up a second point, one which in the last few years has absorbed (unfortunately, perhaps) even more of Christian time and energy than the quest of the historical Jesus. What do we mean by ministry in the Church? What are its necessary features? In other ages these questions have been the instrument of self-criticism by which each community of Christians has measured itself and tested its own resources and its obedience to the constitution required of it; today we look at one another, critically at times, but also with a desire to learn, and look into the future to ask what a Church to which we might all belong could look like.

Well: no one is likely to deny that Peter and the Beloved Disciple form a fair specimen pair of Christian ministers: apostolic ministers. Nothing is said about the outward form of organization of their ministry, but perhaps this was intended and is as it should be. There is a strange contradiction in the attempt to locate what has been called an, or the, essential ministry in what is in fact a form of ministry. Essence and form are not the same thing, and the more one is concerned with what is essential the less dependent one should be on what is formal. Tradition does indeed make Peter a bishop, though I suspect that the first bishop of Rome did not look much like a modern bishop, even in the presbyterian sense; as far as I recall, no tradition makes the Beloved Disciple a bishop. Even towards the end of the second century he is still *Johannes ex discipulis*. The form of their ministry is of no importance to the Evangelist. Ministry, of course, must have form, as must any institution that is going to function in history; but it is its essence – indeed, its function – that matters.

There are two simple but sufficient functions here. 'Tend my lambs,' says Jesus to Peter. This chapter 21 performs a necessary operation, as Hoskyns once observed, in transforming Peter from a fisherman to a shepherd; for fish die when they are caught. The sheep must be fed and cared for. This is not the place to describe the office, better, the work, of a pastor, nor am I the man to do it. It is enough to observe that it is there, and that it is essential. It is described in verbs, not nouns: Tend, feed, not Be a pastor, hold the

office of pastor. And the sheep are Christ's sheep, not Peter's. Not,
Tend your flock, but Tend my sheep.

The other function is that of witness, or better, of witnessing, for
again it is the verb that is used. The Beloved Disciple is the disciple
who bears witness. What that means for the authorship of the Gospel
is neither here nor there. The function is that of witnessing in human
words to the divine Word. Without this witnessing, focused as it must
now be in the written word of Scripture ('. . . who wrote these
things'), there is no Church, for without Jesus there is no Church
and without the word of testimony there is no knowledge of Jesus. In
his written word John does indeed wait for the Lord's coming, his
testimony always at hand.

The two primary indispensable ministries are those of the pastor
and the preacher. They are represented here in the form of two men.
Does this mean that they are distinct, that the two men stand for two
different kinds of minister? There is a good hint to the answer to this
question. Peter is interrogated about his love to Jesus. 'Do you love
me? Do you love me more than these?' It is his affirmative answer
that is the occasion of the charge, 'Feed my sheep.' The other
disciple is – the disciple whom Jesus loved. But does not each
qualification imply the other? Are we to think that Peter loved
Jesus but that Jesus did not love him? Are we to think that the love
of Jesus for the other disciple evoked no answering love? It would
be absurd. Each disciple shared the other's qualification; each was
both loved and loving. Historically it is doubtless true that Peter
was pre-eminent as shepherd, John as witness; that human beings
are different applies to apostles as well as others. But there is one
ministry, and it is the ministry of shepherding and witnessing, of
pastor and preacher. The qualification for it is loving and being
loved, responding in faith to prevenient grace: we love because he
first loved us.

It is time to move to the third inference from the text: the most
practical point, but it may be the briefest, because we have covered
the ground already, and the structure of the Christian life begins to
appear. 'Are all apostles?' said Paul, expecting the answer No. But
all are in the positive, fundamental sense ministers, and the shape
and the basis of the ministry they acquire by being Christians are
before us. Every Christian has a responsibility to his fellow Christians. They are not his flock; it would be absurd to think it. But
each has a duty to the rest: 'Feed my sheep.' And each bears witness

to the truth that has created him. He does this, not by writing gospels, not by preaching sermons, but by being what the Word has made him.

All this repeats on a smaller scale (or is it a larger scale?) what we have already seen; and we have seen too the ground on which the universal Christian ministry rests. It rests upon the love of Jesus for his own, and the derivative love that answers his. To this there is one word more to add: following. Speculation – about our fellows; about the distant purposes of God: 'What is that to thee?' Follow thou me, in trust, obedience, love. There is no other qualification.

It is the occupational disease – no, the occupational crime of theologians to make simple things obscure. But the rest of men are not guiltless. May I use the Turin Shroud once more? Why has it proved so fascinating? I suspect that the answer lies in the fact that it enables men to bring together the interest in Jesus they cannot quite give up, and the interest in natural science they feel to be essential to modern man. Perhaps at last science will prove religion true. Use the new photographic techniques, analyse the fibre and the pollen, and somehow it will tell us that Jesus was right after all. But it won't. It is all far easier than that; and far harder. There is no proof. It is only in hearing the word of Jesus, coming to Jesus, following Jesus, that we ever find out whether he is right or wrong. And when all the arguing is done, the word which is at once invitation and command remains. 'I am the way, and the truth, and the life. Follow me.'

SELECT INDEX

New Testament passages discussed